Kahlil Gibran
Portraits

Salim Mujais

Kahlil Gibran
Portraits

Salim Mujais

Copyright © 2020 Black House Publishing Ltd

All rights reserved. No part of this book may be reproduced in any form by any electronic or mechanical means including photocopying, recording, or information storage and retrieval without permission in writing from the publisher.

ISBN-13: 978-1-912759-32-3

Black House Publishing Ltd
Kemp House
152 City Road
London
United Kingdom
EC1V 2NX

www.blackhousepublishing.com

Email: info@blackhousepublishing.com

Contents

Introduction	1
Parisian Luminaries	5
An American in Paris - Paul Wayland Bartlett	6
Three in Absentia -	7
Claude Debussy	7
Edmond Rostand	9
Henri Rochefort	11
The Master of Clay - Auguste Rodin	13
Boston Interlude	21
The Academia Pontiffs - Dr. Richard Clarke Cabot and Charles W. Eliot	21
A Jovial Baritone - David Bispham	24
Face of American Music - Arthur Farwell	25
A Garland of Poets	27
Ashes of Beauty - Richard LeGallienne	27
Poet with a Hoe - Edwin Markham	28
The Poet of the Sierras - Joaquin Miller	30
From the Mist of Ireland -	31
William Butler Yeats	31
Lady Augusta Gregory	35
Man of Big Spectacles - Percy MacKaye	36
Childless Son - Witter Bynner	37
War Poets -	40
John Masefield	40
Siegfried Sassoon	42
The Orphan Angel - Elinor Morton Wylie	43
Where the Prophet was Born - Marie Tudor Garland	46
Music and Poetry - Leonora Speyer	48
The Beautiful Voices of the East and the Prairies	50
George William Russell	50
Vachel Lindsay	50
Fellow Artists and Writers	53
The Recluse Symbolist - Albert Pinkham Ryder	53
A Portraitist Herself - Eliza Cecilia Beaux	57

    Symbolist to Modernist - Kenneth Hayes Miller ... 59
    Drawing the Archetype - Adele Watson ... 60
    Writing Scheherazade - Laurence Housman ... 62
    Drawing with a Chisel - Johan Bojer ... 64
    The Maya Death Bell - Alma Reed ... 67
    Between Faust and the Prophet - Alice Raphael ... 69
    The Chronicler of Poetry - Howard Willard Cook ... 72

A Constellation of Luminaries ... 75
    The Divine Sarah - Sarah Bernhardt ... 75
    The Dance of Flames - Ruth St Denis ... 80
    A Socialist in the Mix - Charles Russell ... 83
    Rogue Grandson - Giuseppe Garibaldi II ... 85
    Thirst for the Absolute - Thomas Raymond ... 86
    The Blind Baritone - Vladimir Resnikoff ... 87
    The Splendor of God - Abdul Baha ... 91
    Underground of the Soul - Carl Jung ... 93

New York Elite, Friends and Companions ... 95
    Matron of Songs - Julia Ellsworth Ford ... 95
    Beautiful People - The Erdman Family ... 96
    She herself is Art! - Rita de Acosta ... 99
    Women Friends and Lovers - ... 103
        Margaret Lee Crofts ... 103
        Marie-Luise Schloss ... 104
    Fellow Syrians - ... 105
        Ameen Rihani ... 105
        Mikhail Naimy ... 108
        Nasib Arida ... 109

Silent Faces ... 110
Lost Shadows ... 111

Speaking in Color ... 113
    The Dying Lioness - Kamileh Gibran ... 113
    The Sad Mona Lisa - Sultana Gibran ... 116
    The Suffering Mary - Marianna Gibran ... 117
    Invented Self ... 118
    L'Amante - Micheline Emily Michel ... 119
    Not Even If... - Charlotte Teller ... 121
    Colorful, but Silent ... 122
    A Gallery of Heads ... 123

Bibliography ... 125

To Tija,
For the easel,
The brushes,
The paint,
And the journey.

Acknowledgement

My daughter Ayat provided order and balance to the present work. I am most fondly grateful.

Introduction

During his apprenticeship in Paris, Kahlil Gibran embarked on an artistic project that occupied him for many years to come and positioned him as a talented portraitist to the elite of the American cultural and social establishment. Little of this artistic pursuit is evident in the common general biographies about Gibran[1] or in the occasional retrospective exhibits of his artwork. At best, only a few illustrative examples of the most famous portraits are reproduced, or displayed, giving the impression that portraiture may have been an episodic or ephemeral interest of the artist. Yet in his first public show in New York in 1914, Gibran exhibited seventeen portraits from what came to be known as the *Temple of Art* series. Further, Gibran's correspondence with Mary Haskell is replete with the names of artists, writers, and members of the intellectual elite that he had met and drawn[2]. It was not unusual to encounter his portraits of poets or artists in the periodicals of the time and his fame and skill in this pursuit was occasionally featured in fictional works[3].

Portraiture had always been Gibran's medium for connecting with people. It featured prominently in his courtship with Josephine Preston Peabody and Emilie Michel, in his attempted courtship with Charlotte Teller and Miss Marie Moro, in his expression of love towards Mary Haskell, and in his expressions of gratitude towards various benefactors, long before it became an artistic project. Indeed, while in Paris where the artistic project germinated, Gibran drew the portrait of a Syrian lady that took care of him during an illness: "I have finished the portrait of Hasiba Rahaim, the noble Syrian lady who has been more than kind during my illness and who gave me a royal reception some weeks ago. She and her husband are more than pleased of the portrait."[4]

A study of the art of portraiture of Gibran, however, is not a simple undertaking. The published general biographies offer only meager examples and tracking his activities through the periodicals of the period is subject to the hazards of publishing. While the correspondence of Gibran with Mary Haskell offers some record of this activity, it merely provides a list of names

---

1   Jean Gibran and Kahlil Gibran: *Kahlil Gibran: His Life and World*, Interlink Books, New York, 1998; Suheil Bushrui, Joe Jenkins: *Kahlil Gibran: Man and Poet*, Oneworld Publications, Oxford, 1998; Robin Waterfield: *Prophet: The Life and Times of Kahlil Gibran*, St Martins Press, New York, 2000.

2   Annie Salem Otto (Editor): *The letters of Kahlil Gibran and Mary Haskell; visions of life as expressed by the author of The prophet*, 1970, (hereafter *Letters of Kahlil Gibran*).; Virginia Hilu (Editor): *Beloved Prophet: The Love Letters of Kahlil Gibran and Mary Haskell, and Her Private Journal*, 1972, (hereafter *Beloved Prophet*); Mary Haskell's diary, University of North Carolina Library.

3   Anzia Yezierska: *All I could never be*, Brewer, Warren & Putnam, NY, 1932.

4   *Letters of Kahlil Gibran*, page 23.

that is limited to the period between 1910 and 1920. The difficulty is compounded by the dispersion of Gibran's works after his death. This dispersion has particularly affected this series of portraits because either as an act of goodwill or to further the financial value of Gibran's estate, several portraits were either donated to museums or given to their protagonists for a fee. Further, the lack of identification of the identity of the people in these portraits meant that many are languishing in the various collections of Gibran's works with the generic label of 'portrait of a man' or 'portrait of a woman.'

After the death of Gibran, Mary Haskell invited the photographer Juley to make a photographic record of all the artwork in Gibran's studios. This blessed event meant that scholars who wish to study certain aspects of Gibran's art have a rich compendium of this art in a singular source.[5] The portraits included in this collection should be considered as a minimum estimate of Gibran's endeavors in the field of portraitures because many may have ended up with the protagonists during Gibran's lifetime either as gifts or as commissions. The available portraits, however, generally lack any indications of the identity of the individuals. The effort to ascertain these identities is far from simple for although these individuals represented the intellectual and social elite of the period, many have lapsed into obscurity with the passage of time or identified portraits of them are not readily available.

In the present work, I have undertaken to offer a detailed survey of Gibran's portraiture work through identification of the individuals in the portraits retrieved from the Juley collection or other sources, as well as through exploration of intersections of the lives of these individuals with the life of Gibran. Both the identification and exploration have been laborious and necessitated recourse to multiple sources of information and extensive reviews of printed and electronic media. The fruits of this labor have been unique and the present work offers a robust evaluation and display of the art of portraiture by this versatile and talented artist. A natural derivative of this work is that these portraits also capture the characters that populated the cultural and social environment in which artists and poets thrived in the early part of the 20th century in New York and, as such, this collection is a visual record of the cultural life of that period.

Readers are naturally led to the comparison between this collection and the portraits by other artists of the period such as Cecilia Beaux (an acquaintance of Gibran whose portrait also features in the present collection), John Singer Sargent, or Maurice Fromkes (who had painted a portrait of Gibran).[6] The main distinguishing feature is the sensitivity of the portraitist to his subject and his understanding of their character and distinguishing traits.

---

5   Smithsonian American Art Museum photo archives, Washington, DC.
6   *New-York Tribune*, May 09, 1920.

Introduction

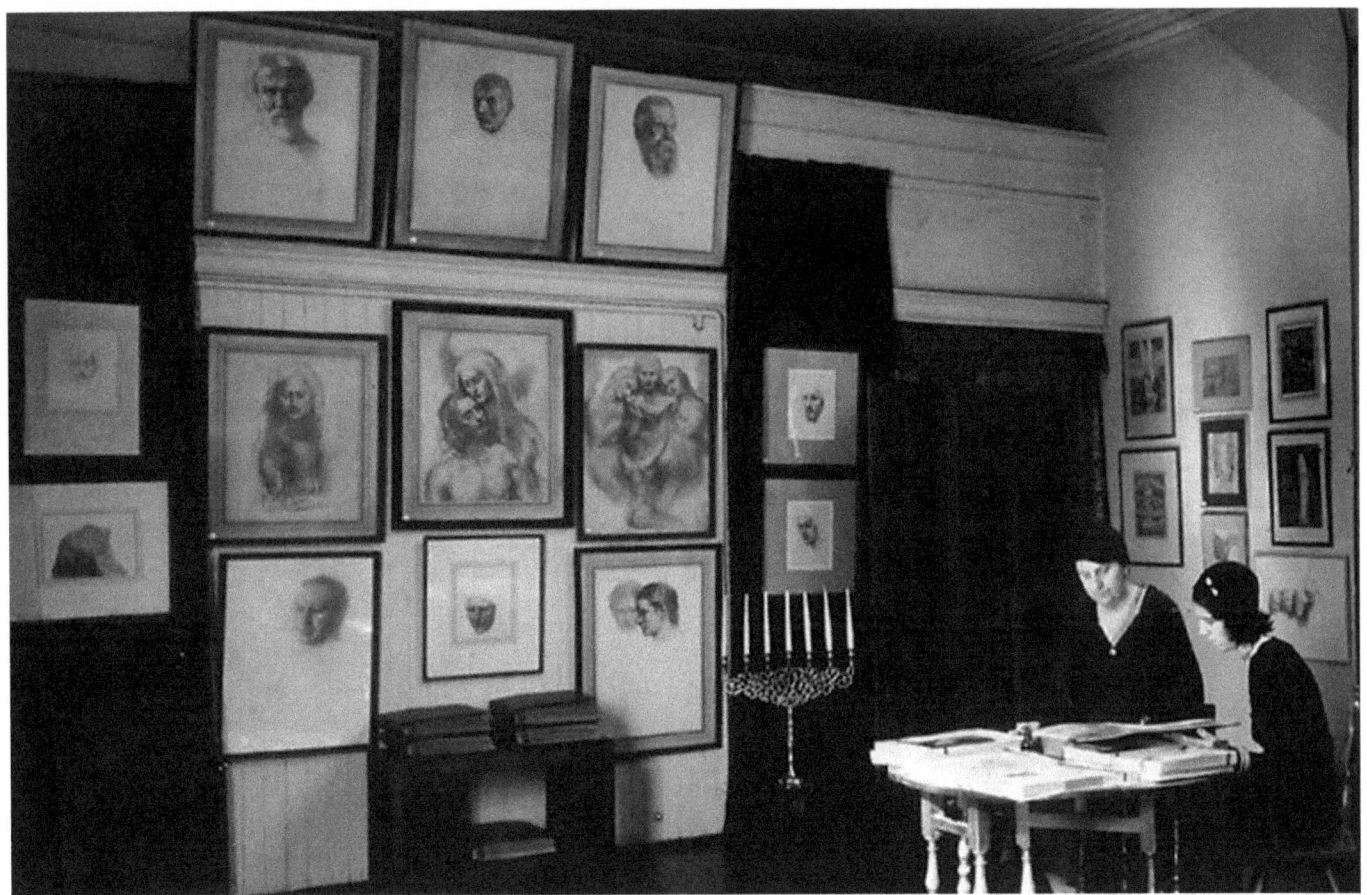

Kahlil Gibran's New York Studio

When Gibran first displayed his collection of portraits in December 1914, a critic remarked: "Mr. Gibran takes pleasure in portraiture, in which, in every case, he idealizes or frankly beautifies his subject, seeking apparently to paint what his subject aspires to be rather than what he or she is."[7] If this collection of portraits is to be viewed as a pictorial representation of a segment of the cultural elite of New York City in the early part of the 20th century, it is certainly a representation through the eyes and special sensitivities of a unique member of that elite.

---

7   Xanthus: New York art letter. *Star Tribune*, January 13, 1915.

Parisian Luminaries

We can trace the gestation of the project of a Temple of Art containing the portraits of great contemporary artists to Gibran's stay in Paris between 1908 and 1910. In a letter to Mary Haskell dated December 19, 1909, Gibran confides to his sponsor that he is undertaking this project and that he had already secured one portrait, that of the American sculptor Paul Wayland Bartlett: "And I want to tell you of a wonderful scheme. I am trying very hard to make drawings of the great artists of our time - the pillars of modern Art and culture... Two weeks ago, I made the first drawing of the series. It was a drawing of the great American Sculptor, Mr. Paul Bartlett."[1] He goes on to boast that all he needs is thirty minutes from his subjects' time! He hastens to stress that the series would include famous women as well citing Sarah Bernhardt and Ellen Terry. It is clear from this early correspondence that Gibran's concept of this series and his criteria for the inclusion of candidates is subject to compulsive choices and hazards of chance and opportunity.

Gibran's work on the series, however, was erratic and inconsistent. In a city brimming with cultural elite, Gibran's slow start is puzzling. By March 29, 1910, he had done no additional portraits and bemoans his inability to secure time with Rodin for a portrait of the great French artist.[2] By May 10, 1910, He tells Mary that he has an appointment to see Debussy in a week's time.[3] Finally, in September he laments to her about the lost opportunities due to his procrastination and that he had added only two additional portraits those of Rostand and Rochefort.[4] The net result is that by the time he joins Mary in Boston in November of 1910, he had only five portraits: Bartlett, Debussy, Rostand, Rochefort, and Rodin.[5]

Gibran is uniquely silent about the circumstances of executing these portraits, particularly his portrait of Rodin. There is reason to believe that for a few of these portraits Gibran may have used available photographic portraits of his subjects.

---

1 *Letters of Kahlil Gibran*, pp 36-37.
2 *Letters of Kahlil Gibran*, page 41.
3 *Letters of Kahlil Gibran*, page 45.
4 *Letters of Kahlil Gibran*, page 50.
5 Jean Gibran & Kahlil Gibran: *Kahlil Gibran*, page 196.

An American in Paris - Paul Wayland Bartlett

Paul Wayland Bartlett (1865-1925) was the first artist Gibran included in his series, and it may well be that the praise that the portrait received from Bartlett may have encouraged Gibran to conceive of his project. Bartlett was the doyen of American artists in Paris where he was a frequent visitor having studied under Rodin, participated in many exhibits and Salons, and honored repeatedly by the art societies and French government. He produced a number of public monuments, sculptures, and historical portraits including the figures of Columbus and Michelangelo for the Main Reading Room of the Library of Congress, and the pediment for the House wing of the U.S. Capitol, The Apotheosis of Democracy, begun in 1908 and was completed in 1916. His latest French endeavor was a statue of Lafayette donated by the subscription of five million American students as a gift to France. Bartlett was commissioned by the Daughters of the American Revolution to create a monument to the Marquis de Lafayette as a reciprocal gift from the United States to France in thanks for Bartholdi's Statue of Liberty. The first casting of the bronze was given to France and was installed in the *Cour du Louvre* where it remained until I. M. Pei's *Pyramide du Louvre* was built. The Parisian cast of Lafayette with its pedestal were moved to the *Cour La Reine* in Paris, where it stands today. A second casting of the equestrian monument to Lafayette was ordered for the city of Hartford, Connecticut.

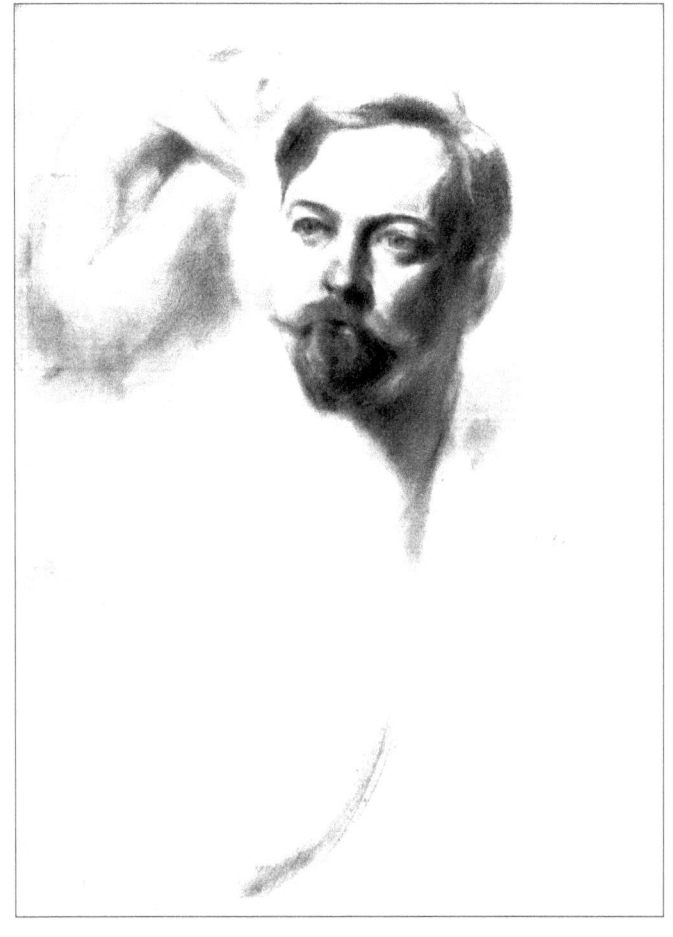
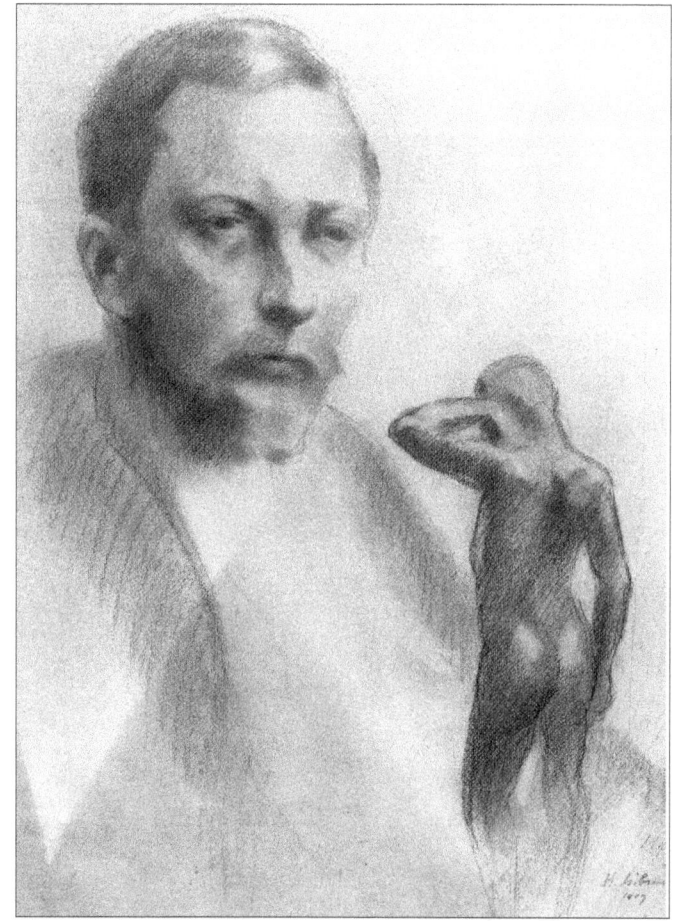

Gibran drew two portraits of Bartlett: the original dated to 1909 and was of a significantly lower quality and skill level[6] than the subsequent portrait drawn in 1912 in New York. In both portraits, Gibran adds a sketch of a symbolic statue in the background. In the 1909 portrait, the symbolic statue does not resemble any of Bartlett's own works, but rather echoes the statue *The Age of Bronze* by Rodin! In the 1912 portrait, there is an implication of creative imagination in the intensity of the gaze. Gibran apposed a sculptural nude, in this case one of Bartlett's own creations.

THREE IN ABSENTIA - CLAUDE DEBUSSY

It was not, however, until May of 1910 before Mary heard of any further progress in the plan when Gibran announced to her: "Next Saturday I shall meet Debussy, the great French composer, and I will make a drawing of his head. Claude Debussy is at the head of the modern French school of music. I hope the drawing will be successful."[7] Circumstantial evidence leads us to suspect that Gibran may have resorted to earlier photographs in his execution of the portrait of *Claude Debussy* (1862-1918). The portrait is very similar to known photographs of the younger Debussy. Further, 1910 was the year in which Debussy's colorectal cancer

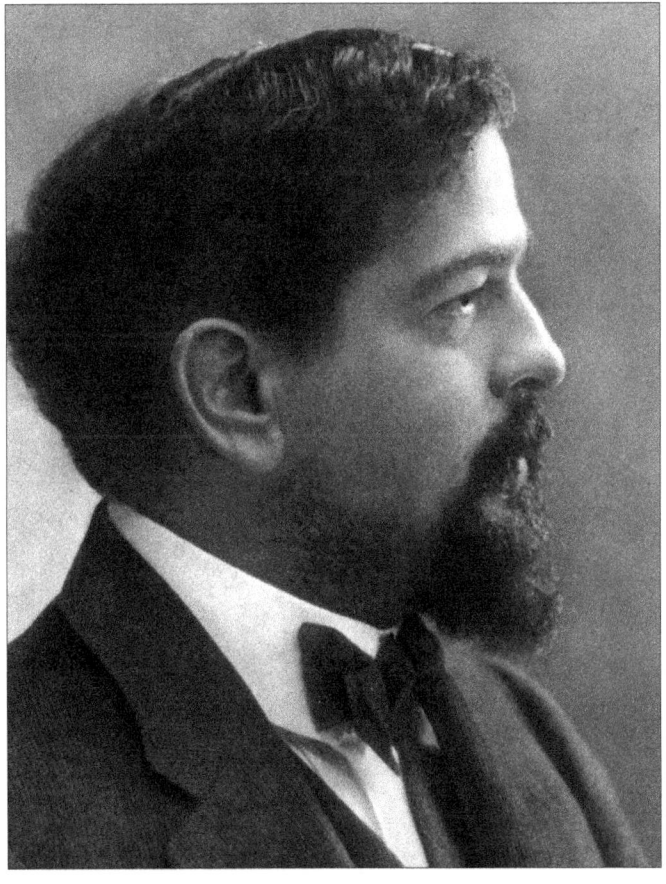 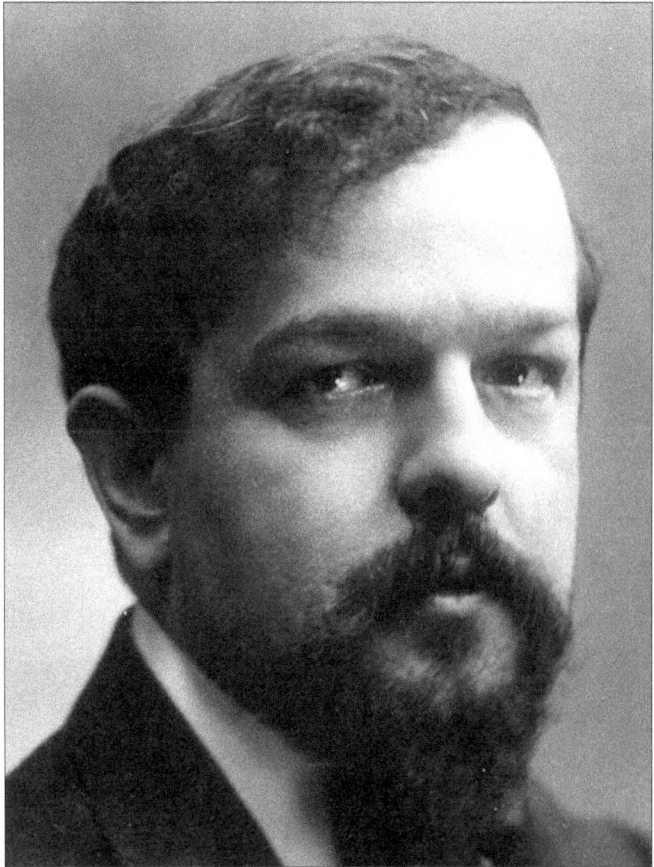

---

6 Aram Saroyan: *Kahlil Gibran: paintings & drawings*, 1905-1930. Vrej Baghoomian Gallery, New York, 1989.
7 *Letters of Kahlil Gibran*, page 45.

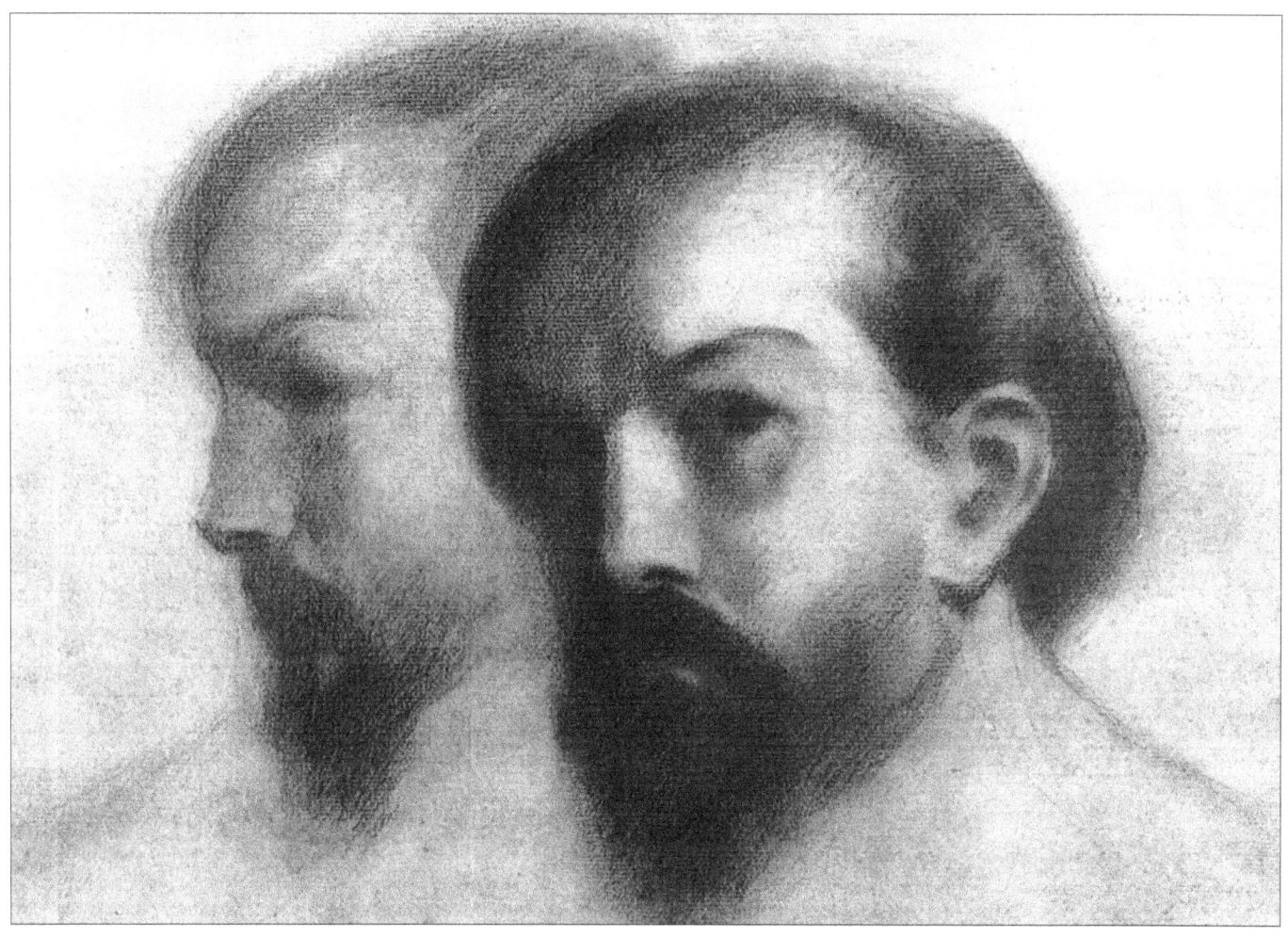

was diagnosed and the composer spent significant time in seclusion, which may have reduced access to him. Gibran will claim that the musician had indeed posed for him one afternoon in his Paris studio and "inquired eagerly of Mr. Gibran about the Oriental scale, a subject vital to the musician in his present method of introducing Oriental themes into his compositions."[8]

The portrait of Debussy is of very low technical proficiency and skill and is far from a true likeness of the subject. The profile in particular is merely an approximation. The treatment of the eye area, however, foreshadows Gibran's future successful portraits. The treatment of the hair is cursory and inaccurate. Several months again elapsed until the next update. In September 1910, just a few weeks before Gibran's departure from France, he writes to Mary: "Last week I made two drawings, one of Rostand, the poet, and the other Henri Rochefort, the great writer and critic. And I am yet waiting for a word from Rodin. Sarah Bernhardt is playing in London, but I hope she will come back before I leave Paris. Most of the great artists are not to be found in Paris during the summer, and I have made a great mistake in not doing more during the winter."[9]

---

8   Ruth Danenhower: Artist puts Roosevelt, Wilson and Edison in his Temple of Fame. *The New York Press*, June 7, 1914.
9   *Letters of Kahlil Gibran*, page 50.

Edmond Rostand

Edmond Rostand (1868-1918) was a natural choice for the Temple of Art series. His fame in the French capital was well established; his signature works *Cyrano de Bergerac* and *L'Aiglon* were constant staples in Parisian theatres. In 1902, Rostand became the youngest writer ever elected to the *Académie française*. He relocated to Cambo-les-bains, in the Basque Pyrenees, in 1903 for health reasons seeking a cure for his pleurisy. Here he built himself a villa, now a Rostand museum, and worked on his next play which was not produced until February 1910. It is therefore likely that he fell in the category of "the great artists not found in Paris" and that Gibran's portrait of him was based on a photograph. Gibran characterized Rostand "as clever, but artificial; one who started as a dreamer and continues as a money maker."[10] Gibran's expressed opinion of Rostand is consonant with contemporary evaluations of the poet seeking material success and pandering to prevailing political currents that led him for example to pen *L'Aiglon* in parallel with the strong Napoleonic nostalgia movement gripping France at the end of the nineteenth century.

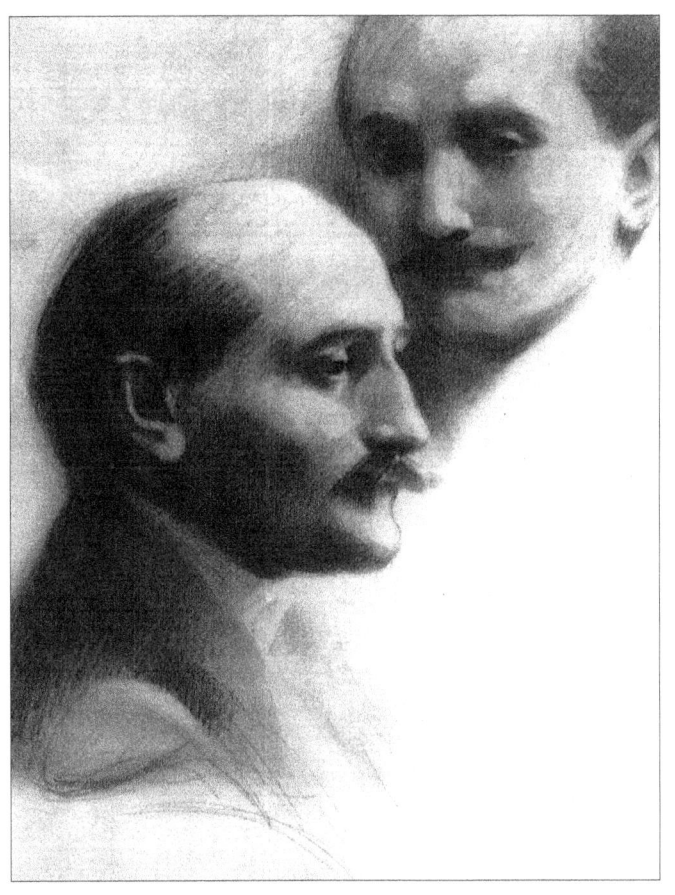 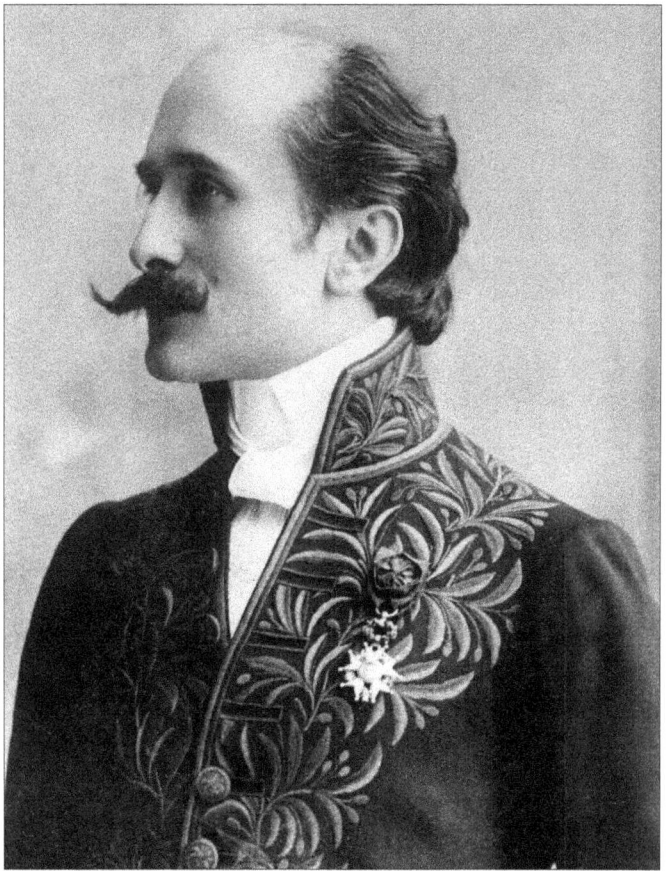

---

10 Ruth Danenhower: Artist puts Roosevelt, Wilson and Edison in his Temple of Fame. *The New York Press*, June 7, 1914.

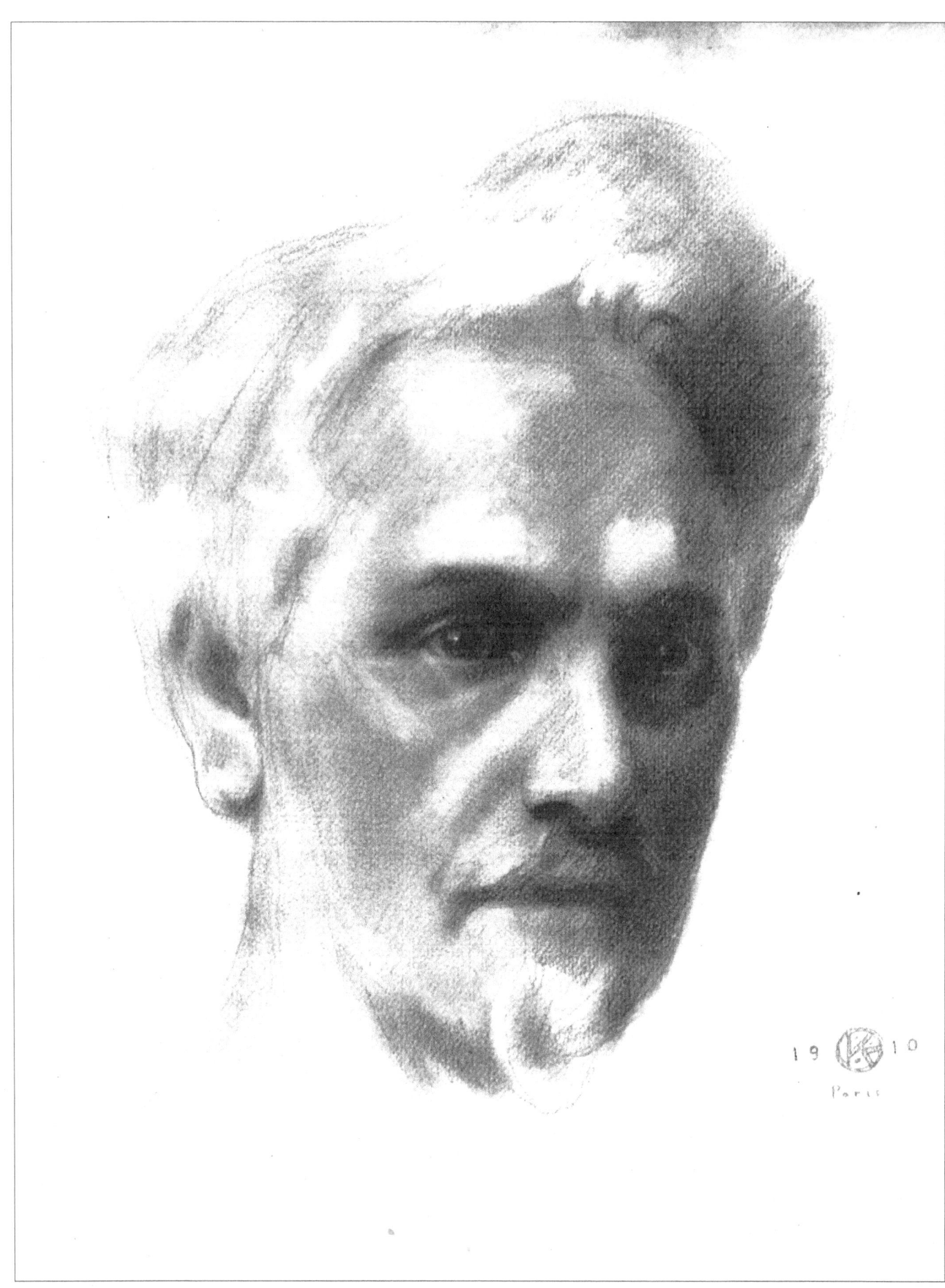

Parisian Luminaries

HENRI ROCHEFORT

Henri Rochefort (1831-1913) on the other hand was in the waning phase of his career when Gibran produced his portrait. The staunch opponent of Napoleon III, who earned for his accomplishments a statue of his likeness by Rodin, had become significantly marginalized after his anti-Semitic stance in the Dreyfus Affair. Victor-Henri Rochefort was a gifted polemical journalist under the Second Empire and the Third Republic who distinguished himself, at first, as a supporter of the extreme left and later as a champion of the extreme right.

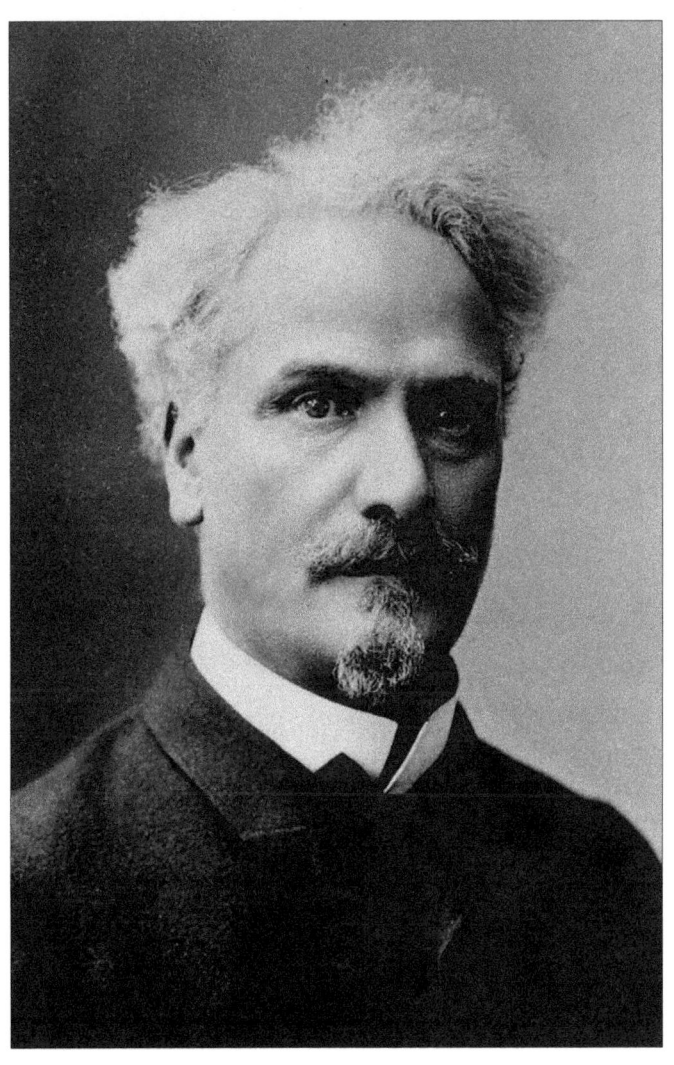

Gibran credited Rochefort with the idea of the Temple of Arts: "The idea was suggested to this Syrian by his very good friend, the late Henri Rochefort, world famous as a journalist and duelist in Paris. Rochefort's idea was to have the portfolio include the twenty-five greatest living contributors to the creative arts and to publish it under the title 'The Temple of Art.' Mr. Gibran immediately started the portfolio with a drawing of the journalist himself, and now counts himself fortunate to have made it before the death of his friend two months ago... The study of Rochefort, with his noble brow, [has] all the beauty of splendid heads of sculpture."[11] Gibran's portrait of Rochefort captures the fierce intensity of his subject and his wild hair, and echoes Manet's celebrated portrait of Rochefort in 1881 and Rodin's bust of him in 1884.

The portraits of both Rostand and Rochefort by Gibran display a remarkable improvement in draughtsmanship, and remarkable resemblance to photographic portraits of both by the famed photographer Felix Nadar!

---

11 Ruth Danenhower: Artist puts Roosevelt, Wilson and Edison in his Temple of Fame. *The New York Press*, June 7, 1914. Rochefort actually died in 1913.

Kahlil Gibran - Portraits

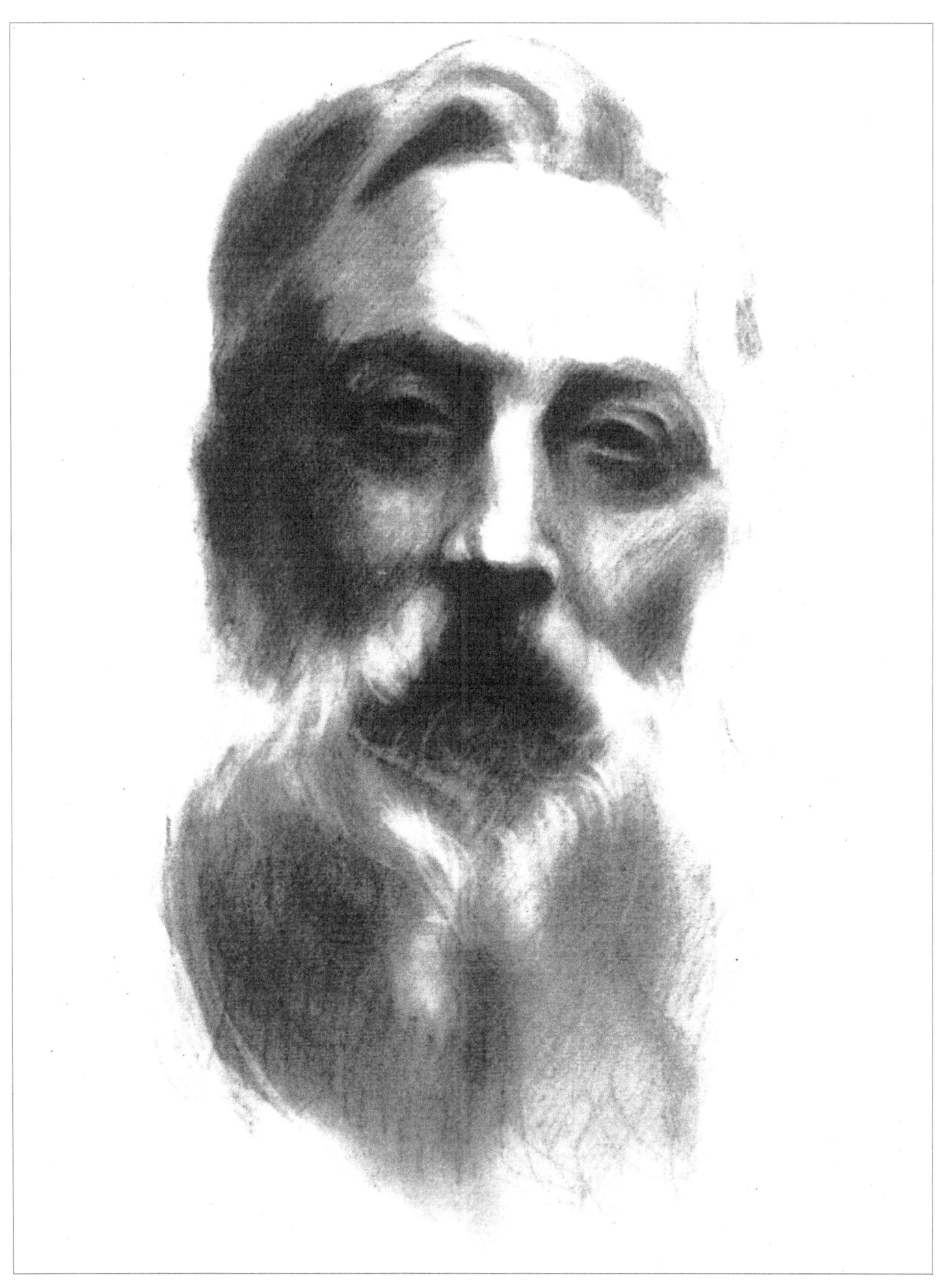

Parisian Luminaries

The Master of Clay - Auguste Rodin

Rodin was pre-eminent in the formation of Gibran's artistic concepts and approaches. It is sufficient to examine Gibran's series on The Centaurs to realize how a single small marble figurine by Rodin could inspire a body of work by Gibran in pencil, watercolors, and oils. This influence was articulated by Gibran freely and recurrently in his conversations with Mary Haskell, and starkly expressed in the prose-poem he penned as a tribute to Rodin. Gibran was devoted to Rodin and his work. His correspondence with Mary[12] and her diary are replete with references to Rodin's work and to portraits of Rodin by Carriere[13] and others.[14]

When news of Rodin's death in November of 1917 reached Gibran in New York, he rushed to pen an elegy of the French artist in English and sent it to Mary on November 25 to polish:[15] "Beloved Mary - Will you not read, correct, change and make whole this prose-poem to Rodin? I would like to have it back soon … so that I may try to publish it together with my drawing of the great man." Mary dutifully made some corrections, but it is not clear if the text was ever published at the time.

"To August Rodin

Master of Clay, to what element more chaste than clay have you turned your versed hands? And what nobler form than man does now hold your searching eyes? And what higher dreams you dream today?

Master of Clay, what substance more yielding than clay has claimed your art? What light, what shadow, what lines more certain have arrested your vision? And what bolder dreams you dream today?

In my youth, while wandering among those ancient hills, where mallet and chisel have long been dumb, I uttered your name. And it seemed as if an invisible being spoke through my lips to break the uneventful silence. Then the veil was lifted, and I beheld you in that thrice-hallowed company of master-men chose to build the house of God that man may be sheltered and man's soul may dwell in knowledge of itself. And I was comforted and my heart knew that Life was not the shattered memories of yesterday, nor the dim hopes of tomorrow; but that all time, all space, all earth, all spirit were one urging wave of

---

12 Suheil Bushrui and Joe Jenkins: *Kahlil Gibran: Man and Poet*, page 128; *Beloved Prophet*, page 130; *Letters of Kahlil Gibran*, page 445.
13 Mary Haskell's diary, entry for December, 1910, University of North Carolina Library.
14 *Beloved Prophet*, pp 145-146.
15 *Beloved Prophet*: page 292. *Letters of Kahlil Gibran*, page 546.

urging songs. And I was gladdened, for I heard in your voice the murmur of Nineveh and Thebes and Athens and Florence. And I was lifted for I saw in you the golden thread upon Life's eternal loom.

Master of Clay, would that you have stayed longer. Would that you have waited through this roaring night for earth's second dawn. Would that you have tarried to see the fuller face of France and to fashion her freer body that man may gaze upon the image of his own freer self."

Gibran submitted the piece to the *Century Magazine*, [16] which declined it. The periodical did publish in March of 1918 a reminiscence of Rodin by Judith Cladel whose father was a friend of the artist, and with whom she had been associated for 15 years.[17] Cladel had recently published a book about Rodin replete with excerpts from his notebooks to which he had given her access.[18]

August Rodin (1840-1917) was Gibran's idol. Gibran emulated the great French artist and his style in many of his works, an aspect noted by American reviewers of Gibran.[19] Gibran had met Rodin twice while in Paris, and both times in a public forum: the first during a visit to Rodin's studio[20] and the second during the annual April exhibits at the 1909 Salon.[21] Gibran tells Mary that the first visit was with a friend who introduced him to Rodin without identifying who the friend was. In his biography of Gibran, Mikhail Naimy places this visit to Rodin's studio in the context of a visit by the students of the Academy Julian at which Gibran was enrolled. He further tells us that it was during this visit that Rodin spoke to the students of Blake and sparked Gibran's interest in the British poet-artist.[22] Indeed, Naimy claims that it was Rodin who inspired Gibran to study Blake. In the aforementioned visit to Rodin's studio, the French sculptor answered the questions of the visiting art students about various topics in the arts and in the course of his remarks, he mentioned Blake and how the muses of Poetry and Art cooperated to enrich his talent making his drawings more poetic and his poetry more artistic. After the visit, Naimy tells us, Gibran hastened to a used bookstore and bought an edition of Blake's work. Fate seemed to have led Gibran to Rodin who in turn led him to Blake!

---

16 *Letters of Kahlil Gibran*, page 548.
17 *The Century*, volume 95, No. 5, March 1918, pp. 694-696.
18 Judith Cladel: *Rodin: The Man and His Art, with leaves from his notebooks*, The Century Company, NY, 1917, translated from the French.
19 'A Poet-Painter of Lebanon' *American Monthly Review of review*, volume 59, 1919
20 *Letters of Kahlil Gibran*, page 18.
21 Jean Gibran and Kahlil Gibran: *Kahlil Gibran: His life and World*, page 183; *Letters of Kahlil Gibran*, page 21.
22 Mikhail Naimy: *Kahlil Gibran: a Biography*, Philosophical Library, NY, 1950, pp 88-89.

Parisian Luminaries

This association between Rodin and Blake will be conflated later into the marketing legend used by the Knopf publishing house to claim that Rodin called Gibran the 'Blake of the Twentieth Century,' or other variants of the same. The claim first appeared with the publication of Gibran's book *The Madman* and was reiterated with every subsequent book by the Syrian writer.

Early reviewers of *The Madman*, while seeming not to contest the veracity of the claim, noted that the apposition was farfetched and that Gibran appeared to draw more from Rodin and Nietzsche than from Blake. A reviewer in *The Dial* conceded: "It is not strange that Rodin should have hoped much of this Arabian poet. For in those parables and poems, which Gibran has given us in English, he curiously seems to express what Rodin did with marble and clay. Both sculptor and poet show an imagination that goes to the mountains and the elements of strength, a desire to give human things a universal quality, a mellow irony, and a love of truth which is not afraid of platitudes. Rodin compared Gibran to William Blake. But the parables collected in *The Madman* are more reminiscent of Zarathustra's maskings and unmaskings, of the long rising rhythms of Tagore."[23] This was similarly affirmed in *The American Review of Reviews*: "Mr. Gibran is a follower of Blake and Rodin. With Rodin, he joins his definite patterns in art to the infinite by direct symbolism; with Blake, he is a lover of the free bounding line. The human form is to him the one eternal perfect symbol."[24]

Soon, however, commentators became tired of the assertion and cast significant doubt as to its veracity and relevance. Aleister Crowley commented in the *Equinox*: "It is not very sensible to compare Mr. Gibran with Blake, because Blake was a genius whose every act was wrought from the white heat of passion. This is a smaller fish swimming in shallower and calmer waters."[25]

A review of *The Madman* in the *New Republic* quipped: "How much English Rodin had in hand for his Blake, whose prophetic works his own countrymen find hard enough to make out is uncertain… Set against Blake Kahlil Gibran lacks Blake's awe, Blake's aspect of a prophetic titan in a bewildered cosmos."[26]

Harriet Monroe in the journal *Poetry* had this to say: "If August Rodin actually called this Syrian poet 'The William Blake of the twentieth century,' as the slip-cover reports, I can only smile in remembering from personal acquaintance with the great Frenchman, his serene

---

23   *The Dial*, November 30, 1918, page 510.
24   'A Poet-Painter of Lebanon' *American Monthly Review of review*, volume 59, February 1919, page 212.
25   *The Equinox*, volume 3, No. 1, March 1919, pages 296-297.
26   *The New Republic*, May 3, 1919, pages 29-30.

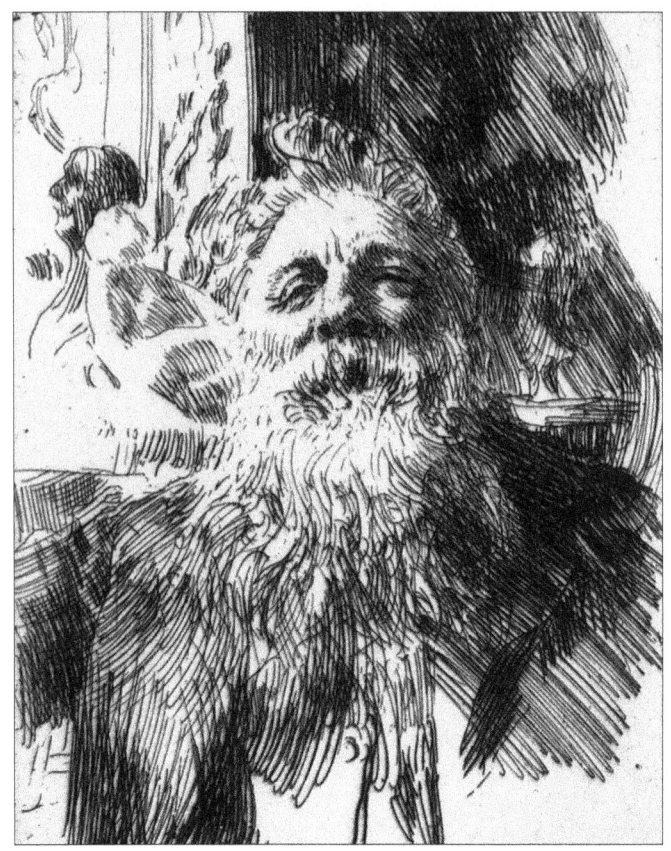
Portrait of Rodin by Anders Leonard Zorn

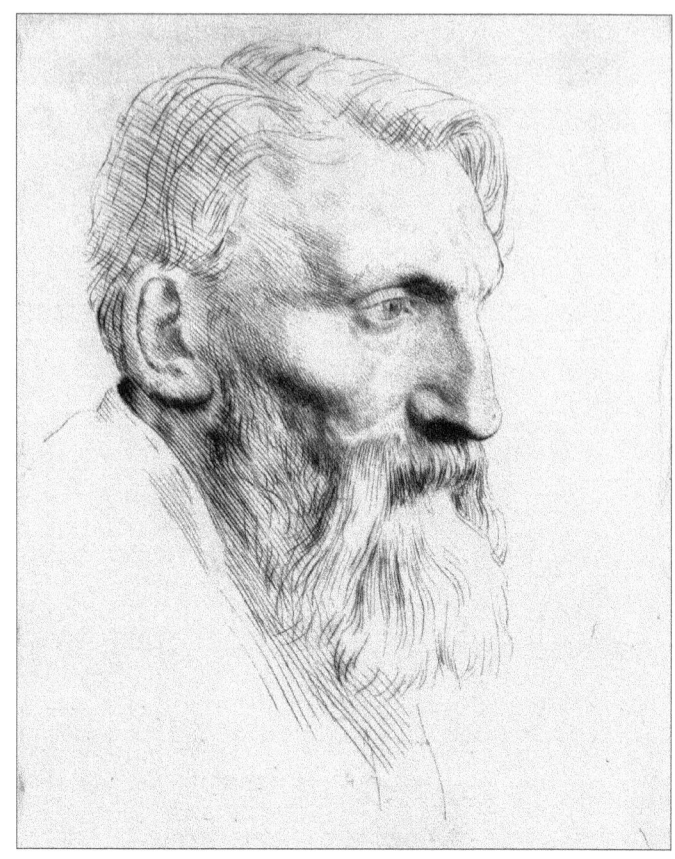
Portrait of Auguste Rodin by Alphonse Legros

amiability toward all fellow artists; and in this case it was the fellow artist – the limner, not the poet – that Rodin's alleged remark must have referred to. But even Mr. Gibran's drawings, though much more interesting than his parables, are a long way off from William Blake."[27]

Doubts about the verdict continued unabated. "August Rodin is said to have called Gibran "the William Blake of the Twentieth century," but the judicious will dispute that verdict. Blake had something like a definite and constructive philosophy. He conveyed an overpowering sense of vision and other-worldliness. We fail to find these in Kahlil Gibran. He arrests with striking imagery and sometimes he seems to be near the heights of symbolism, but his poetry and his drawings would never compensate us for the loss of Blake."[28]

The most severe criticism of the claim of Rodin's comparison came in *The Nation* in 1920 on the publication of Gibran's book *Twenty Drawings*.

Rodin is reported to have said of him: "I know of no one else in whom poetry and drawing

---

27 HM, Journeymen Poets, *Poetry*, volume 14, No. 5, August 1919, pages 277-281.
28 *The Argonaut*, volume 85, August 30, 1919, page 136.

are so linked as to make him a new Blake." This remark is hardly worth serious consideration. To the thoughtful student who knows his Blake, the conceptions of Gibran are tepid indeed by comparison. In Blake the atmosphere is charged with electricity – the symbols leap and swim in pools of sidereal fire… In Gibran's art … the symbols are as lifeless as a cluster of dull bubbles on still water."[29] The article continues in this vein contrasting Blake and Gibran.

It is curious that the most notorious of Gibran's acolytes, Barbara Young, went against the marketing claim stating in her hagiography of Gibran that she "can think of no two artists more unlike in reality."[30] The statement comparing him to Blake is not the only allegation that Gibran ascribed to Rodin. The French artist is also reported to have nicknamed Gibran "the sculptor who paints." [31]

The idea that Gibran was Rodin's pupil reverberated among Gibran's social circle. In her book *Remembering*, Nathalie Sedgwick Colby describes him as a guest at her Sunday salon events:

> "Kahlil Gibran, the Syrian painter and poet, once Rodin's pupil, a powerful little man who later became my friend. Immense tragic eyes he had to pity the world with, and a laugh at it in the corner of his mouth. An Arabic rasp edged the soft depth of his voice when he got annoyed. He got annoyed at American slapdash ways, for he demanded a ceremonious give-take in his friendships. He had a right to set his terms, for his greatest book, *The Prophet*, a volume of prophetic reverberations, was then in its ninth year, and is still gaining impetus.
>
> "I was told that it had reverberated as far as Queen Mary, who was put into complete reverse by the chapter which begins, "Your children are not your children.""[32]

It is important to put to rest in a definitive way the myth that Rodin called Gibran "the Blake of the 20th century". The claim is patently false, as it carries no documentary evidence, is not consistent with Gibran's description of the circumstances of his encounters with Rodin. Further, it is extremely unlikely as the oeuvre of Gibran on which such a claim might be based would have been totally unknown to the French artist. Knopf, and by inference Gibran who we suspect intimated to Knopf that the story did happen, are practicing what the French adage clearly describes: "*A bon mentir qui vient de loin!*"[33] It is utterly impossible for Rodin to have

---

29 Glen Mullin: Blake and Gibran. *The Nation*, April 10, 1920, volume 110, Spring Book Supplement, pp. 485-486.
30 Barbara Young: *This Man From Lebanon*, Knopf, New York, 1945, page 22.
31 Ruth Danenhower: Artist puts Roosevelt, Wilson and Edison in his Temple of Fame. *The New York Press*, June 7, 1914.
32 Nathalie Sedgwick Colby, *Remembering*, Boston, Little, Brown and company, 1938, page 238.
33 Lies best who comes from afar!

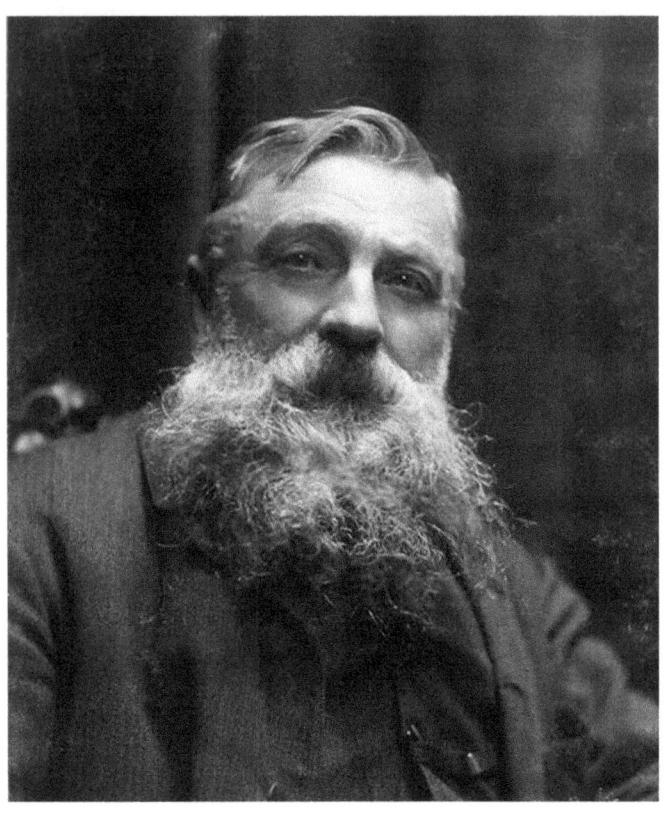
Photograph of Rodin by Jacques Moreau

made the remark: Gibran's opus by the time he met Rodin deserved no such a label and Rodin was completely ignorant of Gibran's work. Alice Raphael, likely with Gibran's consent, compounded the falsehood by expanding its context claiming in the introduction to Gibran's book *Twenty Drawings* in 1919 that Gibran "worked with Rodin and he exhibited at the Salon a series of portraits, which included Debussy, Rostand, Sarah Bernhardt, and Rodin himself."[34]

Refuting the claim should not be construed as a denial of any similarities between the work of Gibran and that of the British poet. Josephine Preston Peabody, Gibran's first muse and love, compares Gibran's early works with those of Blake. She was evidently referring to drawings lost in the fire that consumed Fred Holland Day studio in Boston in 1904. Photographs of the exhibit in the local papers do allow such a comparison as the drawings have metaphysical symbolic representations. Mary Haskell also invoked the theme in her letters to Gibran and her diaries. Many scholars and commentators have since delved into the topic. The similarities between Gibran and Blake are probably imitative and stem from a body of work that Gibran produced mostly after the date of Rodin's alleged statement.

When we reconstruct the encounters between Gibran and Rodin, we find a narrative inconsistent with the claim. On February 7, 1909, Gibran writes to Mary Haskell:

"Few days ago I had the great pleasure of meeting Auguste Rodin the — greatest sculptor of modern time, in his own studio. He has the head of a wise Jew and the expression of an honest Christian. He was indeed very kind to me and to the friend who took me to him. He showed us many wonderful things both in marble and in plaster. I shall not try now to describe his work to you, for you have already seen great deal of it and understood its depth and its height and its strange bold beauty. I am sure, dear Mary, that you remember my telling you once of an Arab who went to Italy from the desert and saw the work of

---

34 *Twenty Drawings*, Knopf, 1919.

Parisian Luminaries

Michel – Angelo and was so moved by its power that he wrote a beautiful poem called "The smiling Marble." When I came home from Rodin's studio I had the same feeling of that Arab, and I too wrote a sonnet on "Man the Creator." Rodin is indeed a creator. His work is a very great step towards the Unknown."[35]

A second chance encounter occurred in April of the same year.

"April is a month of Salons and Exhibitions in Paris. One of the great Salons was open few days ago and of course I went to see it. All the artists of Paris were there looking with hungry eyes on the shadows of the Souls of Men… Great Rodin was there. He recognized me and spoke to me about the work of a Russian sculptor saying "This man understood the beauty of form."

"I would have given anything to have that Russian hear what the great Master said of his work. A word from Rodin is worth a great deal to an artist."[36]

We find it unlikely that Gibran had the opportunity to have Rodin actually sit for the portrait. It is probable that Gibran produced the portrait based on commonly obtained photographs of the French sculptor. Gibran acknowledges the difficulty of securing a time with Rodin. "I love to draw the head of Rodin, but Rodin's time is given to great things. Only kings and princes can find a way to his studio. And yet a poor little artist might be able to find a way also."[37]

Indeed, by September 26, 1910, just a few weeks before Gibran's return to the US, he was still "waiting for word from Rodin."[38]

While there is serious doubt that Gibran executed his portrait of Rodin during an actual encounter, Gibran does not shy from embellishing the alleged encounter. In 1914, we find Gibran regaling a reporter with the circumstances of the drawing. "Perhaps Mr. Gibran's most interesting recollection of the work he did in France is of Rodin, a giant of genius whom he considers will be known and honored in future ages when most of the great ones of the portfolio will be forgotten. Before Mr. Gibran considered the drawing of the sculptor finished, Rodin insisted he should not touch it further. "Don't you know the saying that it takes two artists to make a picture?" the sculptor demanded. "One to do the work and the other to chop off his head at the point where he should stop!" Gibran also claimed that Rodin wrote to a Paris newspaper "that he considered Mr. Gibran's drawing the only adequate likeness of himself ever made. Mr.

---
35 *Letters of Kahlil Gibran*, page 18.
36 Jean Gibran and Kahlil Gibran: *Kahlil Gibran: His life and World*, page 183. *Letters of Kahlil Gibran*, page 21.
37 *Letters of Kahlil Gibran*, pp 41-42.
38 *Letters of Kahlil Gibran*, page 50.

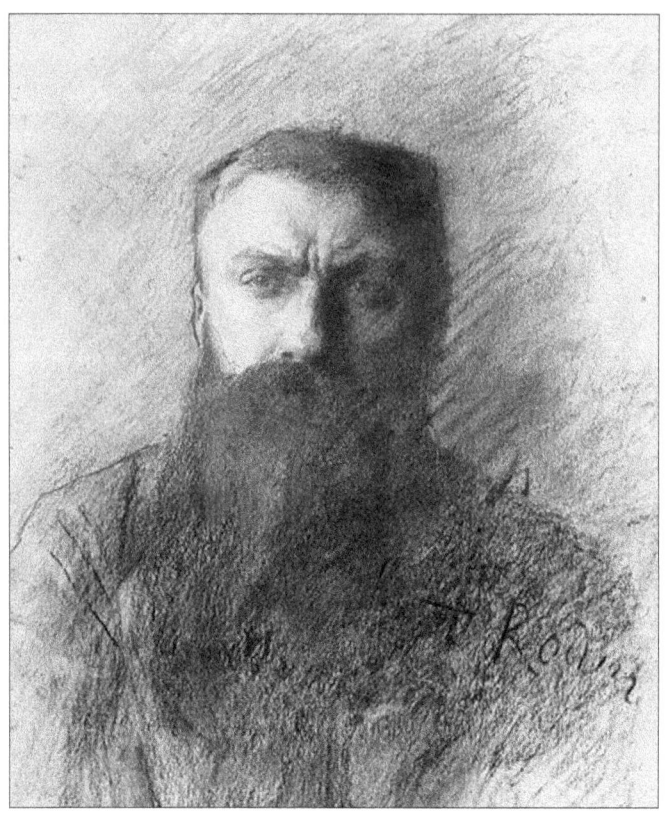
Auguste Rodin Self Portrait

Gibran says this is not so much a compliment to him as a true statement of the inadequacy of all other portraits, drawings and photographs of Rodin."[39]

On a visit to the studio of Davies in September 1913, Gibran asks the American artist to show him and Mary Haskell his drawing of Rodin. Mary remarked in her memoirs: "I could not have had a better object lesson in what Kahlil talks of as the life, the reality of great art. Kahlil's Rodin burst with growth. Davies is simply decorative, by the side of it, 'tapestry work' as Kahlil put it."[40]

Gibran's portrait of Rodin possesses exceptional power and depth and conveys to the observer the brilliance and creativity of the French artist. It also conveys the view of the portraitist himself who held his subject in such heroic awe. The correspondence makes it clear, however, that it is based on a photograph and Gibran's few personal encounters with the great Frenchman. Gibran seems to have channeled Michelangelo's image of the creator God in the panel on the creation of Adam to imbue his portrait. The calm assuredness of a great creator permeates this portrait. Gibran has stylized his subject's hair and beard into a classical form remote from the reality or attributes of his subject. He represents a subject with no flaws.

---

39 Ruth Danenhower: Artist puts Roosevelt, Wilson and Edison in his Temple of Fame. *The New York Press*, June 7, 1914.
40 *Beloved Prophet*, pp 145-146.

Boston Interlude

As soon as he settled back in Boston, Gibran resumed his pursuit of portraits. He drew relatives, friends of Mary Haskell, and teachers at her school. For the *Temple of Art* series, he drew on the contacts of his friends: Mary Haskell, Charlotte Teller, Fred Holland Day, and Ameen Rihani to introduce him to desired subjects.[1] On the advice of Day, he broadened the range of the series to include men of science, industry, politics, and academia. It is in the academia that he found his first American subjects.

THE ACADEMIA PONTIFFS - DR. RICHARD CLARKE CABOT AND CHARLES W. ELIOT

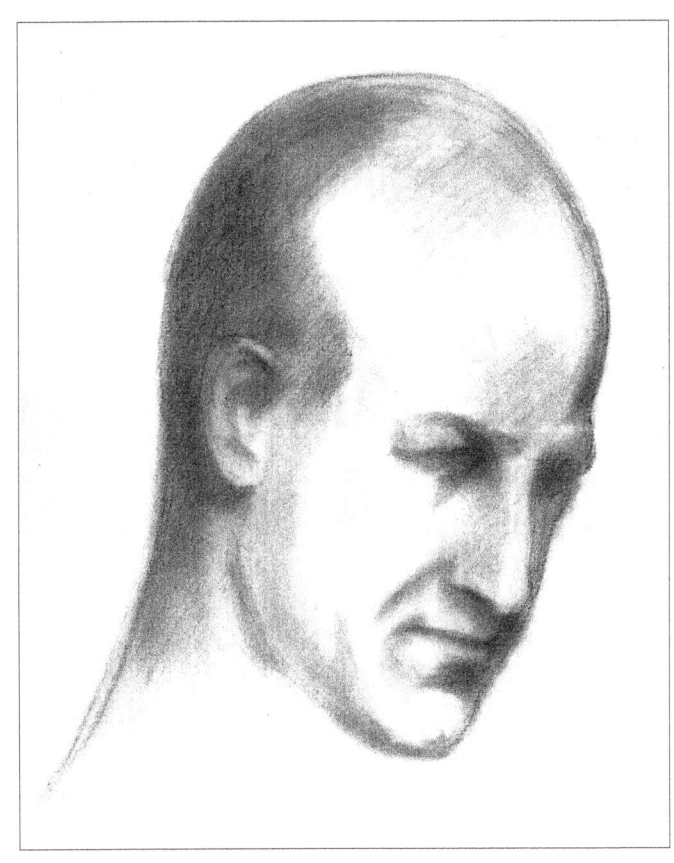

The first extant portrait for the *Temple of Art* series that Gibran drew in Boston was that of Dr. Richard Clarke Cabot, chief of staff at Massachusetts General Hospital, to whom he had been introduced by Mary Haskell.[2] Dr Cabot was one of the pioneers of clinical pathologic correlations in medicine and a renowned educator.[3] His wife, Ella Lyman Cabot, was a member of the Massachusetts Board of Education[4] and by virtue of this position well acquainted with Ms. Haskell's school and person. Gibran drew Dr. Cabot in early December 1910 in his office while he was at work and the portrait was a true likeness of the subject. Dr. Cabot liked the portrait and agreed to introduce Gibran to the illustrious president of Harvard, *Charles William Eliot* (1834-1926).

---

1 Unlike the portraits executed in Paris, the portraits drawn in America have ample documentary evidence of being drawn during actual encounters with their subjects.
2 *Beloved Prophet*, page 23.
3 *Boston Globe*, February 10, 1915.
4 *Boston Globe*, February 25, 1909.

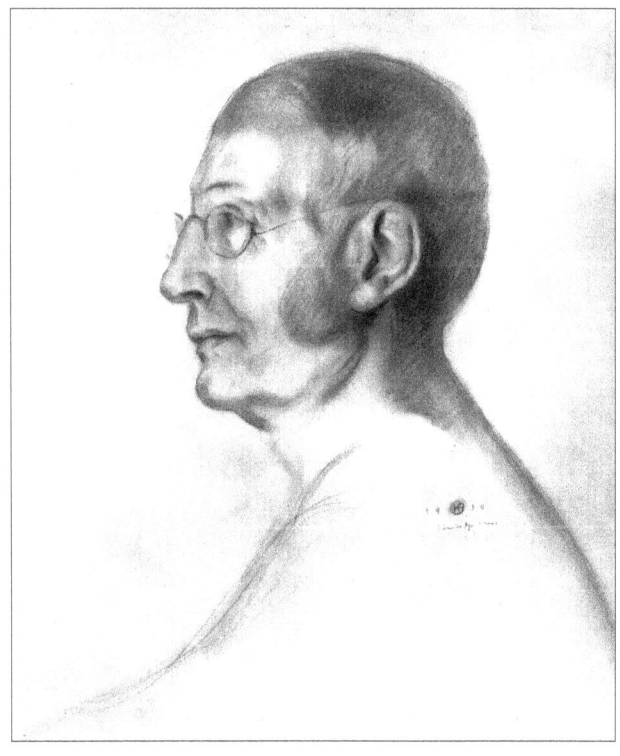

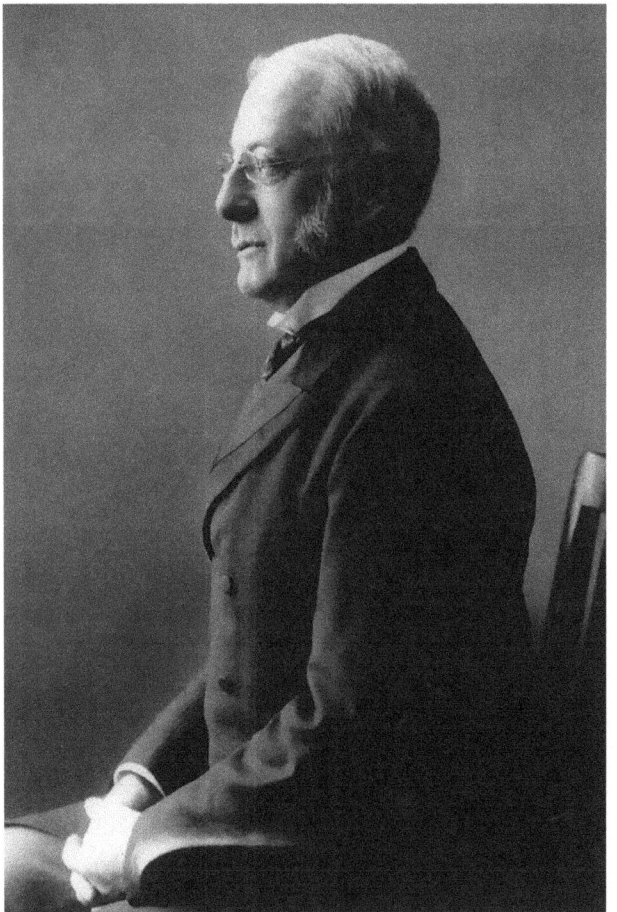

Charles W. Eliot had retired after a forty-year tenure as president of Harvard University. He was 35 years old when he was elected to the post, the youngest man to have ever held that post. He was an analytical chemist, yet is remembered for his stewardship of the university and his contribution to the humanities.

On December 19, 1910, President Eliot received a handwritten note from Kahlil Gibran. The letter follows the same formulaic approach that Gibran adopted, basically declaring the general scope of the project ("I am making a series of drawings of the big men who represent the art and knowledge of this day"); enticing his addressee with a list of prior participants (I have already drawn Rodin, Debussy, Rochefort and others); and defining the parameters of their requested commitment. In future versions of the letter, Gibran updated the list of completed portraits customizing it to the perceived interests of the addressee and in some he listed Eliot as a completed portrait. Gibran included, whenever possible, a note from a supporting figure known to the addressee; in Eliot's case, a note from Richard C. Cabot was enclosed.

Eliot agreed to be drawn, but not before quizzing Gibran as to the eventual use he may make of the portrait. Gibran assured him in a subsequent letter that he would eventually publish the series in a book, but it "will require some time for completion."[5]

Gibran and Eliot's meeting on December 28, 1910, exceeded the allotted half hour for the portrait

---

5 Paul M. Wright: The President meets the Prophet: Charles W. Eliot's 1910 encounter with Kahlil Gibran. *Harvard Library Bulletin*, volume 21, No. 3, 2010, pp. 79-92.

execution as the two engaged in conversation about the Near East. Recalling their meeting almost four years later, Gibran confided in Mary Haskell of the change in his evaluation of Eliot:

> "I remember so well my morning with Charles Eliot—how I spent half an hour drawing him and he kept me for two hours after, talking to me. And I listened with respect—and thought with surprise how much he knew about the Near East—And afterwards I realized he knew nothing—that it was all gleanings—two + two put together to make four—I realized he was cold & dead—and that I who had listened to him as to a big man, and admired him, was a little flame, a little bit of real life. Those hours with him opened a great many other people to me, after I understood them, but I did not understand until a little while after I had been in New York." [6]

Contrary to Gibran's later assertions, Eliot was well acquainted with international affairs and had traveled widely on behalf of the Carnegie Peace Foundation.[7]

The portrait on the opposite page shows Eliot in profile. Eliot, whose right cheek was disfigured by a large birthmark, always presented his left profile for portraits and photographs. In the portrait, Gibran conveys to the observer a softer and warmer impression of the venerable scholar than the formal magisterial image of a university president in an austere suit. Indeed, the bare shoulders hark more to statues of Greek philosophers than to a Harvard professor.

During this period in Boston, Gibran hoped to draw Frank Sanborn through the intervention of Mr. Day,[8] but when this did not materialize, he called on his friend Ameen Rihani for an introduction.[9] It is not known, however, whether he ever succeeded in this endeavor. Charlotte Teller wrote to her friends in the performing arts the director producer David Belasco (1853-1931)[10] and the operatic singer Bispham soliciting their approval to be drawn. In surviving copies of her letters, she echoes the formulaic approach of Gibran's own letters with a personal touch exhorting Belasco for example to let Gibran's Syrian talent, trained to its task in Paris, gaze upon Belasco's Portuguese, Spanish and Jewish features and reveal his true self![11]

---

6   Mary Haskell papers.
7   *Boston Globe*, March 20, 1914.
8   Mary Haskell's diary, entry for January, 1911, University of North Carolina Library.
9   Letter to Ameen Rihani, April 5, 1911. In Gibran Khalil Gibran: *Complete Works: Letters* (in Arabic), page 95.
10 Mary Haskell's papers, letter dated April 23, 1911, University of North Carolina Library.
11 Letter from Charlotte Teller to David Belasco, April 23, 1911. Mary Haskell papers.

A Jovial Baritone - David Bispham

David Bispham (1857-1921) was visiting Boston to perform at an oratorio for Easter and had been approached by Charlotte Teller and persuaded to have Gibran draw his portrait for the series. She had given Bispham Mary Haskell's address as a person to contact which Bispham duly did and through her arranged an appointment during his short stay in the city.[12]

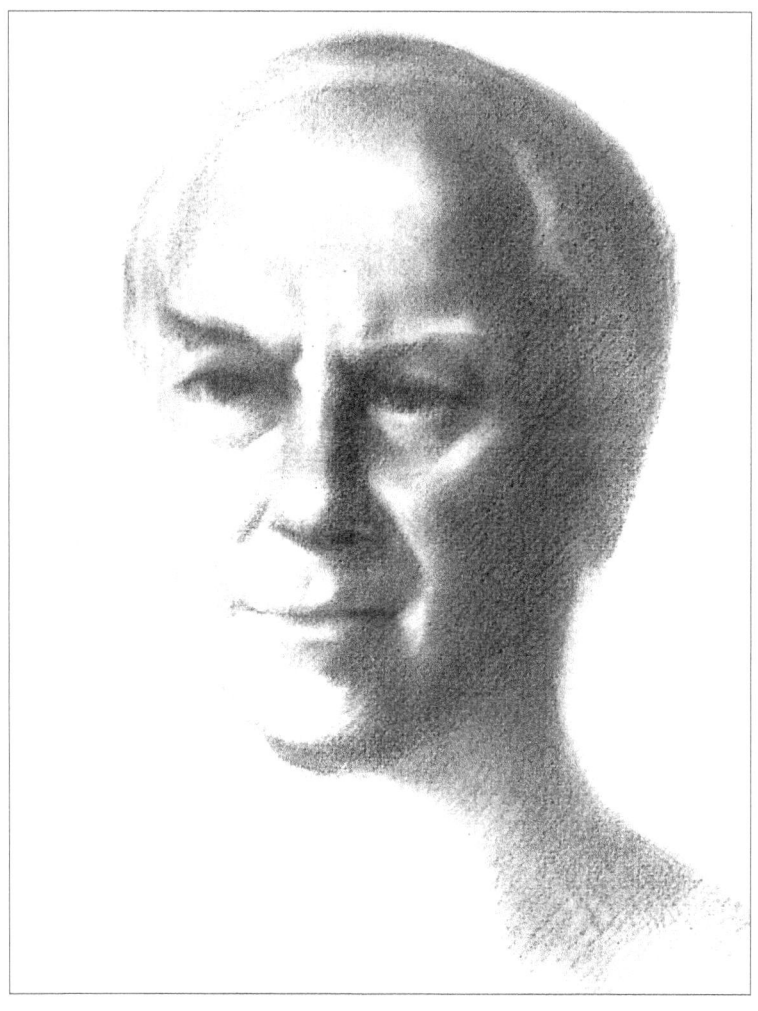

Bispham was renowned for his interpretive power, and as a singer of dramatic moods with "the ability to take a musical phrase, a line of melodic thought, sculptured as clearly as thought in marble, to expend labor, intelligence and art upon it and to endow it with a serene, a purifying loveliness in which the mind and the soul may bathe." [13]

The sitting took place on April 14, 1911, in Gibran's modest studio in the presence of Mary. Gibran enjoyed meeting Bispham immensely and was greatly amused by the singer's impersonations and colorful character.[14] Bispham apparently liked the portrait and would later entreat Gibran to give him a photograph of the portrait. Charlotte, however, suspected that Bispham was going to use the portrait for promotional purposes and warned Gibran not to provide a copy as it would taint the series, but Gibran was torn between his admiration of Bispham and Charlotte's warning [15]. The baritone is depicted as a powerful character, intent and serious with a slight frown. Mary commented in her diary that Gibran succeeded in capturing the multifaceted moods of Bispham's visage and the tragic and comedic roles he has personified on stage.

---

12 Letter from Bispham to Mary Haskell, April 12, 1911. Mary Haskell papers.
13 *The Boston Globe*, April 15, 1911.
14 Mary Haskell's diary, entry for April 1911, Mary Haskell papers. University of North Carolina Library.
15 *Letters of Kahlil Gibran*, page 106.

Boston Interlude

FACE OF AMERICAN MUSIC - ARTHUR FARWELL

Feeling constrained in Boston and encouraged by Charlotte to visit New York where he could stay at her place while she was on tour with a theatre group, Gibran headed to New York in May. In New York, he was reunited with his friend Ameen Rihani and through him and through Charlotte accessed a string of literati to add to his series.

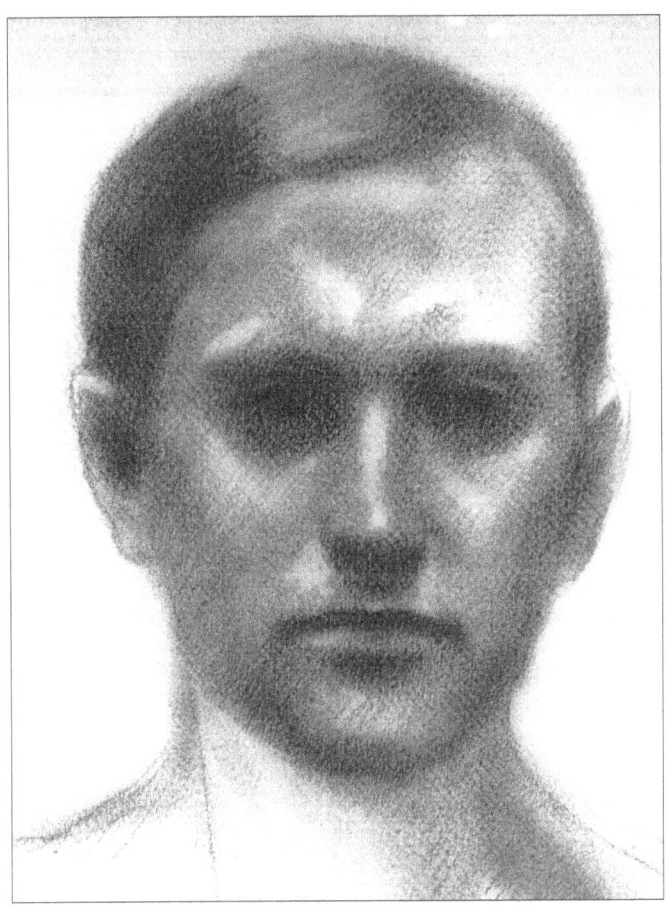

Arthur Farwell (1872-1952), the famous American composer and the President of the American Music Society, was his first subject during his exploratory visit to New York. Mary had provided Gibran with a letter of introduction to her friend,[16] and Gibran wrote to him on May 2, 1911 asking for an appointment and offering to show him the portfolio of his prior work on the series. The endeavor succeeded and he drew the portrait on May 5. "The drawing I made of Mr. Farwell is among the very best. He said it expresses his whole inner being, and he must have a Photograph taken from it." Indeed, in the portrait the composer appears dreamy, yet his gaze conveys a determination and power. Haskell saw in the portrait of her friend "the seer, the life beyond ordinary life, the inward being."[17]

As a composer, Falwell was a pioneer in championing a genuinely 'American' approach in music incorporating elements from American Natives tradition and attempting to lessen reliance on European forms. In addition to African-American and North Indian songs,[18] Falwell used material from Central America such as the legend of creation in his *The Domain of Hurakan* to mixed reviews.[19] He had recently written and composed a 'Hymn to Liberty' to be featured at the Fourth of July celebrations.[20]

---

16 Jean Gibran and Kahlil Gibran: *Kahlil Gibran*, page 209.
17 Mary Haskell's papers, June 1, 1911, diary entry.
18 *The New York Times*, April 16, 1911.
19 *The Brooklyn Daily Eagle*, February 13, 1911; *The Evening World*, February 13, 1911.
20 *The New York Times*, July 2, 1911; *The Brooklyn Daily Eagle*, July 30, 1911.

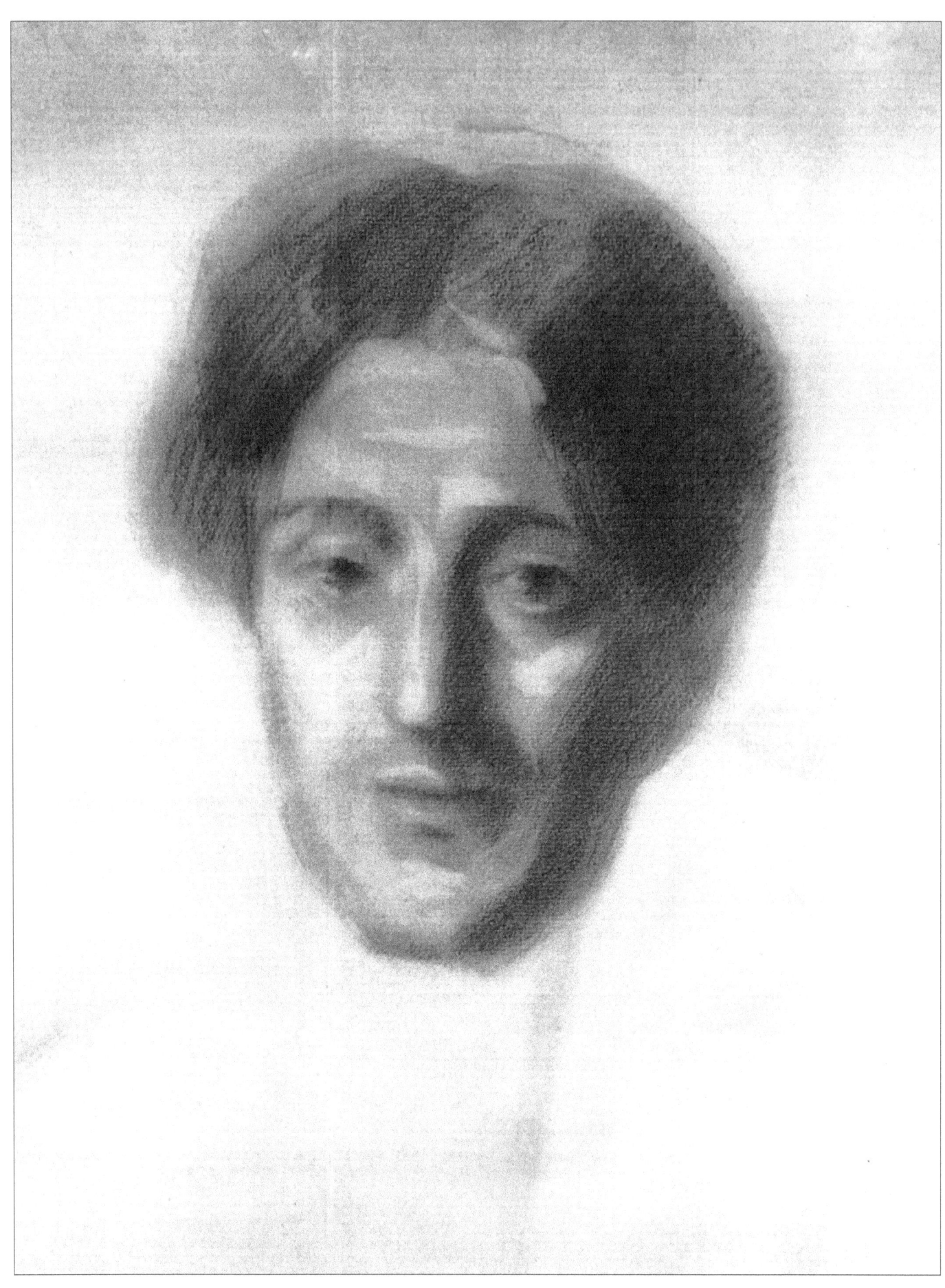

A Garland of Poets

On Sunday, March 26, 1916, *The New York Times* published a photograph of poets gathered at a farewell dinner given in honor of the English poet John Masefield who had just completed a tour of the US.[1] Featured in the photo were the poets Laurence Housman, Witter Bynner, Percy Mackaye, Edwin Markham, Cale young Rice, Louis Untermeyer, Vachel Lindsey, Amy Lowell, Josephine Dodge Daskan Bason, John Masefield, and Alfred Noyes. Gibran had drawn portraits of at least half of the poets present and was well acquainted with all.

Ashes Of Beauty - Richard LeGallienne

Richard LeGallienne (1866-1947), the prolific English poet living in New York, was a friend of Ameen Rihani. The two may have met because of LeGallienne's interest in eastern poetry (he had translated the quatrains of Omar Khayyam and odes from the Divan of Hafiz to some acclaim),[2] a common ground with Rihani who had translated to English the quatrains of the blind Syrian poet al-Maari. Rihani introduced Gibran to the English poet and a portrait ensued.[3] The fellow poets Markham and Russell commented that someone finally captured the real LeGallienne. The poet himself was saddened by the portrait's realism, an understandable reaction if we consider Mary Haskell's characterization of the portrait as depicting the "ashes of burnt beauty" and that it would make the angels weep![4] In a prose fancy titled *The Burial of Romeo and Juliette*, LeGallienne had written: "For indeed life has no beauty so wonderful as the beauty of death."[5]

Gibran's portrait of LeGallienne carries shades of ashes and weeping. Gone is the youthful beauty that had seduced Oscar Wilde. The poet's face is marked by the tragedies of his life. His first wife and second daughter died in 1894 in childbirth and he will carry with him, even in his second marriage, an urn containing her ashes. He remarried in 1897, but his second wife left him in 1903, on the grounds of alcoholism and womanizing, taking with her all his children. Le Gallienne's career had paralleled the tragic course of his personal life with critics dismissing his prolific output as "of no value to anyone."[6]

---

1   *The New York Times*, March 26, 1916.
2   *The Brooklyn Citizen*, February 16, 1902.
3   *Letters of Kahlil Gibran*, pp 73-75.
4   Mary Haskell's diary, entry for June 1, 1911, University of North Carolina Library.
5   LeGallienne, Richard: *The Burial of Romeo and Juliette*. The Blue Skye Press, 1904.
6   *Buffalo Courier*, May 1, 1904.

A great sadness appears to permeate the portrait. The once Adonis-like beauty of the poet has faded and the labors of life have left their traces on his forehead and around his eyes.

POET WITH A HOE - EDWIN MARKHAM

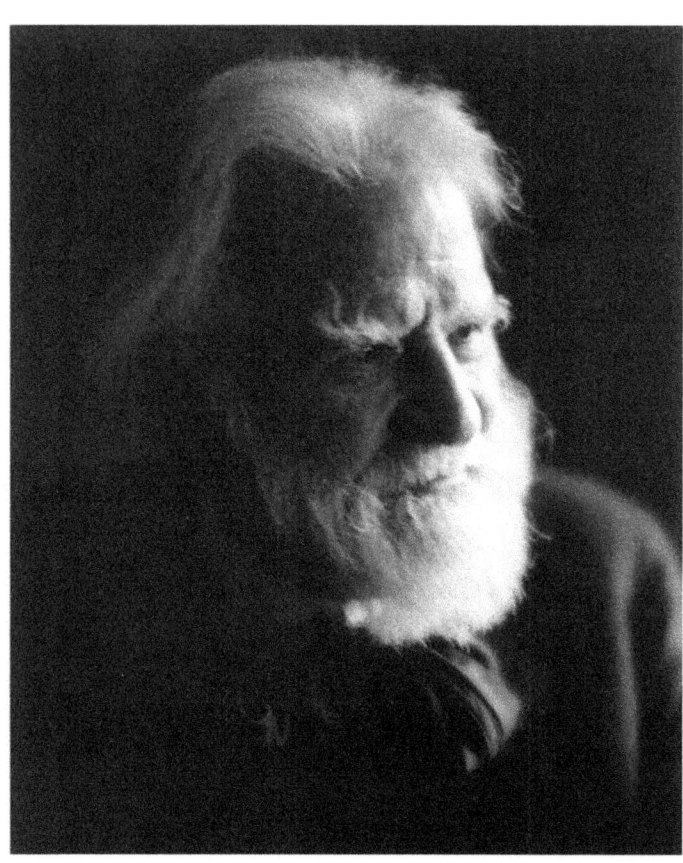

Edwin Markham (1842-1940), famed for his poem *Man with the Hoe*, and a supporter of Christian Socialism, was the next poet Rihani introduced Gibran to.[7] Markham admired eastern literature and was later to write favorably about Rihani's *Book of Khalid*[8] and Gibran's *The Prophet*. On May 21, Gibran accompanied Rihani on a visit to Markham, but could not execute the portrait.[9] He returned on May 23 and succeeded in not only capturing Markham's likeness, but also extracting from him a pledge to help secure for him his friend the poet *Joaquim Miller* whom Gibran also drew[10]. The poet of the working man is shown as a compassionate and caring elder. The elongated face has a sweetness to it.

It is curious, however, that both Rihani and Gibran remained silent about Markham publicly embracing the cause of Italy against criticism of the atrocities the Italian army was committing against Libyans in Tripoli.[11]

---

7   *Letters of Kahlil Gibran*, page 75.

8   "In *The Book of Khalid* Mr. Rihani writes a critique of our Western civilization as it appears to the wisdom of the East, ambition against contentment, activity against sweet idleness. Mr. Rihani is a man of ardent poetic temperament, a clever poet, and a man of unwordly ideals. He thinks nobly of life and writes with ease and grace. His hero, Khalid, explores many creeds seeking to find a way through the labyrinth of human thought."

9   *Letters of Kahlil Gibran*, page 75.

10 Salem Otto: *The letters of Kahlil Gibran and Mary Haskell*, page 76.

11 *The Brooklyn Daily Eagle*, November 28, 1911.

A Garland of Poets

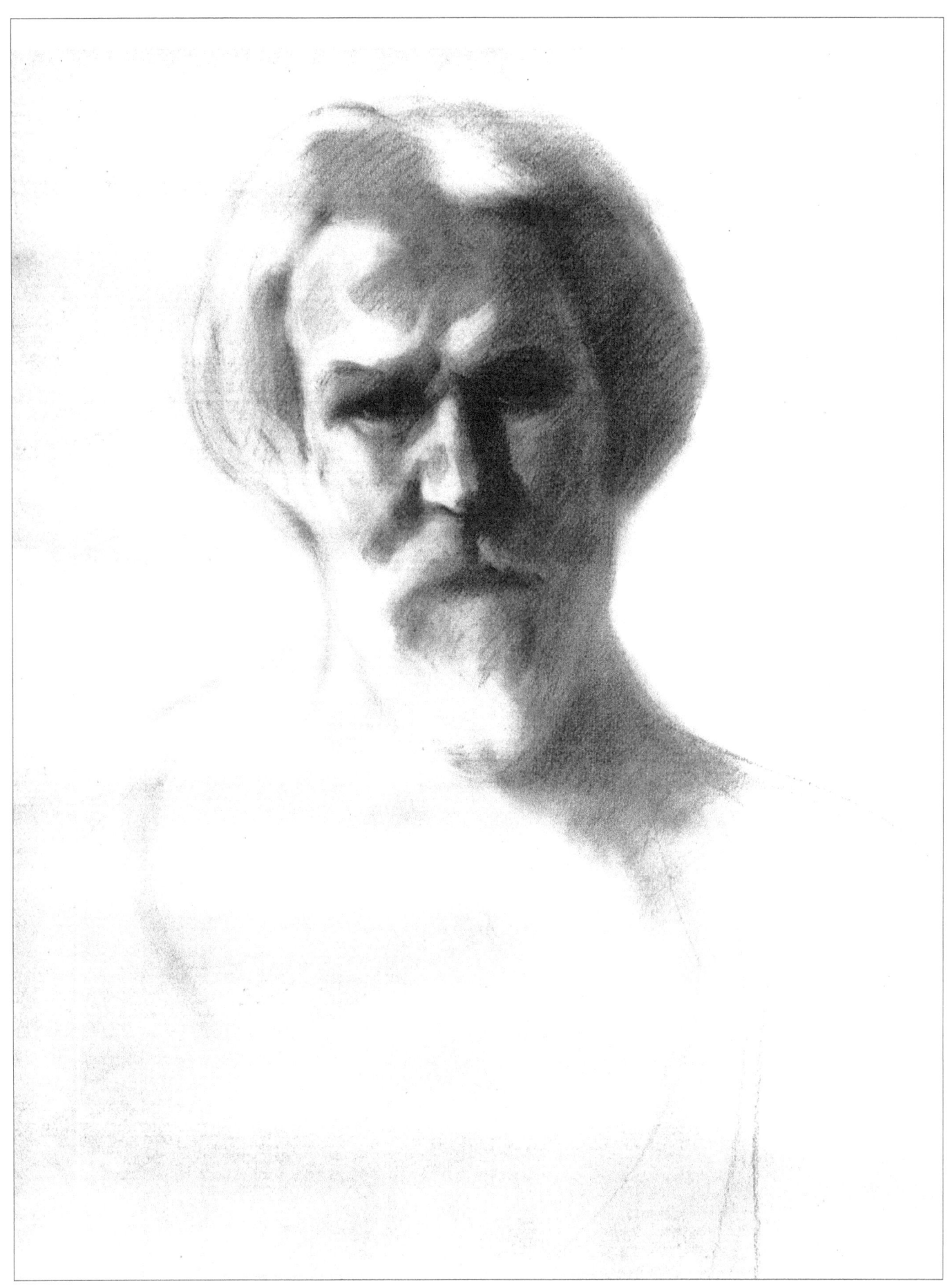

The Poet of the Sierras - Joaquin Miller

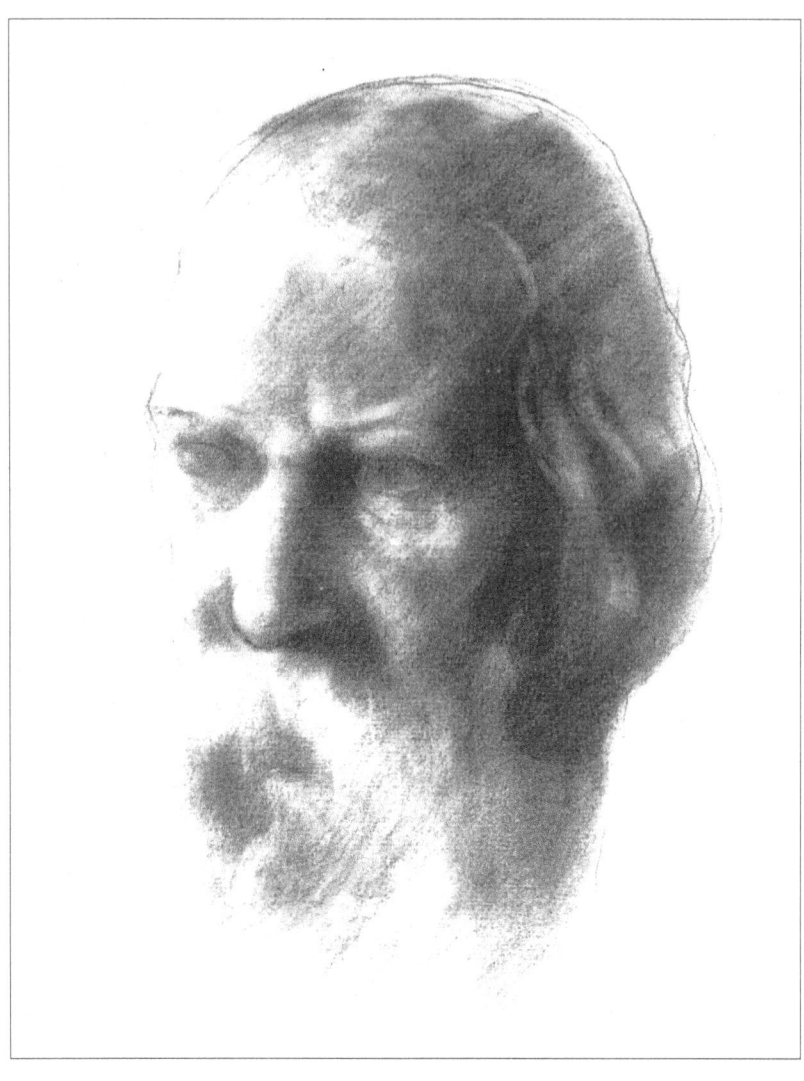

Markham did succeed in convincing his friend *Joaquin Miller* (1837-1913) to allow Gibran to draw his portrait. Miller was known as the 'poet of the Sierras' and was in his seventies when Gibran drew him. His original name was Cincinnatus Heine Miller, but he used Joaquin Miller as his pen name after he defended Joaquin Marietta, the famous Spanish-American outlaw who had been the terror of California for 10 years. He had spent a tumultuous life in the West before turning to law and literary pursuits. In 1870, Miller went to London where he published his collection *Songs of the Sierras*, which established his literary reputation. He was a very prolific writer publishing in excess of twenty books of poetry, essays and plays.[12] Miller's love of nature would have resonated with Gibran. Miller was an avid conservationist who called trees "God's first born."[13] We have, however, no testimonial of the sitting nor of any further association between Gibran and the elder poet. There is a wildness to the portrait of Joaquin Miller commensurate with his life story.

---

12 *Green Bay Press – Gazette*, November 10, 1911.
13 *The San Francisco Call*, April 3, 1905.

From the Mist of Ireland - William Butler Yeats

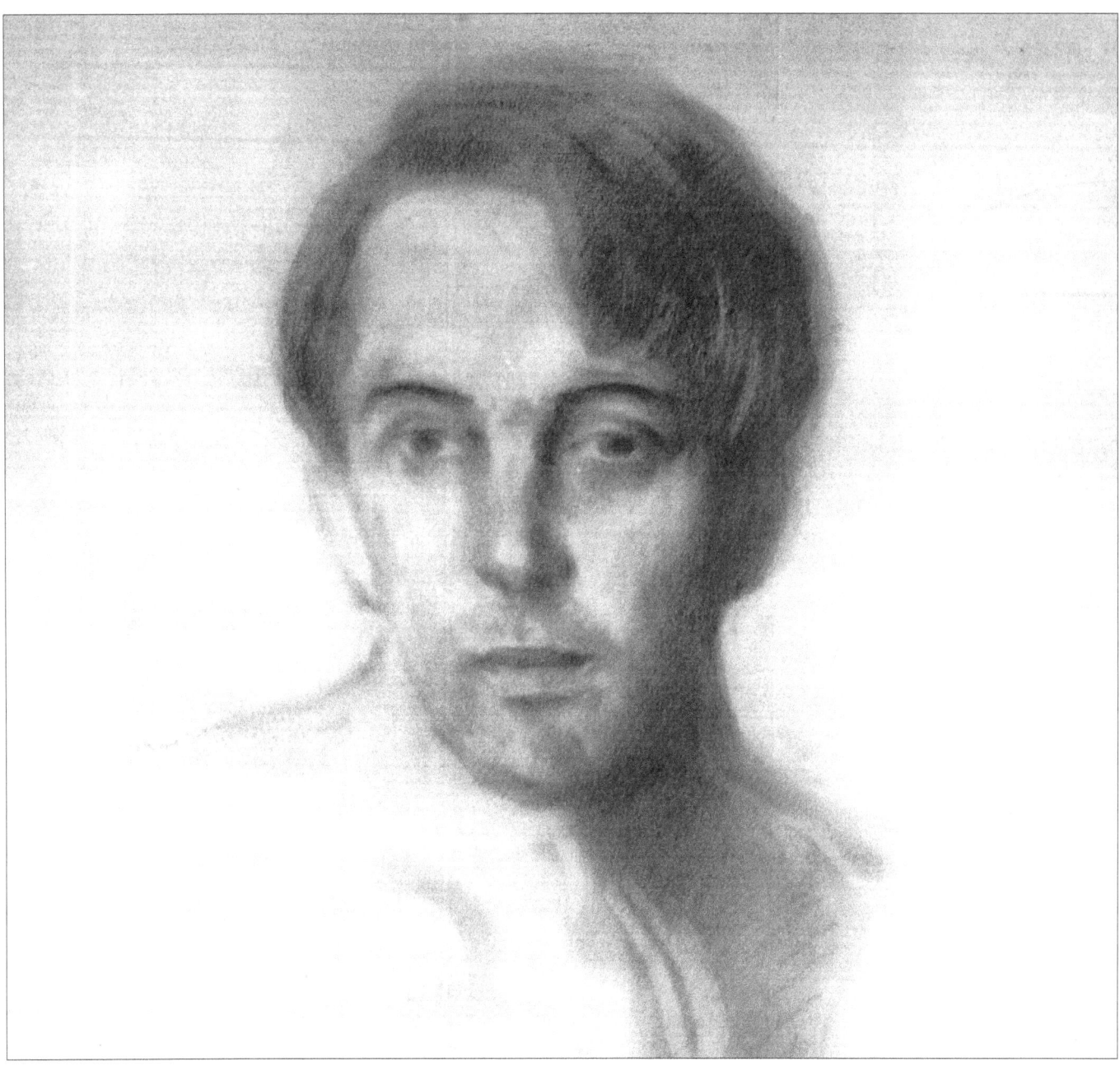

Gibran returned to Boston later that summer and had the opportunity to meet and draw *William Butler Yeats* (1865-1939). The Irish poet was visiting Boston along with the theatrical group The Abbey and was lecturing in Boston on various topics about the renaissance of Irish poetry and literature in general.[14] In September, Gibran and Mary attended one of these lectures, were introduced to Yeats by one of Mary's acquaintances, and Gibran secured an appointment to

---
14 A. Norman Jeffares: *W.B. Yeats: a new biography*, Farrar Straus Giroux, NY, 1988.

draw Yeats at his hotel later that week which he did to Mary's delight[15].

"September 28, 1911, Boston, Diary: We heard Yeats address the Drama League at the Plymouth Theatre — incredibly smooth-skinned and boyish looking for all his gray hairs, with manner half stage-struck at times — as if his mind had suddenly gone dry and dark. Then he seeks his notes again. He gesticulates as if by lesson, yet sincerely and peculiarly, with his long straight sensitive and virile hands. And his features are odd — the high nose bridge strangely wide, the warm fullness about mouth and chin, the mouth corners tender and eager and whimsical and sensitive to every beauty, the lips not large, but the lower full like rose in bud. I have never seen anything like it on a man. He's confessed in face as worker, promoter, poet, lover, and I think bachelor, steady minded, luminous hearted, born shy, loftily delicate and considerate, with the dignity of simplest sincerity, exquisitely companionable.

"We sat front. K. was delighted with his face and then we went behind the scenes and Mr. Baker introduced us and K. made appointment with Yeats to draw him at the Touraine [Hotel] at 11 this Sunday." [16]

The lecture that Gibran and Mary attended was at the Plymouth theatre under the auspices of the Drama League of Boston.[17] Yeats lecture was titled 'History of the Irish National Theatre and its purposes." He presented the national theatre as a manifestation of the intellectual movement in Ireland to draw on the imaginative beauty of Irish language, traditions and customs distinct from being overshadowed by English preconceptions.[18] Yeats declared, "We have succeeded because we have based our art on the life of Ireland."[19]

The two poets seem to have found some common ground as they conversed for three hours after the drawing was finished.

The portrait has many imperfections involving the pupils, the nose, the skewed chin, and imbalance between the cheeks. One side of the face plumper than the other. Haskell who saw the portrait soon after its execution describes it as "spiritual, real — with the complexity of Yeat's ... with that elusiveness as of one still hovering, not yet quite settled into his complete self."

---

15 *Letters of Kahlil Gibran*, pp 84-85.
16 *Letters of Kahlil Gibran*, pp 84-85.
17 *Boston Globe*, September 21, 1911.
18 *Boston Globe*, September 29, 1911.
19 *Boston Globe*, September 24, 1911.

A Garland of Poets

"The portrait took about 40 - 50 minutes, but they talked 3 hours. Y. is bored in Boston - "He doesn't care for the things they do for him here. There's nobody that interests him. He told me so. He has a great deal to do, but he can't work here. Lady Gregory can. She does not mind it. But he can't and he wants to get away...

"One bad thing is spoiling Yeat's work. He is a patriot — and he ought to be simply an artist. He knows it. I believe he will work out of it."

Gibran criticized Yeats insistence on nationalism in art, for Yeats considered true art as the greatest gift an artist can offer his nation.[20] Gibran's comment about Yeats' nationalism hampering his art is peculiar considering Gibran's own involvement in the national issues of Syria, but may have presaged his future estrangement from such pursuits.

Gibran had opportunity to meet Yeats again in New York in 1914 at the house of Mrs. Ford.[21] They also met at a meeting of the Society of Arts and Science when they both read from their works. By this time, Gibran had already published his book *The Madman* and his English writings were appearing regularly in US magazine. Gibran shares with Mary Haskell his observations about Yeats and his wife:

"I spent an evening with him and his wife, a strange being when he is there. Absolutely dumb – but at the dinner I sat by her, and she was very much alive, interested and well read. No doubt she helps him a great deal. She knows and understands so much and can ask so many questions. And he needs to be helped so much. For instance, he was sitting talking, deeply in earnest and very eager, and just here, say, was his tea. He kept feeling here and there for something. She said: "You want some sugar, don't you? Here it is." His two personalities are active at once and one of them conquers the other."[22]

A curious sidebar in this association with Yeats is the complete antipathy Yeats' father will have towards Gibran. He writes in February 1919 to the poet Jeanne Foster (1879-1970), who admired Gibran, of his mistrust of the genuineness of Gibran's 'hazy mysticism' as expressed in his book *The Madman*,[23]

"Last Monday... amidst all the noise and enthusiasm... sat a quiet man, charming, tactful

---

20 *Letters of Kahlil Gibran*, page 85.
21 *Beloved Prophet:* page 176.
22 Mary Haskell Diary, May 20, 1920.
23 Richard Londraville, Janis Londraville: *Dear Yeats, Dear Pound, Dear Ford: Jeanne Robert Foster and Her Circle of Friends,* Syracuse University Press, 2001, pp 69-70.

and modest amidst the general homage – your Syrian, the artist of "The Madman" – a man endlessly clever and practical, that is to say where art is concerned quite insincere – and all the time I kept wondering how Mrs. Foster could take this man for a genius. Except in organizing a practical success, cleverness is always insincere in poetry as in Religion, because cleverness aims at external success – whereas genius belongs to the inner world of conviction and idea and mood, and vision. I am sure that he is a nice fellow enough and perhaps he believes that he believes."

John Butler Yeats feared that his son's mysticism might adversely affect his poetry. He wrote him a letter in which he offered a clear critique of Gibran:

"Vagueness is always insecurity, and of it are two kinds. When a man does not take the trouble to think or to know precisely, he is vague – and if this comes from human weakness or laziness or because it is so soothing in itself to a disturbed mind, then it is so human as to be likeable or even lovable, and great poets have shown themselves not averse – only with this condition, that as honest men they must not pretend that it is a conviction, or, as some of your second-class mystics, that it is a religion. There is another kind of vagueness which no poet or artist should touch with his delicate and sensitive fingers: that is where there is calculation that vagueness may be of popular advantage to the writer." [24]

Gibran had opportunity also to draw *Lady Gregory*, an associate of Yeats and the director of The Abbey group after she saw and liked his portrait of the poet.[25]. Mary remarked about the portrait:

"Do let me tell you here that I think your sketch of Lady Gregory, delightful likeness -- full of the spirit & strength & ringing quality that one feels in her — & there's something about the work on nose, mouth that enchants me - that nose-tip conveyed so firmly by vacancy! Her face recalls very vividly, too, the beautiful picture of her when she was younger — an added merit!"[26]

---

24 George Mills Harper: *Yeats and the Occult*, Macmillan, 1975, page 25.
25 Jean Gibran and Kahlil Gibran: *Kahlil Gibran: His Life and World*, page 222.
26 *Letters of Kahlil Gibran*, page 94.

Lady Augusta Gregory

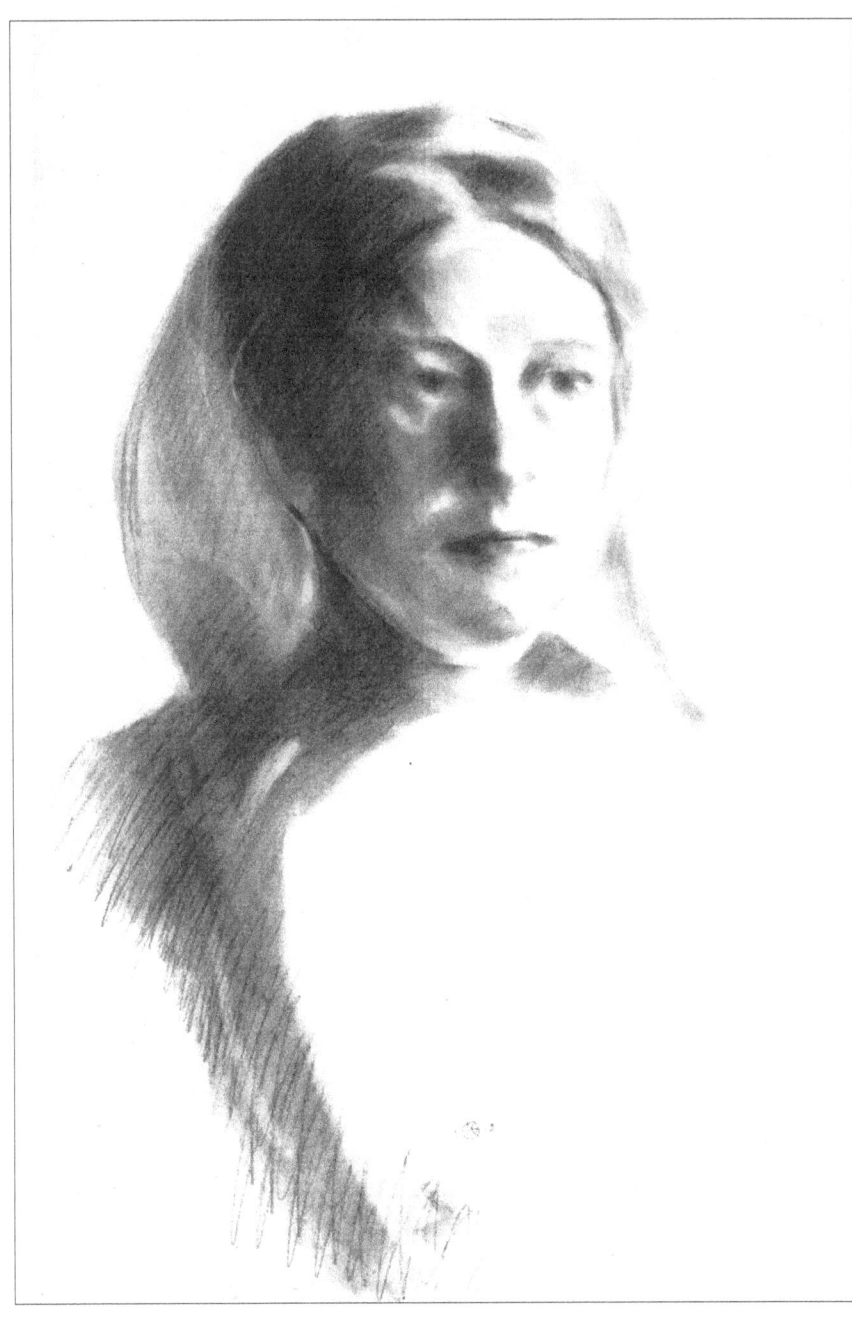

Lady Gregory was a very prolific playwright. On the trip to the USA, she wrote a new play while onboard the steamer.[27] She wrote mostly delightful comedies. As Mary remarks, Gibran's portrait goes beyond the somber note of her photographs that do not do justice to her wit, charm and humor. This may be due to her stately figure and the fact that she dressed entirely in black. Gibran's treatment of Lady Gregory softens the austerity of her photographs and while her strong will comes through in her intent gaze, the general contours of the face and head suggest an approachable person. Her husband, Sir William Gregory, was Governor of the island of Ceylon. Her work as a dramatist did not start until after the death of her husband and her engagement in the affairs of the newly organized theatre company. When asked if she will go on writing comedy, she replied: "All the young writers are so busy writing tragedy that I shall have to go on, as I am the only one old enough to laugh."[28]

---

27 *Boston Globe*, September 30, 1911.

28 *Boston Globe*, September 22, 1911.

Man of Big Spectacles - Percy MacKaye

Many of Gibran's subjects for the *Temple of Art* series would be recurrent visitors to the literary salon of Mrs. Ford (Julia Ellsworth Ford, 1859-1950), the wife of a wealthy entrepreneur in New York. Mrs. Ford was herself a poet and an art critic and her weekly literary gatherings were a sustained medium for intercourse among the literary elite of the city. Among the first people whom Gibran met at her house and drew was the playwright *Percy MacKaye* (1875-1956). Gibran initially admired MacKaye, but thought that he was not destined for greatness despite the fact that he strived for success.[29] Mackaye frequently strived for great displays in his works. He was a prolific playwright, always going for the big spectacle and subjects of wide appeal. In 1907, he produced *Jeanne d'Arc*,[30] and *Sappho and Phaon*,[31] both played by the biggest names in the industry. *The St Louis Pageant* featured a cast of over 1500![32]

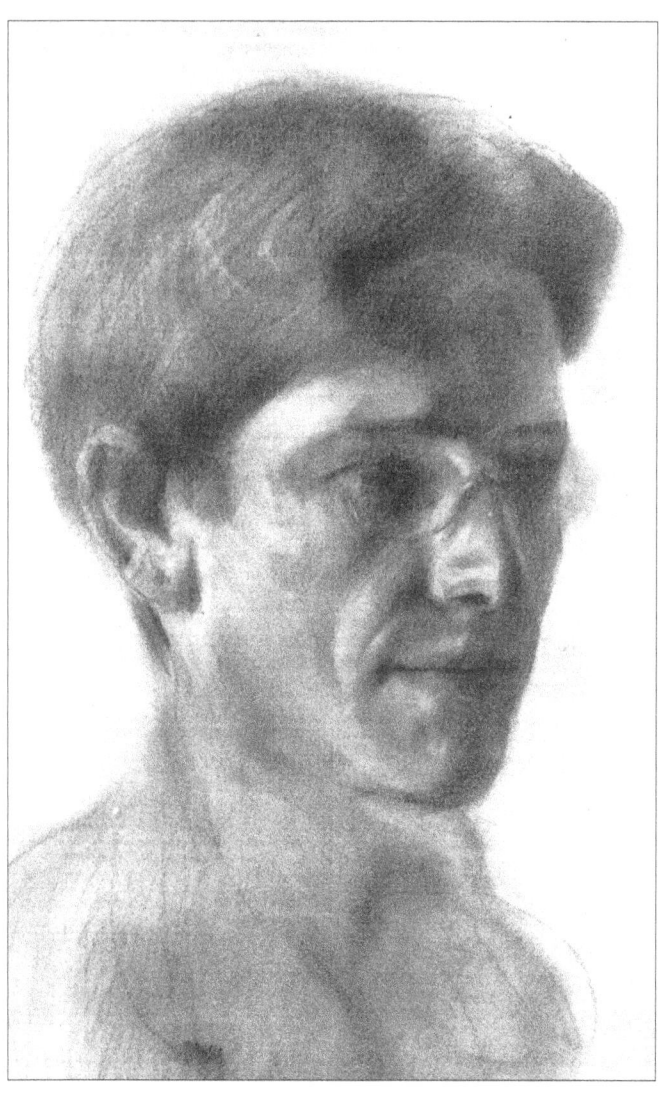

Gibran's portrait of Mackaye appeared in the magazine *The Bookman* at the same time as the staging of Mackaye's *Saint Louis, a Civic Masque*.[33] MacKaye used the portrait as a frontispiece for a special edition[34] of his play published in 1914. The treatment of the neck and shoulder appear whimsical as if Gibran wanted to bring a colossus down to size! Additionally, he 'beautifies' the poet by softening the acute features of his face.

---

29 Mary Haskell Papers, entry for August 29, 1913.
30 *The Boston Globe*, January 2, 1907.
31 *The Sun*, February 20, 1907.
32 *St. Louis Globe-Democrat*, May 26, 1914.
33 *The Bookman*, volume 39, June, 1914, page 377.
34 Percy McKaye: *Saint Louis, A Civic Masque*: Edition de Luxe, limited to 300 copies, signed by the Author: Frontispiece portrait-drawing of the Author by Kahlil Gibran; Doubleday, 1914.

A Garland of Poets

CHILDLESS SON - WITTER BYNNER

Witter Bynner (1881-1968) was Gibran's closest poet friend. They likely met at Mrs. Ford's literary evenings, and Gibran's letters to Bynner, which extend over many years attest to their closeness.[35] Bynner was instrumental in introducing Gibran to the publisher Alfred Knopf and the genesis of the close association that launched Gibran's English books on the American scene. The two poets also appeared together at many gatherings to read from their works[36]. Bynner wrote a short biography of Gibran for an anthology published by Knopf.

In 1922, Bynner published *A Book of Plays* containing a play, originally named Prussia, which he had composed during the First World War. Gibran wrote to him: "I love you for writing 'Prussia'... we all were deeply moved. And you know just what it did to a Syrian from Lebanon... After you publish it, I want to have it translated into Arabic. I assure you that it will find a place of honor in the best Arabic magazine. The Syrians have a right to love you almost as much as I have."

The renamed play, Cycle, was dedicated to Gibran. It opens in the house of a Prussian officer recently returned from the front in Syria. He had been posted there as part of the German contingent to shore up the Ottoman army in their attack on the British in Egypt. His wife accidentally finds photographs of young Syrian women in his luggage that he angrily tore to shreds. An itinerant peddler knocks on the door, a handicapped old Syrian man who when invited into the foyer by the sympathetic daughter of the officer, tells the gathered family of the atrocities perpetrated by Prussian officers who gang raped young Syrian women like his daughter by descending military rank before killing them. He is on a mission of revenge and attempts to kill the officer having identified him as one of the perpetrators. The officer shoots him dead. Horrified by the revelation, the officer's wife shoots him in turn. The narrative line of the play is clearly contrived.

In 1925, while Bynner was preparing to publish his poetry collection *Caravans*,[37] Gibran suggested to him to change the title to The Winged Serpent and offered to design the cover of the book including in his letter a sketch of a winged serpent. Bynner declined. The coincidence is curious. While the title proposed by Gibran caries no direct reference to the contents of Bynner's book, Bynner himself appears as a character[38] in D.H. Lawrence's book *The Plumed*

---

35 Bynner, Witter. Papers. Ms 186. Rio Grande Historical Collections. New Mexico State University Library.
36 *New-York Tribune.* March 7, 1920; *Daily News,* November 8, 1919.
37 Witter Bynner: *Caravan.* Alfred A. Knopf, publisher, New York, 1925.
38 See the biographical introduction by James Kraft in volume one of the works of Witter Bynner: *Selected Poems,* edited with a critical introduction by Richard Wilbur. Farrar, Straus and Giroux, publishers, New York, 1977. Kahlil's portrait of Bynner appeared in this edition.

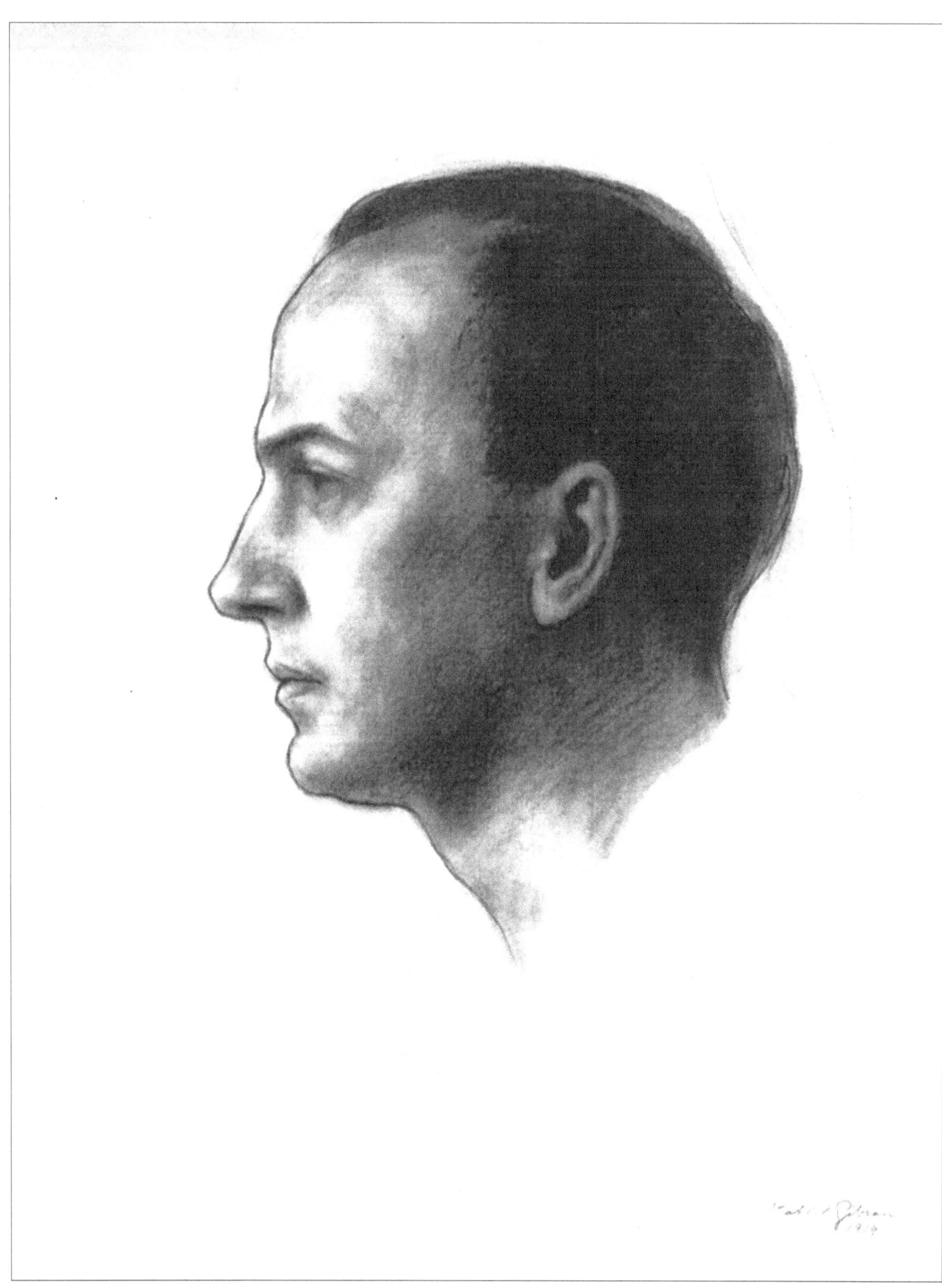

Serpent published a year later! [39] Two of the poems in *Caravans* are dedicated to D.H. Lawrence. Gibran must have introduced Bynner to some aspects of Syrian literature as we find a poem by Bynner reminiscent of the Syrian poet Abu al-Ala al-Maari:

> On a tomb in Lebanon
> Is graven: *This indignity*
> *My parents visited upon me,*
> *I upon none.*
> Why do I then, childless as he,
> Seem to be
> His son? [40]

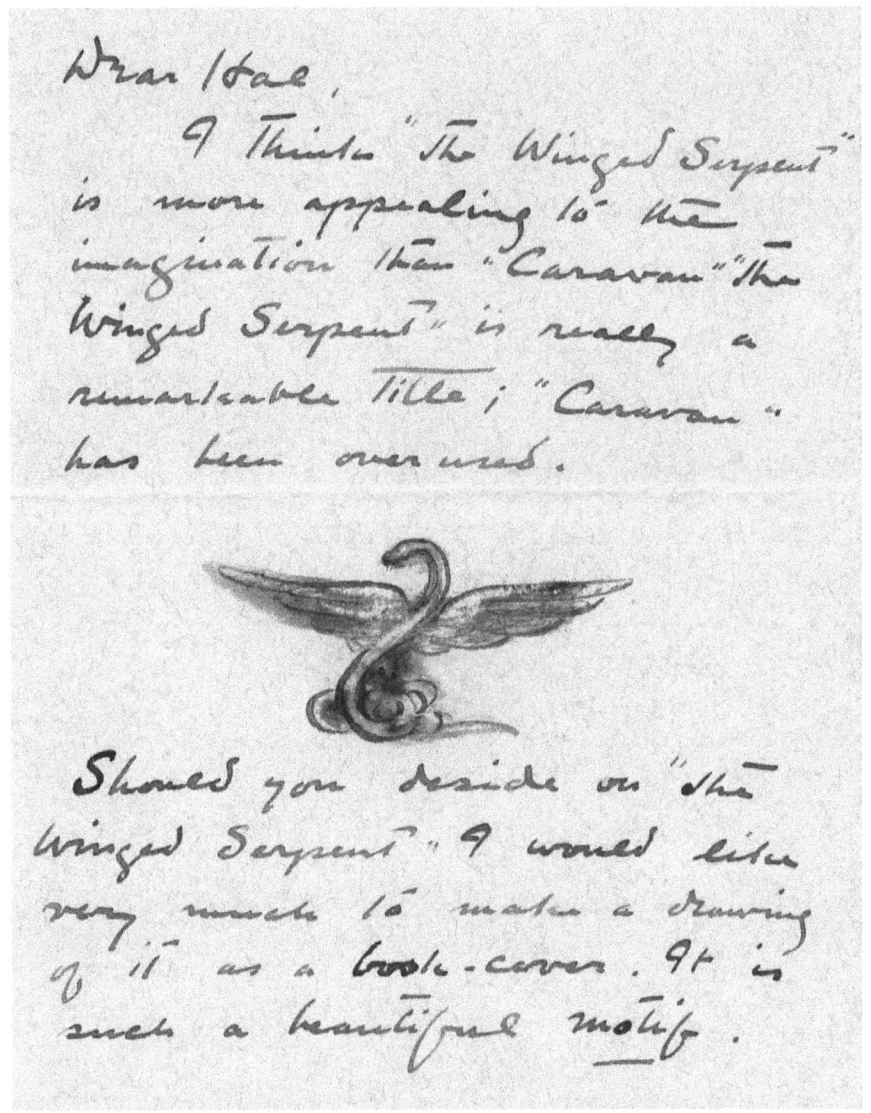

Gibran's letter to Bynner showing the winged serpent

---

39   D. H. Lawrence. *The Plumed Serpent.* Alfred A. Knopf, publisher, New York, 1926.
40   Witter Bynner: *Take Away the Darkness.* Alfred A. Knopf, New York, 1947, page 43.

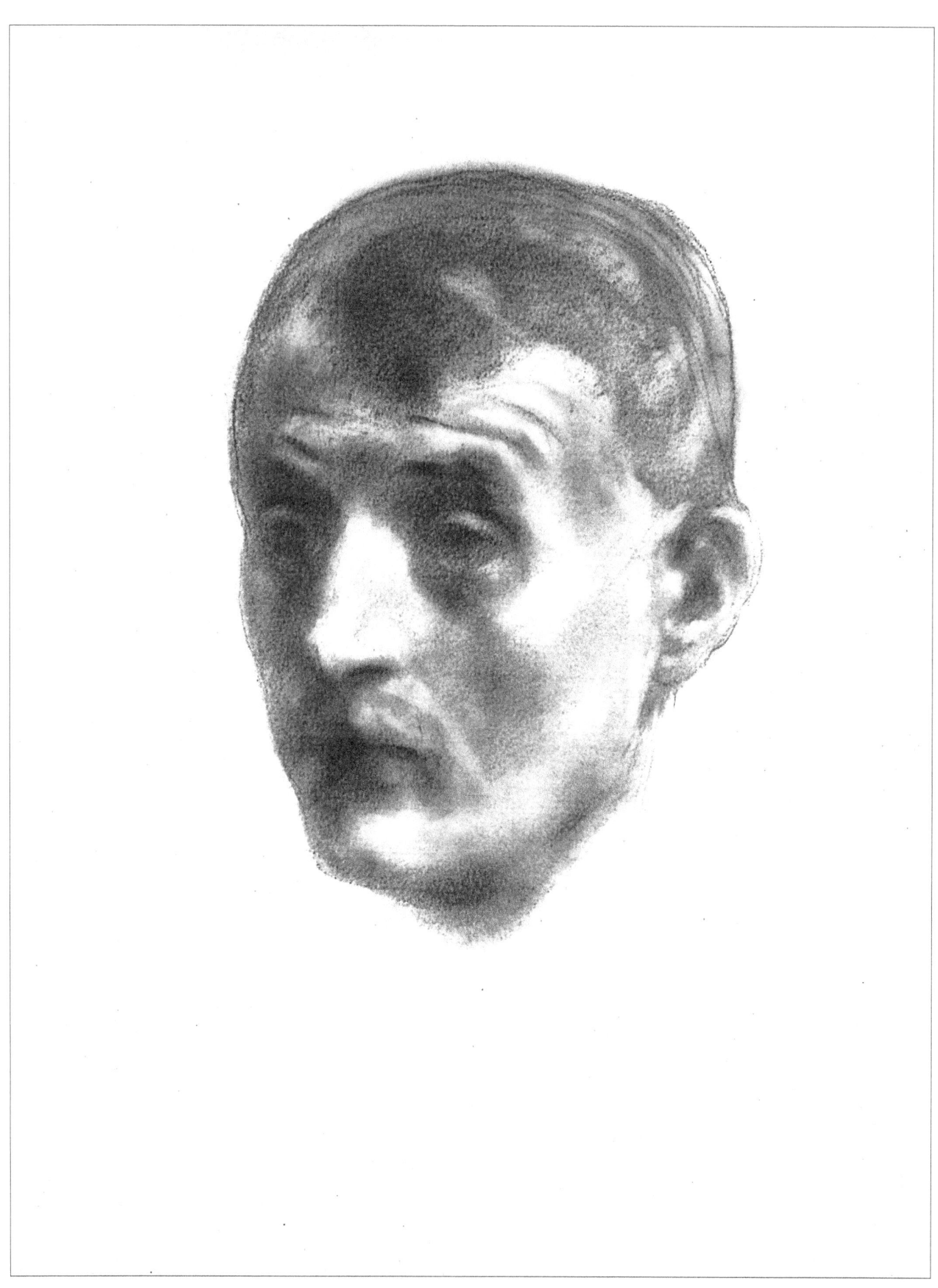

A Garland of Poets

WAR POETS - JOHN MASEFIELD

The cataclysmic events of the First World War and the immense carnage spawned numerous poets around the world, in particular in England where two types of poets appeared to have emerged: those singing the importance of patriotism and support for King and Country, and those advocating pacifism and an end to carnage. Gibran was to draw his subjects from both categories.

The prolific English poet *John Masefield* (1878-1967) had enlisted during the First World War and was assigned a non-combatant position in the war theater in France. His government, however, soon realized that his dispatches describing the carnage of the war, the bravery of the British soldiers and their tenacity under adverse conditions, would serve the war effort more than the clerical job he was performing close to the front in France. The British government dispatched him to the US on several tours to encourage American support of the Allies effort and to sway American public opinion towards America's entry into the war on the side of the Allies. It was during one of these tours in 1916 that Gibran met Masefield and drew him.[41] Masefield had just completed a tour of the American Midwest and East Coast and his lectures in Nashville[42], Lacrosse,[43] Minneapolis,[44] and Boston prominently featured in the periodicals of these cities. He generally lectured about English literature as well as his life experience in the US as a young man and his experiences in the war in France and the Dardanelles.

Masefield was labelled 'the greatest living English poet' by US newspapers and was quoted as blaming the war for the lack of poetry in the world.[45] One reporter described him as "quiet, gentle, thoughtful and wonderfully courteous," a description consistent with the impression we get from the portrait. Masefield appears as if he has just been startled by a thought or a vision and has not yet grasped its meaning. Gibran's portrait of the English poet appeared in the *New York Times* in 1917 at the time of Gibran's second exhibit[46].

---

41   *Letters of Kahlil Gibran*, page 471.
42   *The Tennessean*, February 1, 1916.
43   *The La Crosse Tribune*, February 3, 1916.
44   *Star Tribune*, February 6, 1916.
45   *Boston Post*, April 2, 1916
46   *The New York Times*, February 25, 1917.

SIEGFRIED SASSOON

Siegfried Loraine Sassoon (1886 – 1967) would become the other type of English poets that Gibran drew. Although decorated for bravery on the Western Front, he became one of the leading poets of dissent of the First World War. He had fought three times in France, once in Palestine, and had been promoted and won the Military Cross for an act of valor on the field.

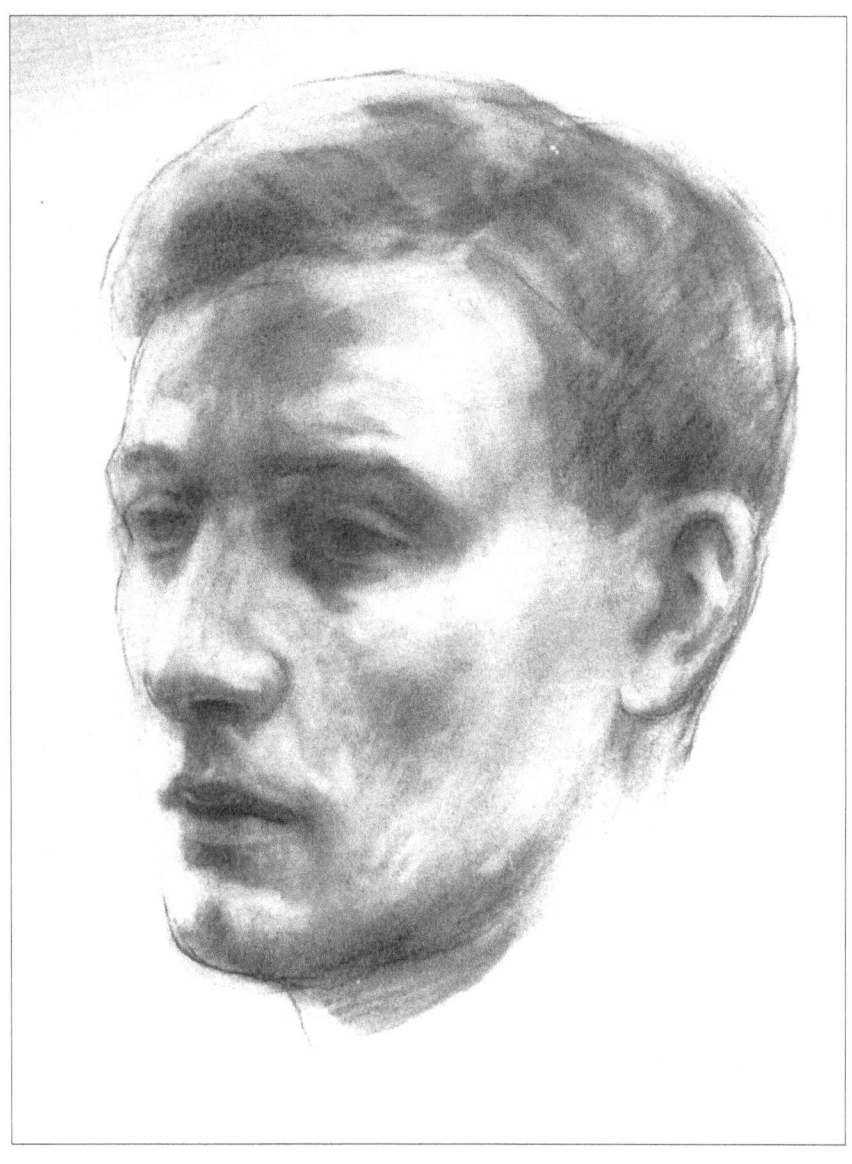

His poetry described the horrors of the trenches and satirized the patriotic pretensions of those responsible for it. He became a focal point for dissent within the armed forces when his poems against the continuation of the war started circulating depicting the bare face of human suffering with biting irony.[47] The American poet Louis Untermeyer described his poems as "revealing a nature that had met the war but had not been conquered by it… These poems do not merely spring from the poet's convictions; they are wrenched from the bleeding core of his suffering."[48]

On January 28, 1920, Sassoon arrived in New York for a lecture tour and Gibran, eager to draw him for his "Temple of Art," got an appointment with him on 10 February. On that cold and snowy Tuesday, the two lunched together and Sassoon agreed to sit for a portrait. Afterwards, he recorded his impression of Gibran in his notebook as "a little Syrian artist & poet… He seems a very nice creature. Nothing commercial about his point of view."

---

47 For examples of popularized poems, see *The Ottawa Citizen*, February 14, March 19, May 26, 1917.
48 Louis Untermeyer: Pegasus Redivivus, *The Yale Review*, July 1919, pp. 858-867.

A Garland of Poets

THE ORPHAN ANGEL - ELINOR MORTON WYLIE

Elinor Morton Wylie (1885-1928) was one of the most famous women poets in America in the early 20th century. She led a very intriguing life and was favored with ethereal beauty and a fascinating personality. She shone among the visitors to the Ford household and was held in awe by the younger women poets such as Mercedes da Acosta, who attended those gatherings.

"I went this winter for the first time to Mrs. Simeon Ford's poetry dinners. These were dinners at which Mrs. Ford gathered poets, and after feeding them well, invited them, still sitting around the table, to read or recite their latest poems. Here in Mrs. Ford's house I met many of the most important poets in America: Edgar Lee Masters, Vachel Lindsay, Robert Frost, Sara Teasdale, Elinor Wylie and Leonora Speyer were often there, and also Charles Hanson Towne, Edna St. Vincent Millay, Dorothy Parker, Ezra Pound and Kahlil Gibran, all of whom I already knew… Mrs. Ford used to say laughingly, "Everyone must sing for his supper." I suffered agonies when I had to recite before any one of these fine poets, but I especially suffered when I had to recite in the presence of Elinor Wylie. She had all of her own poems at the tip of her tongue and could recite them with great charm and a fine delivery. It was a joy to hear her and they were all first-rate."[49]

The "*femme fatale*" beauty of Elinor Wylie, her creative fire, and her frank countenance were paralleled by the particular events of her life, which were to haunt her image throughout her life. Elinor came from an elite family in Washington, DC and married within her class to Philip Hichborn, a Harvard law graduate and poet. After six years of marriage, she abandoned her first husband in 1912 and ran away with her neighbor Horace Wylie, a married man. Elinor eloped with Wylie to Europe, abandoning her husband and young son. They returned to Washington, Elinor to her paternal home and Wylie to his wife briefly, but eloped to Paris again. As they could not be married immediately, they lived abroad for six years and returned to the US only after they were married. Her first husband, his mind unhinged by the disgrace, committed suicide. Elinor married Wylie, but after her literary fame made Wylie appear less relevant, she divorced him to marry the poet and literary critic William Benét.[50] The matrimonial disasters of Elinor, her sister Nancy, and their brother Morton were fodder for frequent coverage in newspapers.[51] Elinor Wylie's startling episodes in early life were resurrected at the time of her death of a stroke in December of 1928.[52]

---

49 Mercedes de Acosta: *Here Lies the Heart*, Reynal & Company, NY, 1960, page 140.
50 *The San Francisco Examiner*, March 6, 1927.
51 San Francisco Chronicle, July 22, 1923; Montgomery Advertiser, July 1, 1923; *Philadelphia Enquirer*, June 10, 1923; *The San Francisco Examiner*, March 6, 1927.
52 *The San Francisco Examiner*, January 13, 1929; *Intelligencer Journal*, December 18, 1928.

Kahlil Gibran - Portraits

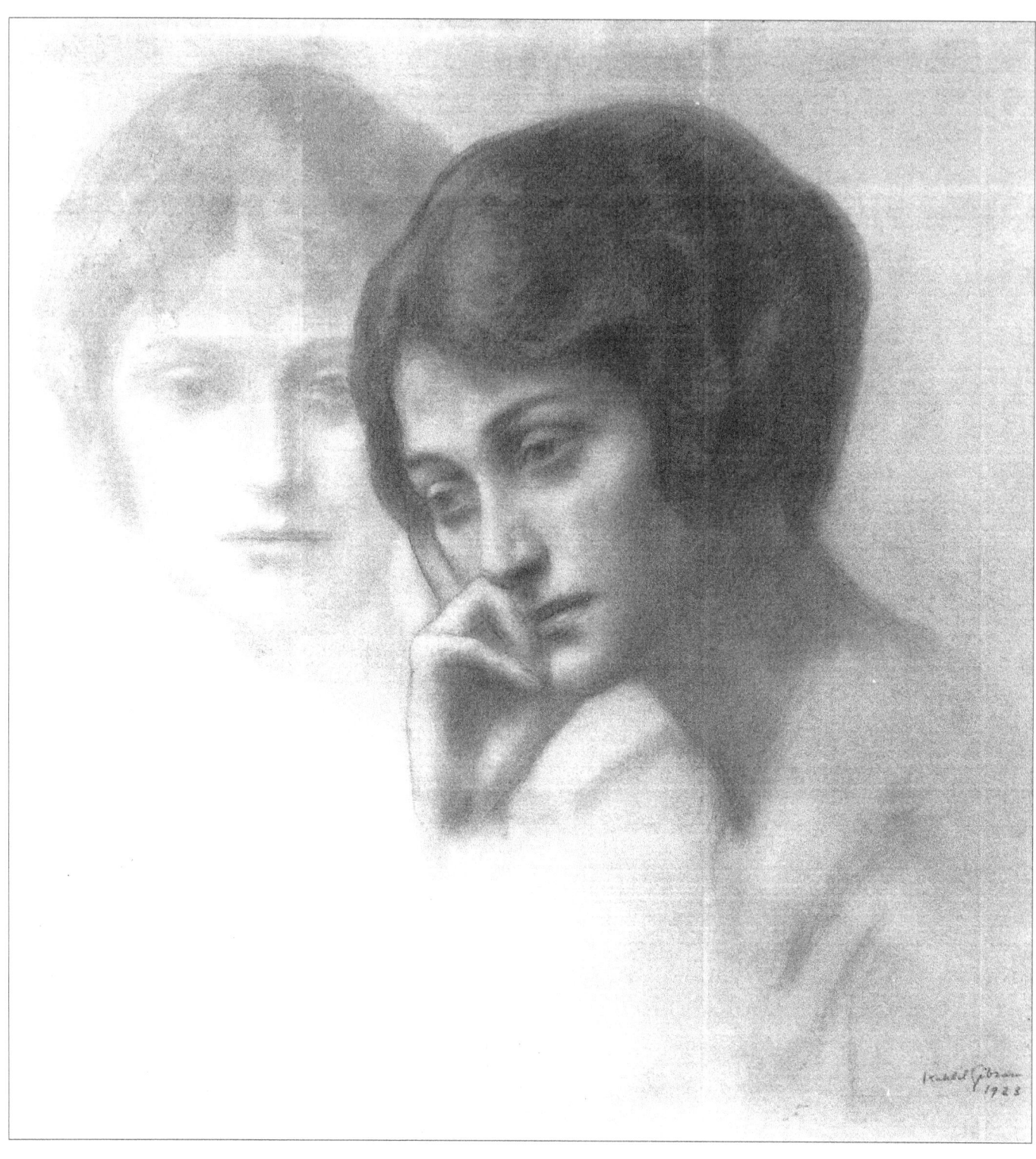

A Garland of Poets

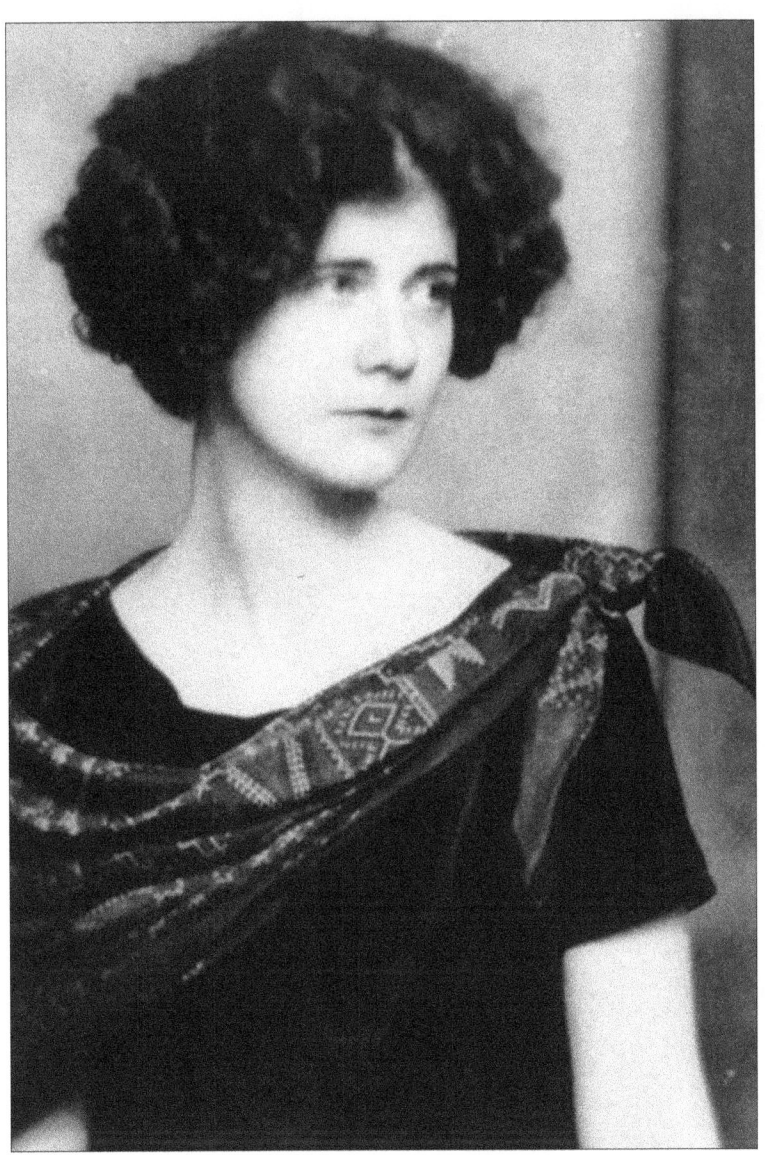

Photograph of Elinor Wylie

Between 1921 and 1928, Elinor published three books of poetry and 4 novels, all to exceptional acclaim. The Poetry Society of America awarded her first book, *Nets to Catch the Wind,* the Julia Elsworth Ford award for the best poetry book of 1921. She dedicated her second poetry book, *Black Armour,* to her third husband William Rose Benét.

Literary critics were unanimous about the beauty of her verse which sang of the bitterness of love incomplete and the beauty of grief. She was considered a singer of unusual grace and beauty.[53] After the *Black Armour*, Elinor seemed to take a break from poetry and embarked on novel writing producing four imaginative novels in the span of 5 years.[54]

She returned to poetry with her collection *Trivial Breath*, and a posthumous book of love sonnets was published in 1929 by Knopf, who also published her collected poetry and prose works in the early 1930s. In the portrait, Gibran captures the elements of grief and thought so dominant in Elinor's poetry and the sad grace of her physical beauty.

---

53 *The Springfield News Reader*, February 15, 1925; *The Evening News*, July 8, 1927; *The South Bend Tribune*, December 23, 1928.
54 These are in turn *Jennifer Lorn* (1923), *The Venetian Glass Nephew* (1925), *The Orphan Angel* (1927), and *Mr Hodge and Mr Hazard* (1927).

WHERE THE PROPHET WAS BORN - MARIE TUDOR GARLAND

In April 1918, *Marie Tudor Garland* (1870-1949) invited Gibran to spend a few weeks at Bay End Farm where she had established a sort of an art colony. He had visited the place the prior year and found the companionship of poets and authors who frequented it most delightful. Artists and writers enjoyed her hospitality and the freedom to do as they pleased. Each was provided with a private cottage. Marie Tudor Garland was a poet and a rich patron of the arts and literature and used her extensive fortune to foster an intellectual life at her various estates.[55] Bay End Farm was only one of a series of abodes where she played hostess to writers and artists. Garland arranged for a group of prefabricated cottages to be delivered and erected on her property. They would house the many visiting painters, writers and poets who enjoyed Marie's hospitality and beautiful farm. Garland supported a few writers and artists financially, among them the American novelist Evelyn Scott (1893-1963) who lived on the property for many years. She replicated the experience in New Mexico with her third husband and hosted Georgia O'Keefe.

Gibran spent twenty-four days at the farm, riding horses, taking long walks and drafting the majority of *The Prophet*. Sixteen of the twenty-one 'counsels' took form during this period. He had been considering the topics of this book for many years. The conversations with Haskell are replete with references to the "Commonwealth' and 'al-Mustafa, the island-man'. At Bay End Farm, these early musings finally took form in *The Prophet*.

When asked by a reporter how he wrote *The Prophet*, Gibran replied that each of the chapters of the book took only 30 minutes to write. Gibran is likely referring to this early draft. It is reasonable to assume that after long contemplation of a concept, a brief period of pen to paper would suffice. The reporter is incredulous: "This was almost unbelievable. Those deep and vivifying passages on love and pain, religion or marriage might well be the crowning achievement of a lifetime effort." Gibran explains that indeed they are the result of a lifetime effort in their genesis, but not in their writing: "I wanted to write *The Prophet* ever since I was a lad of 18 when I began writing it in the Arabic language." His second attempt was in Paris, but that too came to naught. The work gestated in him until he was ready, and then there was no hesitation. "Did you rewrite and polish it?" the reporter asks. "No, but I kept it for four years before I delivered it over to my publishers because I wanted to be sure that every word of it was the very best I had to offer." The fact that he and Mary Haskell chiseled every sentence, debated every nuance, and produced many copies of the manuscript need not be declared![56]

---

55 Marie Tudor Garland: *The Potter's Clay*, Published by G. P. Putnam's Sons, New York, 1917; *The Winged Spirit*, Published by G. P. Putnam's Sons, New York, 1918; *The Marriage Feast*, Published by G. P. Putnam's Sons, New York, 1920.

56 Gladys Baker: Kahlil Gibran, Syrian Poet-Artist tells how, and why he wrote 'The Prophet'. *The Birmingham News*, December 11, 1927.

A Garland of Poets

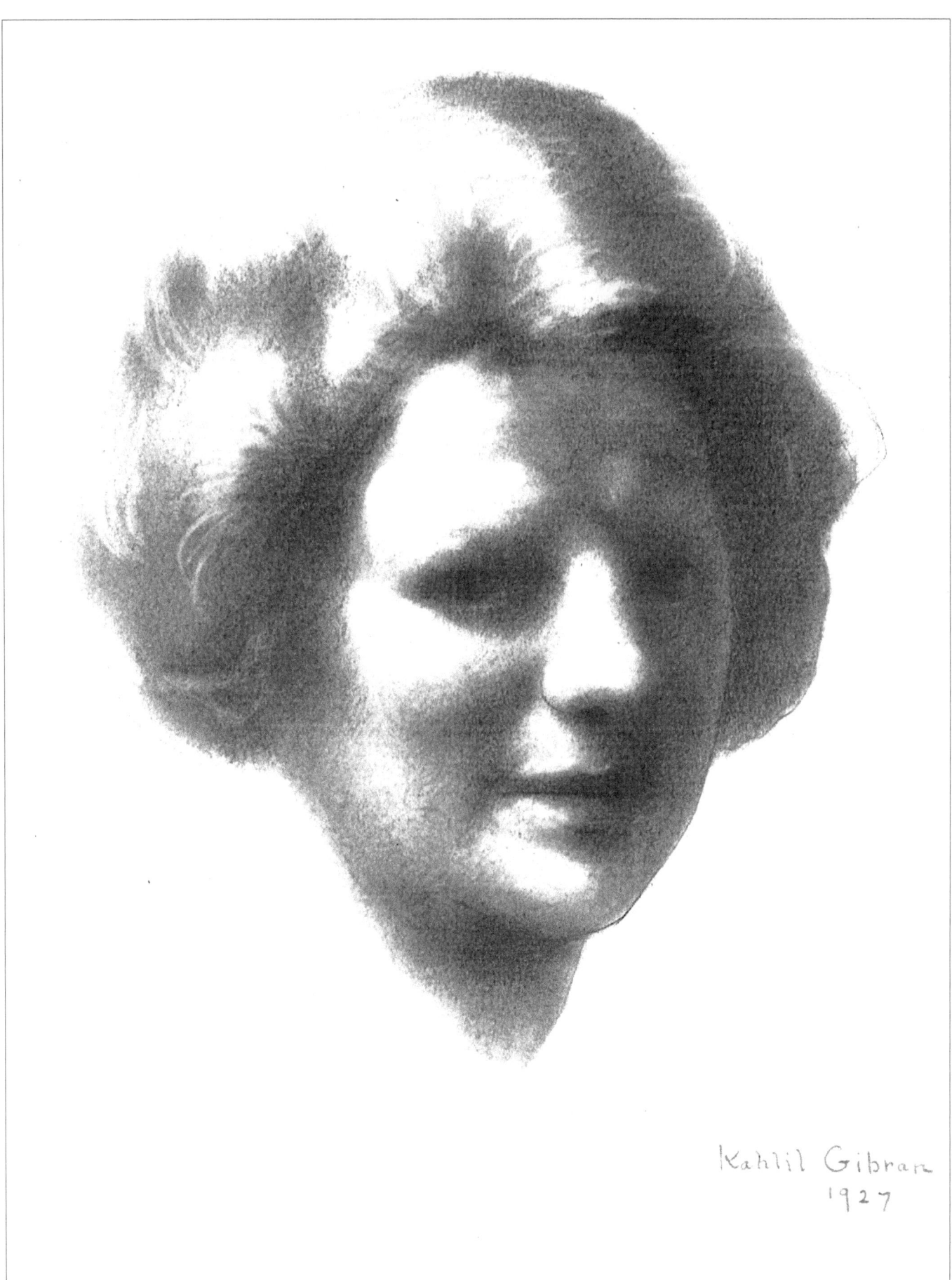

MUSIC AND POETRY - LEONORA SPEYER

Gibran's social charm and talents made him a sought after guest in the homes of artists and socialites. We find him at the home of Mrs. Ford, Rose O'Neill, Leonora Speyer, Alma Reed, and other talented women of the era. It was in the house of Rose O'Neill[57] that Gibran might have first met the poet and socialite *Leonora Speyer* (1872-1956). Leonora was also a friend of Witter Bynner and the latter may have introduced her to Gibran. Lady Speyer was a violinist of some accomplishment and a great beauty. She graduated from the Brussels Conservatory

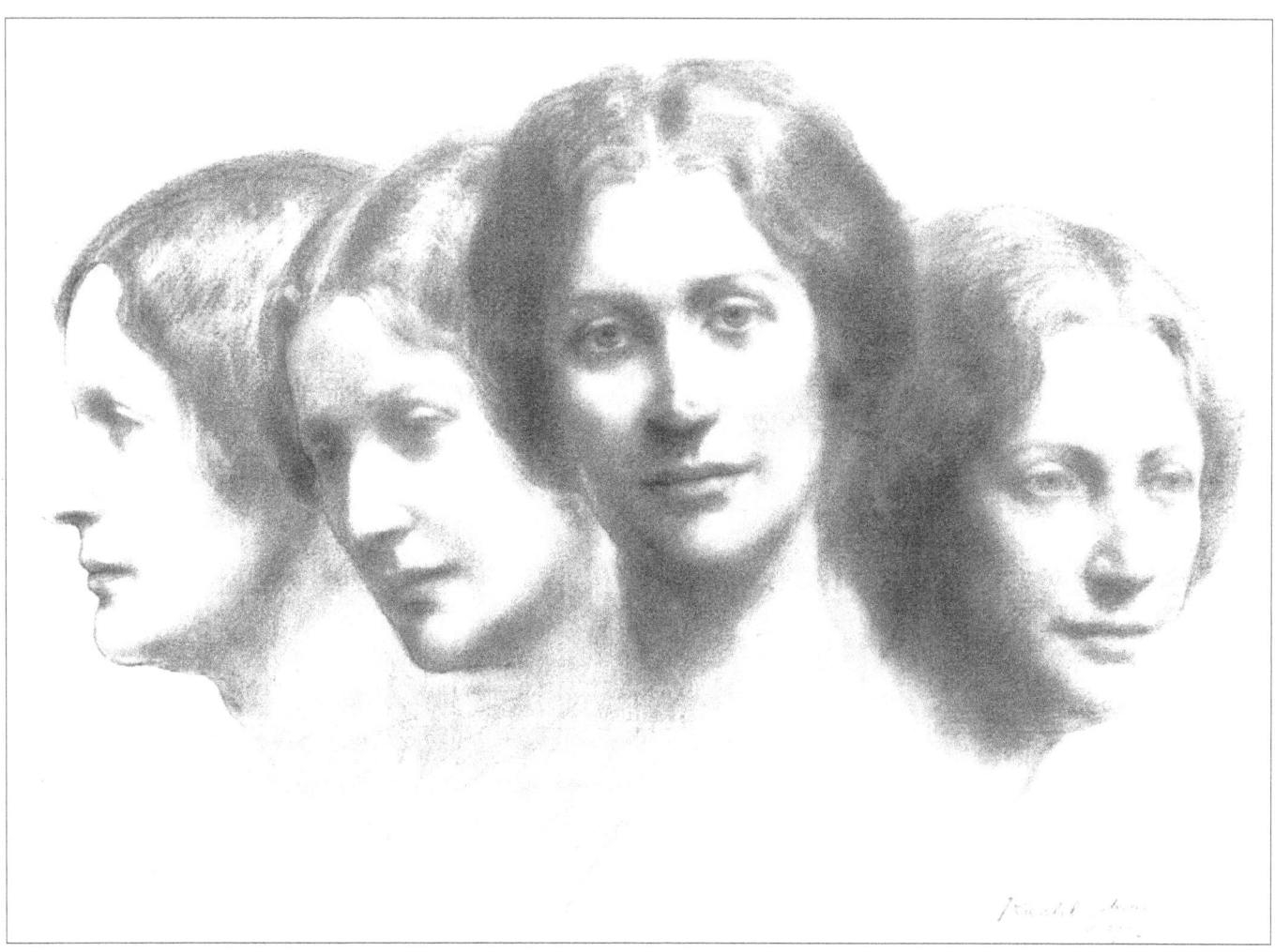

of Music with high distinction and became a concert violinist making her debut at 18 with the Boston Symphony. Sargent painted a portrait of her in 1907 playing the violin. When she married her second husband, Edgar Speyer, a British banker, she moved to England. The German heritage of her husband generated harsh criticism and even a withdrawal of his British citizenship during the First World War forcing the family to move to America in 1915.[58]

---

57 Rose Cecil O'Neill, Miriam Formanek-Brunell: *The story of Rose O'Neill: an autobiography,* University of Missouri Press, Columbia, 1997.
58 *The Brooklyn Daily Eagle,* December 15, 1929.

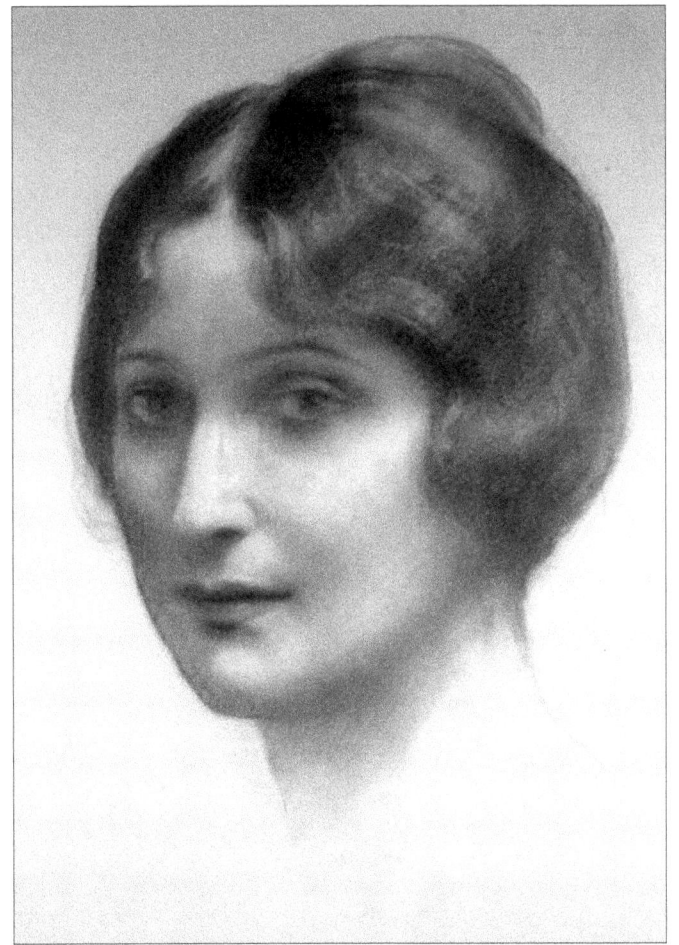

Gibran's portrait of Enid Hewitt

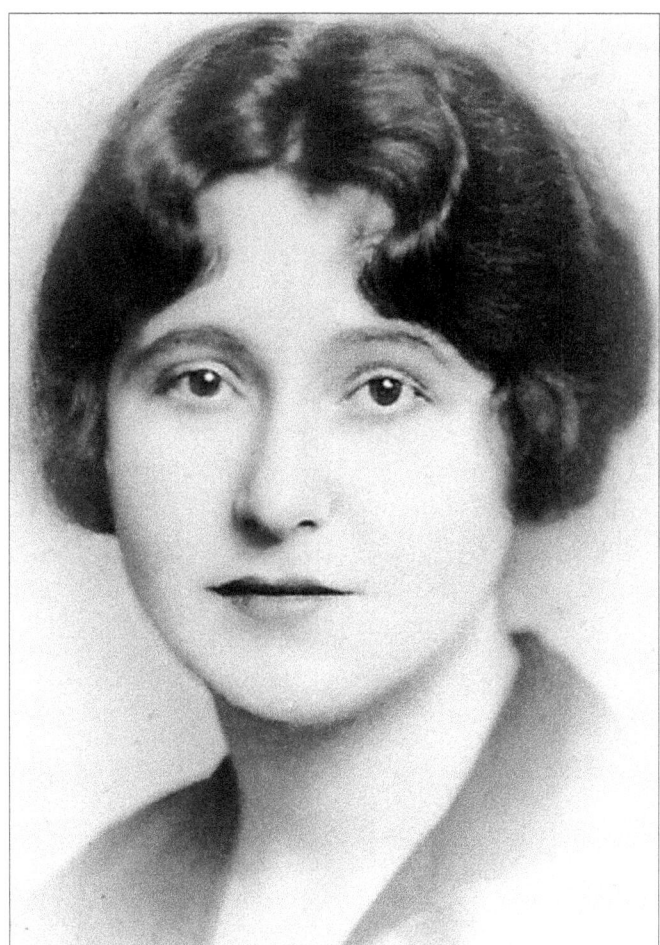

Photograph of Enid Hewitt

After her return to America, she redirected her interest to poetry. Critics frequently commented how her musical training affected her verse, her "metrical cadences [are] without a flaw."[59] Rose O'Neil, famous for the Kewpie Dolls, who is credited with a striking portrait of Gibran, related that Leonora's home was a favored haunt of Gibran, and that he may have executed in her lively salon some of his Leonardo like portraits.

The multidimensional Leonora is symbolized in the composite quadruple portrait as if one or two views were not sufficient to capture the essence of the poet-musician. While a youthfulness characterizes the portraits to the viewer's right, the other two suggest an older thoughtful demeanor. The portrait suggests the stages of her life journey. Lady Speyer used the portrait on the cover of her poetry collections that won the Pulitzer Prize.

Gibran also drew Lady Speyer's daughter from her first marriage, Enid Hewitt, likely as a social courtesy and a sign of friendship.

---

59   *The New York Times*, February 5, 1939.

The Beautiful Voices of the East and the Prairies
George William Russell and Vachel Lindsay

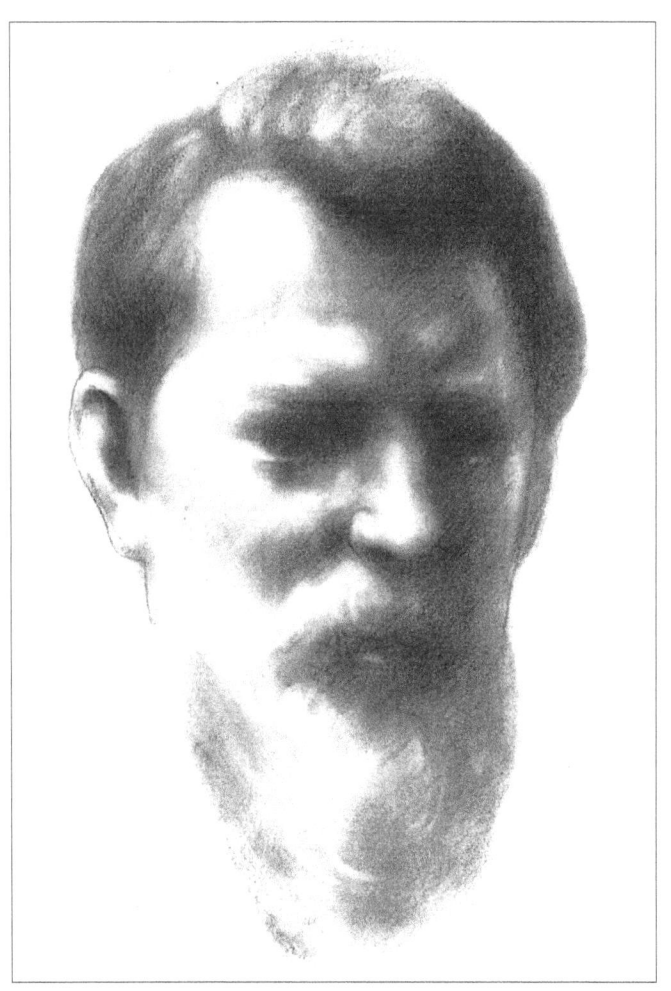 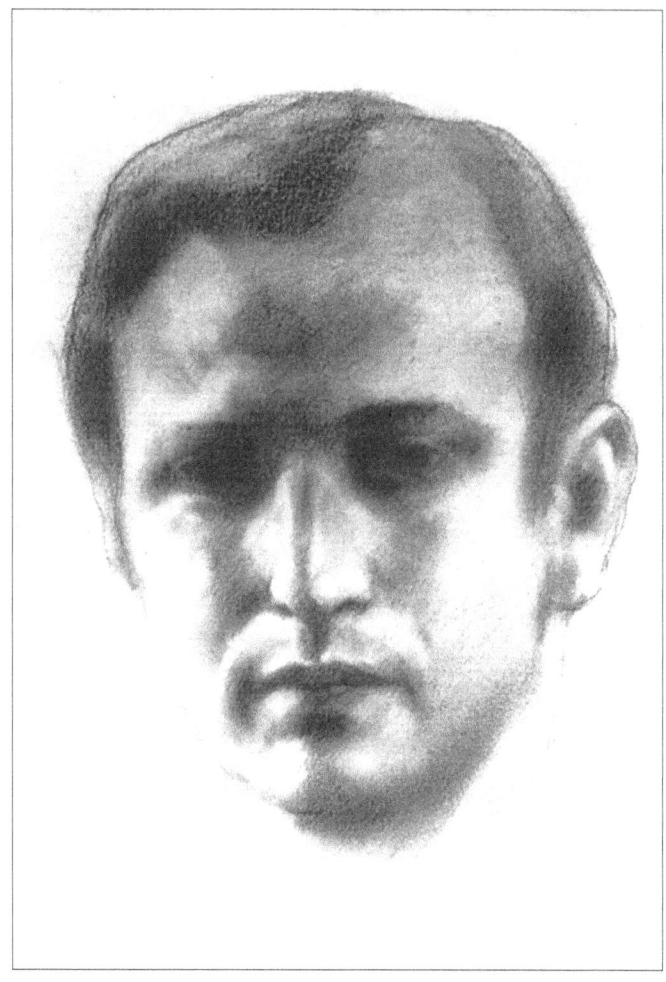

The circumstances of the drawing of the next two writers remain obscure. Both *George William Russell* (1867-1935) and *Vachel Lindsay* (1879-1931) participated in literary activities that Gibran was part of, and common friends can be identified who may have facilitated their meetings.

Russell was an Irish poet and painter, a spiritualist and mystic. He spent most of his life in Dublin so Gibran must have met him during a visit to the US, hence the paucity of information about any relationship between them despite many possibly accidental affinities of interest, such as their interest in the work of Krishnamurti. Writing about the unfortunate youth of Krishnamurti, Russell invokes Gibran: "Kahlil Gibran as well as Tagore have expressed the mystical faith of Asia much better than Krishnamurti, but there is an engaging, boyish innocence in his poems, though I cannot find in them a wisdom or beauty which would lift them beyond the average expression of spiritual life." The mild criticisms of Krishnamurti's poems leads Russell to express his assessment of Gibran: "I do not think the East has spoken with so beautiful a voice since the *Gitanjali* of Rabindranath Tagore as in *The Prophet* of Kahlil Gibran, who is an artist as well as a poet… Two of the drawings are especially moving, one of a lovely drooping figure of a girl, the arms outstretched as in crucifixion with the hands nailed to the hearts of two other figures. I have not seen for years a book more beautiful in its thought, and when reading it I understand better than ever before what Socrates meant in *The Banquet* when he spoke of the beauty of thought, which exercises a deeper enchantment than the beauty of form."[60]

There were many points of intersection between Gibran and Vachel Lindsay. They had common friends (Witter Bynner etc.), frequented similar social circles (Mrs. Ford dinners), and were closely associated with a few literary publications such as *The Seven Arts* and *The Dial*. Lindsay through his 'prairie poetry' shared with Gibran the love of nature. Lindsay's focus on the musicality of poetry may have also found resonance with Gibran, steeped as he was in Arabic poetry and its rich enchanting meters. Gibran, Vachel Lindsay, and Edna St-Vincent Millay were on the Art Committee of the St Mark Church-in-the-Bowery, which hosted literary readings, art exhibits and even dancing. The guidance of the Committee made St Mark a cultural center in addition to a place of worship. Lindsay died the same year as Gibran (December 5, 1931) committing suicide by ingesting a poison.

---

60   George W. Russell: *The Living Torch*, The Macmillan Company, NY, 1938, pp.168-169.

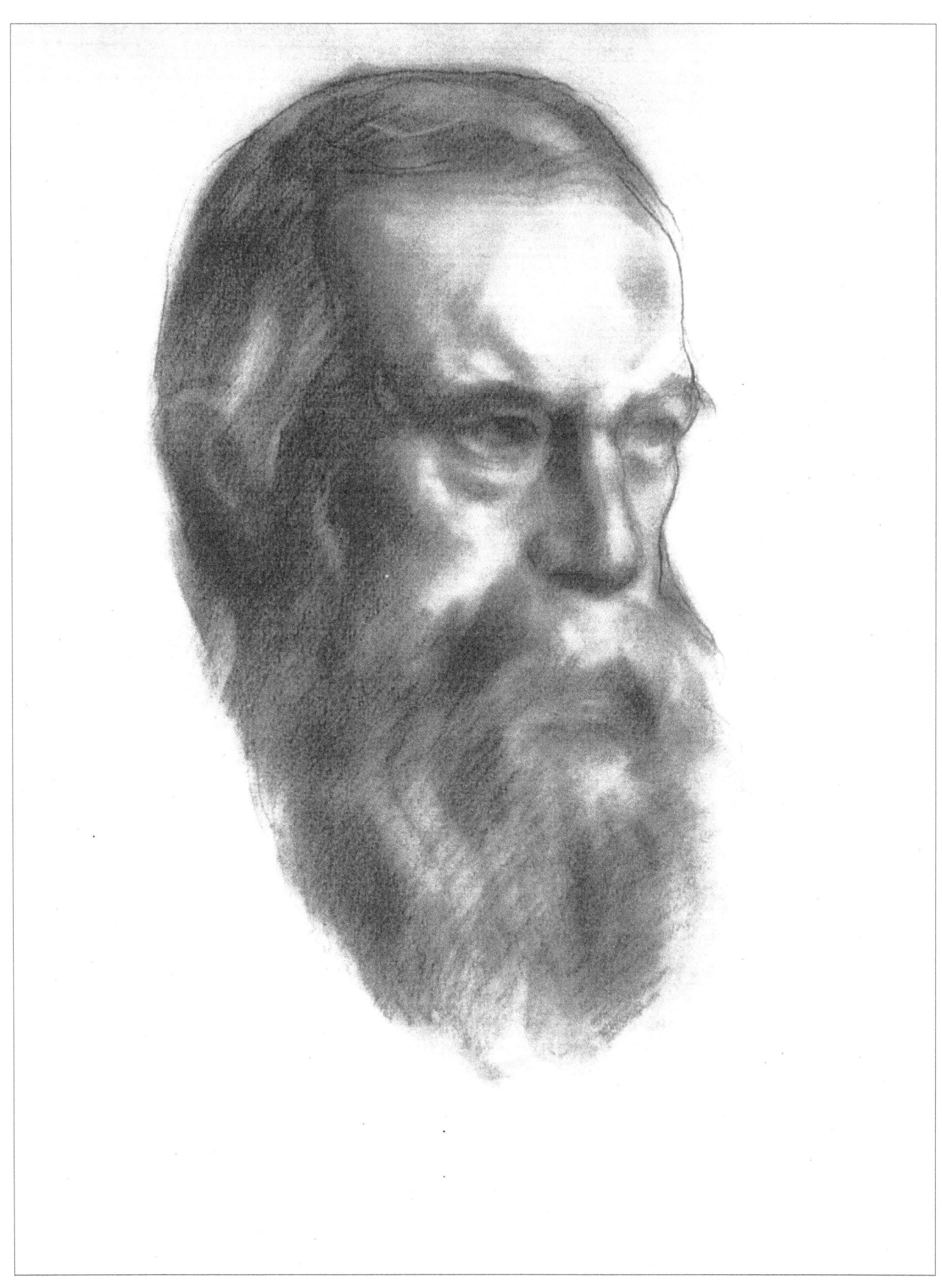

Fellow Artists and Writers

THE RECLUSE SYMBOLIST - ALBERT PINKHAM RYDER

The great symbolist American painter *Albert Pinkham Ryder* (1847-1917) had been leading a life of isolation and utter poverty when Gibran met him in New York. The American artist felled by gout, depression and chronic kidney disease was living in miserable conditions. He visited Gibran's first exhibit in New York in December of 1914 and commented favorably about what he saw.

A report of that visit comes to us from Henry Mcbride, a renowned art and literary critic:

"Almost any of his drawings might be entitled *A Wish*. He seems to aspire for something he scarcely knows what... For my part, I looked at him with new respect when I found that Albert P. Ryder was one of his believers. The only time I ever met the old gentleman was at an exhibition of Gibran's drawings in one of the Fifth Avenue galleries. I myself was somewhat exasperated with the muffled quality of the Syrian's work and so looked with curiosity at an aged man who seemed to be devouring the drawings with study... and taking my courage in my two hands, I spoke to him. Ryder embarrassed me at once by asking me what I thought of the exhibition. I replied, as mildly as possible, that the artist seemed to desire to do vast things, but seemed to be as yet uncertain as to which things were vast. Ryder looked at me wistfully, and a shade disapprovingly, and said, "Well, the main thing is, he tried."[1]

Gibran sought out Ryder and in January of 1915 wrote a prose poem dedicated to the elder painter and had it printed privately.[2]

> To Albert Pinkham Ryder
>
> Poet, who has heard thee but the spirits that follow thy solitary path?
>
> Prophet, who has known thee but those who are driven by the Great Tempest to thy lonely Grove?

---

1 Henry Mcbride: Forward, *The Dial*, July 1920, volume 69, No. 1, pp. 63-64.
2 Jean Gibran and Kahlil Gibran: *Kahlil Gibran: His Life and World*, page 280.

And yet thou are not alone, for thine is the Giant-World of super-realities, where souls of unborn worlds dance in rhythmic ecstasies; and the silence that envelops thy name is the very voice of the Great Unknown.

Thine is the Giant-World of primal truth and unveiled visions, whose days stand in awe of mystic nights, whose nights are big with high lustrous days, whose hills relate the unrecorded deeds of unremembered races, whose seas chant the deep melody of distant Time, whose sky withholds the secrets of unnamed gods.

O, poet, who has heard thee but the spirits that follow thy footprints?

O, prophet, who has known thee but those the Tempest carries to thy lonely fields?

O, most aloof son of the New World, who has loved thee but those who know thy burning love?

Nay, thou art not alone, for we, we who walk in the flaming path, we who seek the unattainable and reach for the unreachable, we whose bread is hunger and whose wine is thirst, we know thee, and we hear thee, and we love thee, and we hold thee high.

Kahlil Gibran, January 1915.

Gibran sent the prose poem to Mary Haskell for edits.[3]

I am sending you this poem to Ryder to read and to correct its English. He is the one painter whom I love and honor with all my heart — and there is no other way by which I can show my love and respect. If you like the poem I will publish it separately on Japanese paper and send it to him. It may warm his old and weary heart.

Mary's comments on the poem illustrate the role she has played in Gibran's English opus:[4]

"And do I like the poem? Why, K.G. - you have said what fills the depths of my soul when I stand even in thought before Ryder — Your poem filled me with it again, and satisfied me. And I had never thought of that's being ever done — he walks so with God in me. It was very wonderful to me to see him on the day you had taken me to your pictures.

---
3 *Beloved Prophet*, page 228. *Letters of Kahlil Gibran*, page 388.
4 *Letters of Kahlil Gibran*, page 389.

Fellow Artists and Writers

Now he will be always warmed with your fire also in my heart. I am so glad you love him as you do. I too care for him only, among living artists whose work I have seen. And I am both personally & impersonally glad beyond expression that you wrote this. Shall I tell you my suggestions on the text - or my questions about it?"

Mary did not like his use of "super-realities," "in rhythmic ecstasies," and "thy name" that she found "unnecessary." She also made several emendations that she would later retract, and the poem as published follows the original text. Gibran shows in the poem, despite its convoluted language, a deep understanding of Ryder's opus and the poem might have received greater appreciation if he had accepted Mary's suggestions.[5] He refers specifically to some of Ryder's paintings (*The Great Tempest*) and some of his published poetry. How closely Gibran's poem comes to Ryder's work can be appreciated by remembering that symbolist artists considered the marriage of poetry and painting as reflecting complete art. Ryder approached paintings as a poet, shunning details and expressing ideas through his canvases liberated in their subjects from time and space.[6] Gibran's prose poem about Ryder was quoted in the eulogies written in several US papers about the American painter after his death in 1917.[7]

When he presented the poem to Ryder, the latter was moved, and a friendship developed between the two men.

> One of the most creative hours in my life was that which I have spent with Ryder the other day. I found him on a cold day in a half heated room in one of the most poor houses on 16th street. He lives the life of Diogenes, a life so wrecked and so unclean that it is hard for me to describe. But it is the only life he wants. He has money - all the money he needs - but he does not think of that. He is no longer on this planet... He is beyond his own dreams.
>
> And he read the poem. Oh what a thrilling moment. His face changed, and there were tears in his old eyes. Then he said, "'It is a great poem. It is too much for me. I am not worthy of it. No, No, I am not worthy of it."
>
> Then after a long silence he said, "I did not know that you are a poet as well as a painter. They did not tell me that you are a poet when I went to see your exhibition. I have been wanting to write a letter to the lady who wrote to me about your work. I wrote many

---

5 It was published in *The Evening Mail*, February 4, 1915.

6 Elizabeth Broun: *Albert Pinkham Ryder*, Smithsonian Institution, Washington DC, 1989 page 99. William Homer and Lloyd Goodrich: *Albert Pinkham Ryder: painter of dreams*, Harry N. Abrams, Inc., New York, 1989, pages 51-52.

7 'The Most Imaginative painter this Country has yet produced', *Current Opinion*, volume 62, May, 1917, pp 350-351.

letters to her but I burned them. One must wait for the spirit to move before one can write a letter."

And it gave him such a joy to know that I was born on Mount Lebanon. He said, "Mt. Lebanon, Mt Lebanon, that is the place where every poet and painter should be born. I should have known that you came from Lebanon after seeing your pictures."

He promised to sit for a drawing. I shall go to him tomorrow. And if I do not find him I shall go again and again until I make a drawing. It must be done. His head is wonderful — very much like that of Rodin... only it is unkempt. [8].

To capture a portrait of the great recluse, Gibran almost had to stalk him, waiting for him outside restaurants and taverns until finally Ryder felt comfortable in Gibran's familiarity and allowed him to draw his likeness.[9] Gibran was to make two portraits of Ryder that he compared to his portrait of Rodin in their power and expressiveness. On seeing the drawing, Ryder had commented that Gibran had drawn what is inside his head, his brain and his bones.

"I have made two drawings of Ryder. To me they are finer than anything I have done. One of them is not finished yet and I must go to him again. But oh, Mary, how tired and weary he is - and how aloof. He told me the last time I saw him that he is painting pictures in his mind. He can use his hands no more."

Gibran's treatment of Ryder is reminiscent of his portrait of Rodin. The infelicities of life and dishevelment have been erased by the artist's pencil and we are left with a noble and powerful intellect and creative genius. Haskell describes the scene:

When Kahlil had finished drawing him, he looked at the picture carefully. 'It was a great revelation to me – such looking – as he was – to see what life was in it. Then he said: Wonderful work. You've drawn what's inside me – the bones and the brain.[10]

Years later, on reminiscing about the encounter with the now dead Ryder, Mary records: "Of Ryder's face, when I said it had the look of a deserted house where even the glass is broken out of all the windows, "But empty is not what you'd call it. Rather the life is remote, withdrawn. It is not absence of life, but he could give little manifestation…"[11]

---

8   *Beloved Prophet*, pages 232-233. *Letters of Kahlil Gibran*, page 399.
9   Jean Gibran and Kahlil Gibran: *Kahlil Gibran: His Life and World*, page 280.
10 *Beloved Prophet*, page 243.
11 *Beloved Prophet*, page 334.

Fellow Artists and Writers

A Portraitist Herself - Eliza Cecilia Beaux

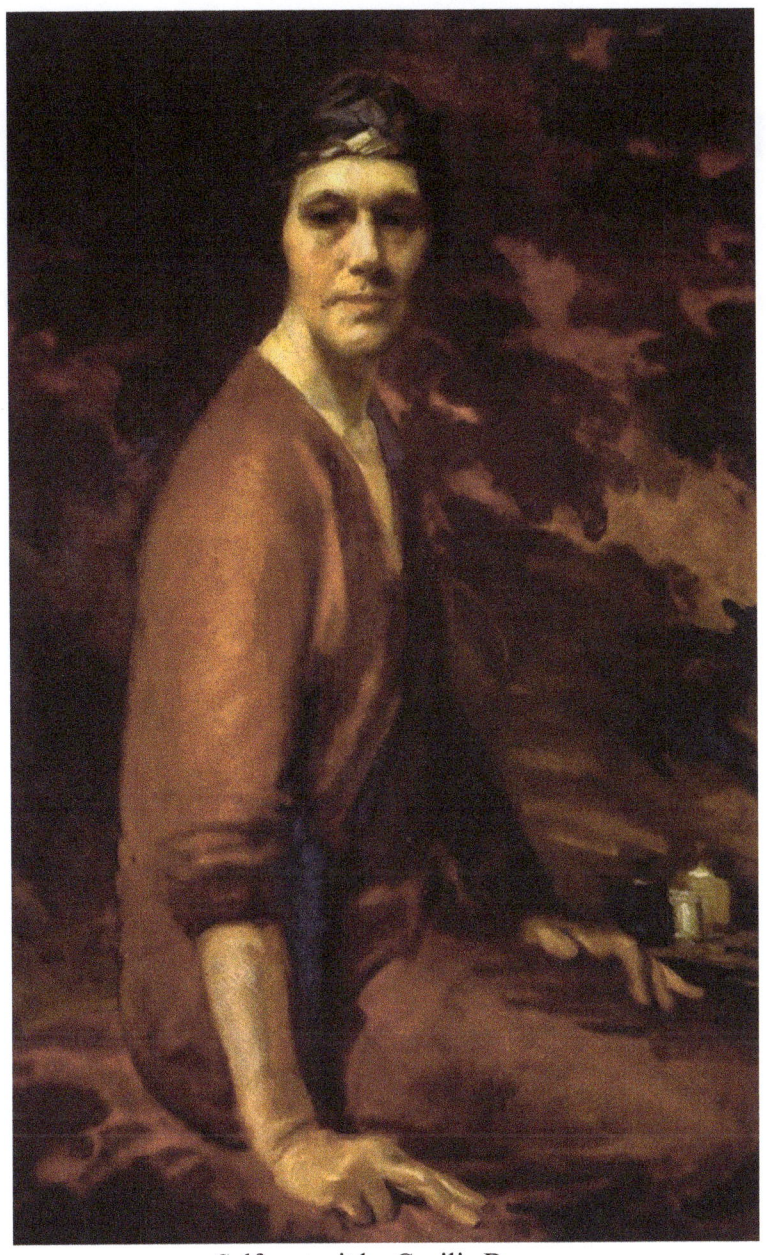
Self portrait by Cecilia Beaux

Eliza Cecilia Beaux (1855–1942) was one of the first American artists to acquire a painting by Gibran at the time of his first exhibition in New York in 1914. Gibran may have met her that December for by March 14, 1915 he told Mary that he had drawn her portrait[12]. Cecilia Beaux was a portrait artist herself, but her oil portraits were more extravagant than what Gibran was attempting, and were comparable to the works of John Singer Sargent. Her subjects were the aristocratic elites of America and Europe.

Cecilia was one of the most talented and famous portrait painters in America at the beginning of the 20th century competing with the likes of John Sargent. She had studied at the *Académie Julian* and had among her instructors famed artists like William-Adolphe Bouguereau.

She started exhibiting at the *Salon* in 1890. Her portraits were rapidly recognized and she had six shown at the Salon of the *Champ de Mars* in Paris in 1896.[13] She had a very successful and lucrative career affording her the ability to pay a generous sum for a Gibran painting in 1914.

The League of Women Voters chose her in 1923 as one of the 12 greatest living American Women. Newspapers described her portraits as "unique and distinct from tradition. She aims for the big, sweeping, dramatic effect." [14]

---

12 *Letters of Kahlil Gibran*, 1970, page 93.
13 *Birmingham News*, July 25, 1926.
14 *The Boston Globe*, June 24, 1923.

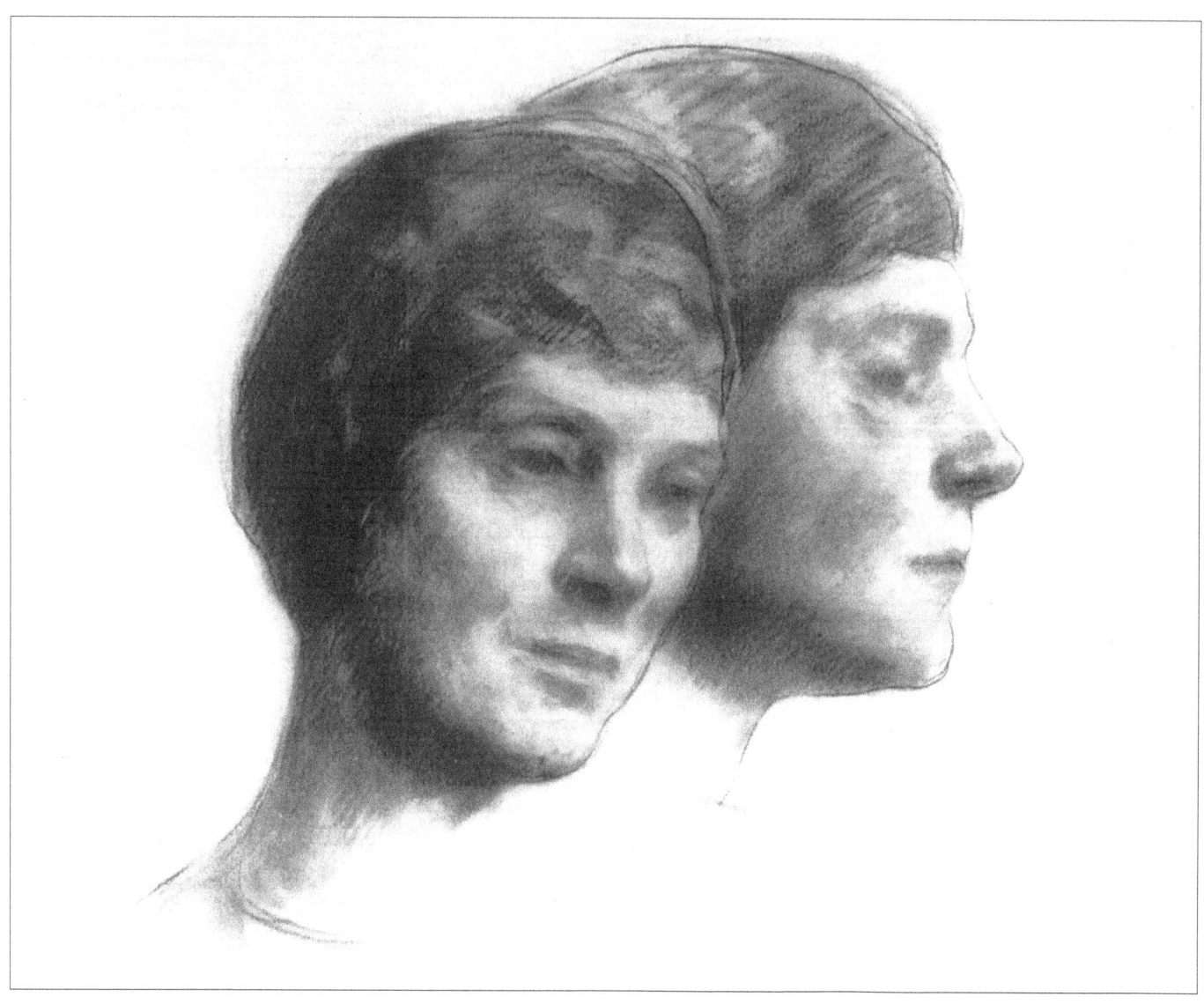

Gibran produced a composite dual portrait of Cecilia Beaux, a standard profile and a slightly off-center frontal view. The artist is shown in her characteristic head wrap; her gaze is directed downward with an air of dreaminess.

Symbolist to Modernist - Kenneth Hayes Miller

Kenneth Hayes Miller (1876-1952) was another American artist that Gibran drew in 1915 and found affinity with his work[15]. This is not surprising for Miller's work at that time was heavily influenced by Ryder and one art critic even compared Gibran's symbolist paintings to the work of Miller. Miller frequently depicted dreamy nudes in a hazy undefined environment, an approach readily recognizable in Gibran's work. Miller, however, would later change his approach and adopt a more modernist style depicting urban scenes reflecting the dynamics of modern life. It is for this later style that he is most remembered.

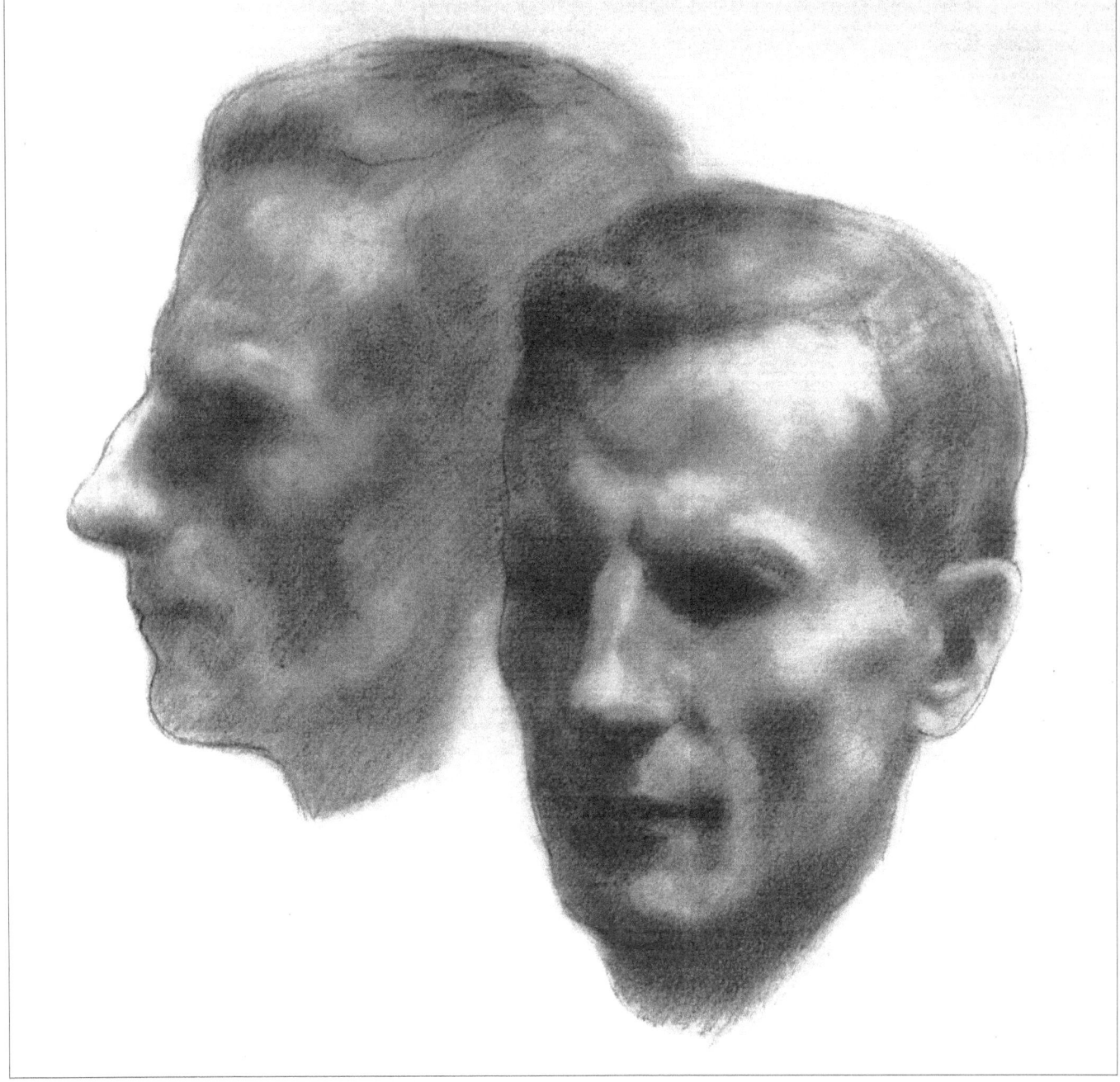

---
15   *Letters of Kahlil Gibran*, page 93.

Drawing the Archetype - Adele Watson

The American painter *Adele Watson* (1873-1947) had a lasting friendship with Gibran and was greatly influenced by his artistic style and his worldview. They seem to have spent as much time together discussing Zarathustra[16] as they did painting styles. Gibran's influence on her work is evident in her symbolist approach and frequent use of naked figures in a natural environment reflecting the vital ties between man and nature.

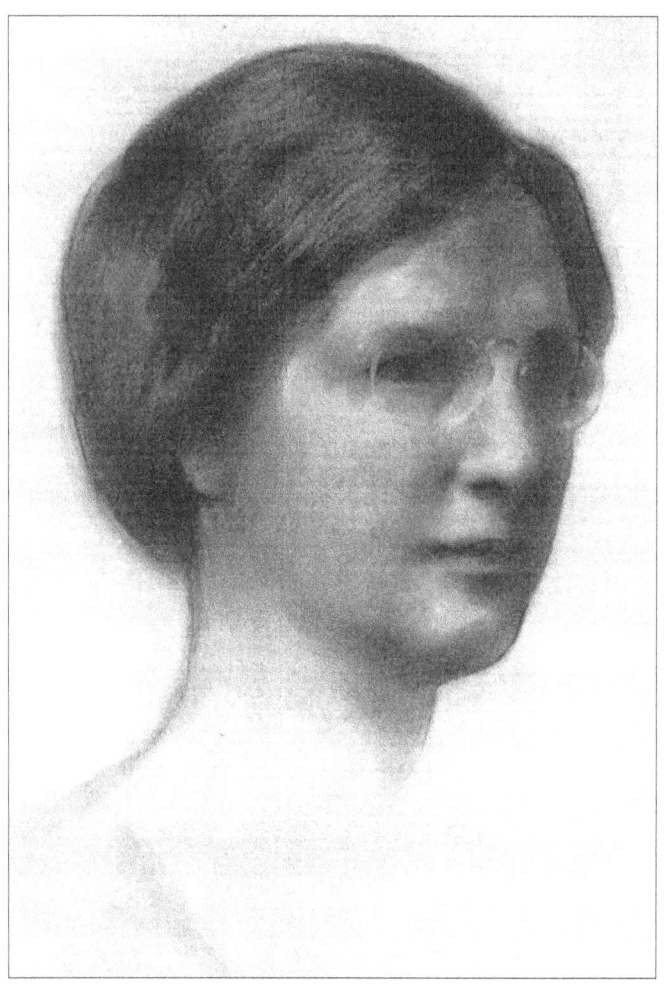 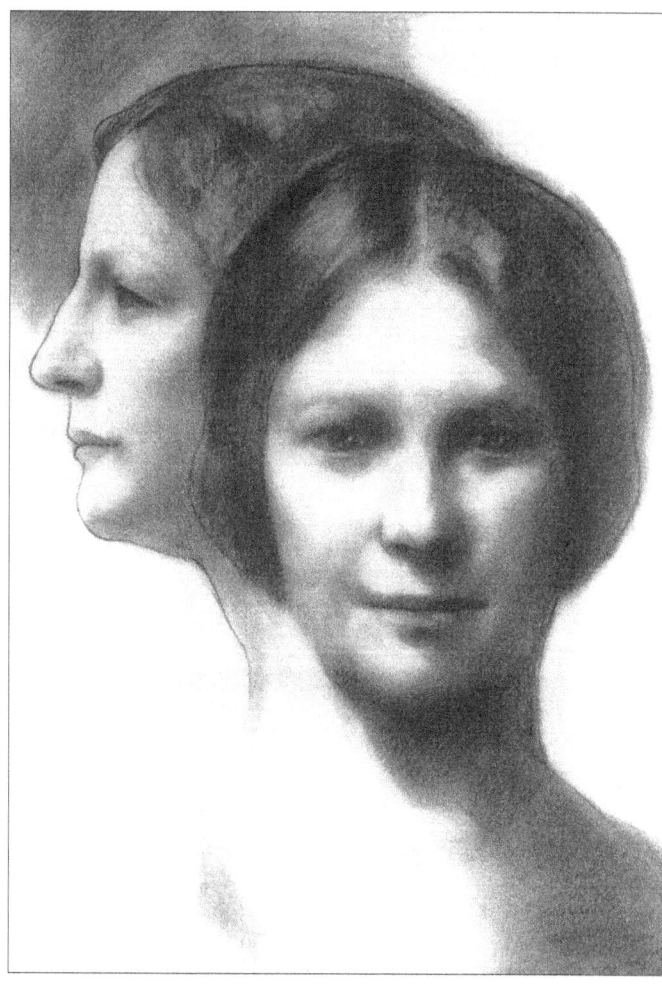

Watson traveled from her home in California to study art in Paris and New York and continued her journeying to the East Coast throughout her career. Her first exhibition in New York in 1917 consisted of landscapes "filled with rhythm of poetry and music," populated by nudes of classic mythology.[17] [18]

---

16 Mikhail Naimy: *Kahlil Gibran: a Biography*, page182.
17 *Brooklyn Daily Eagle*, December 10, 1916.
18 *LA Times*, January 17, 1917; *The Brooklyn Eagle*, December 10, 1917.

Fellow Artists and Writers

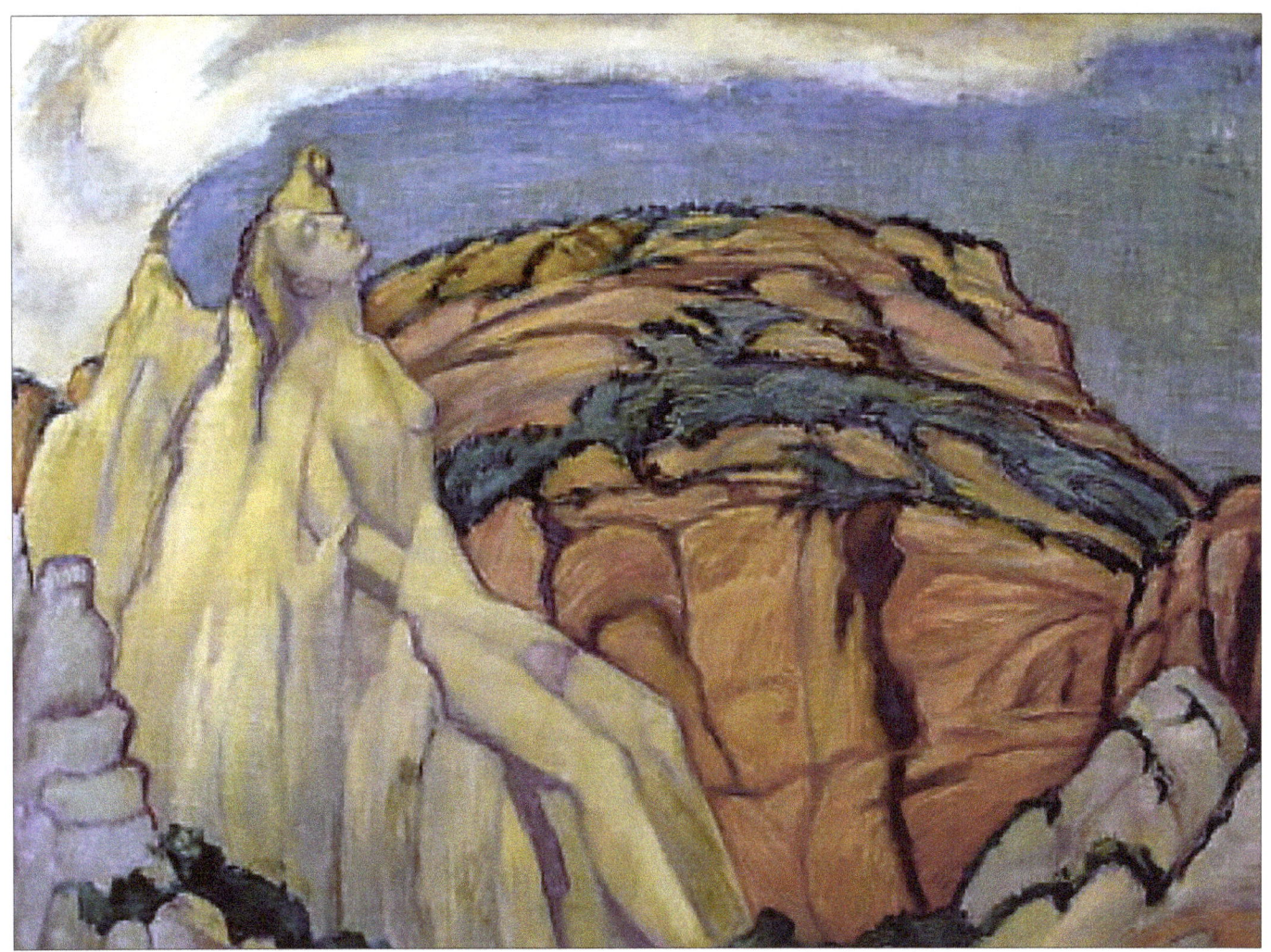

An example of the work of Watson illustrating Gibran's influence.

Examination of Watson's artwork clearly reveals the influence of Gibran, particularly in her symbolic use of the human figure in depictions of nature and the anthropomorphic rendering of landscapes, a symbolic testament to the unity of man and nature. Human figures in Watson's work share the same facial features and body type, something akin to Gibran's own focus on depicting the human archetype.

Critics continued to link her to Gibran for many years to come, and frequently noted that Watson's work was inspired by the work of Ryder, Davies, Blake, and Kahlil Gibran.[19] Gibran drew several portraits of Watson, two of which are reproduced on the left. The portraits are simple, realistic and convey very little of the character of the subject.

---

19 *Brooklyn Times*, January 18, 1931.

Writing Scheherazade - Laurence Housman

Another British writer that Gibran drew in the same period was *Laurence Housman* (1865-1959). Housman had rewritten the tales of *One Thousand and One Nights* (also known as the *Arabian Nights*) in an elegant edition illustrated by Edmond Dulac, which may have been reason enough to seek him out and obtain his portrait.

The portrait of the writer is very intense. The subject appears in deep meditation on a weighty subject reflected in his intent gaze. Gibran's depiction of a thoughtful and serious Housman is fully consonant with the author's character and personality.

Housman was a prolific writer purported to have published over 100 books on subjects as varied as women's emancipation, socialism, anti-war, in addition to plays, epistolary novels, and collections of poetry.

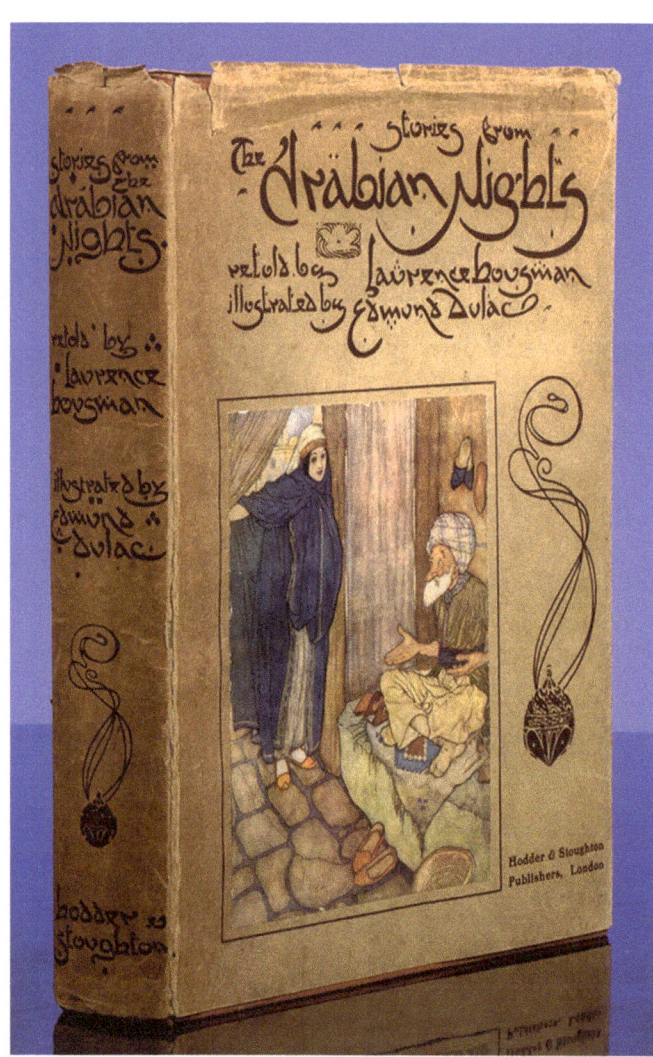

The Arabian Nights by Housman

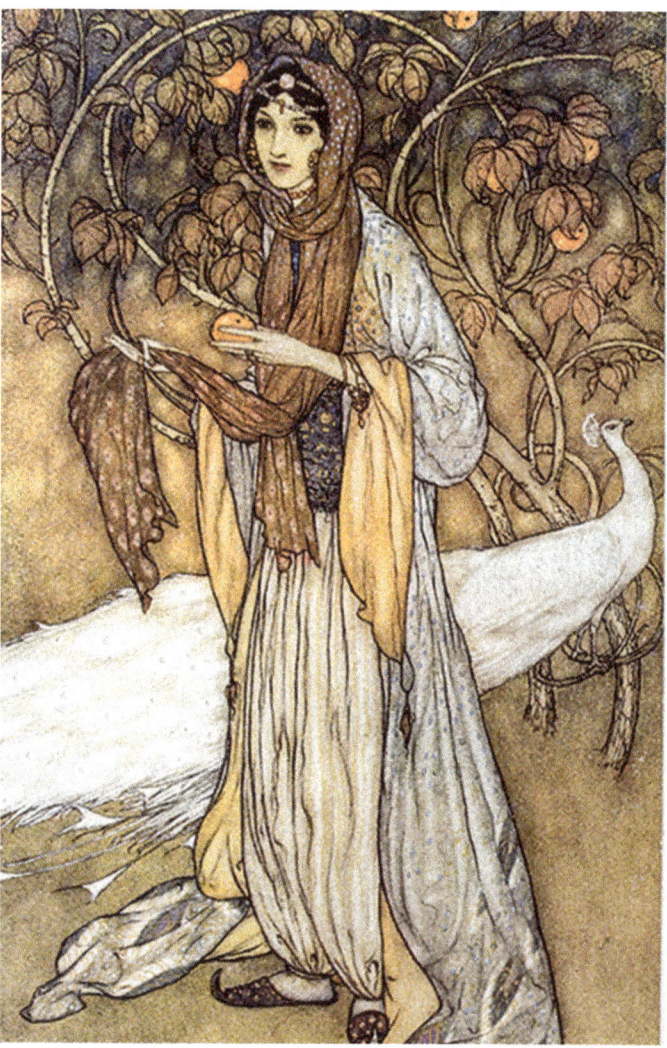

The Arabian Nights illustration by Edmond Dulac

Fellow Artists and Writers

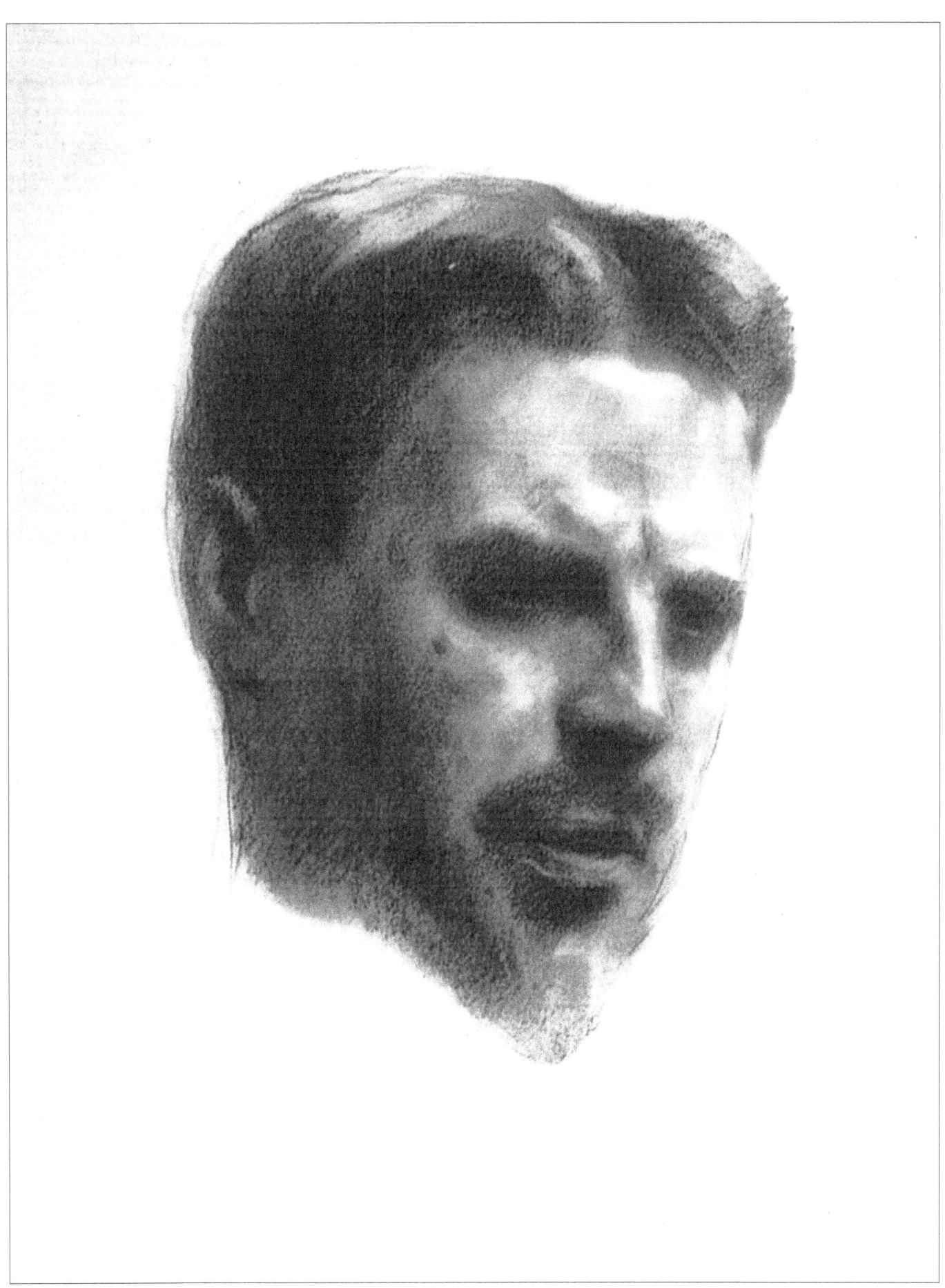

Drawing with a Chisel - Johan Bojer

In 1920, the Norwegian writer *Johan Bojer* (1872–1959) visited the United States to study the conditions of Norwegian immigrants in the American west. Bojer had been acquiring a reputation in America with the translation of his works that dealt with the struggle of poor fishermen and other paupers to secure a decent life for themselves and their families. Bojer was considered at the time as the most significant writer to come out of Scandinavia since Henrik Ibsen. He was described as the 'Maupassant of the North'[20] who had depicted the human condition among his countrymen with deep pathos and subtle insight.[21] Bojer had arrived in early April and Gibran drew his portrait soon after arrival.

Gibran's portrait of Bojer appeared in the press at the time[22] and in a book dedicated to Bojer.[23] Indeed, an opening chapter in the book was titled 'Bojer and Gibran' and describes the execution of the portrait and the exchange between the two men.

Howard Willard Cook, a devotee of both men, was present in the studio when Gibran drew Bojer, and contended that Gibran succeeded in creating a "marvelously intelligent companion piece" to the essays in the book.

> Kahlil Gibran, the painter and poet of Lebanon, aroused my sincere admiration some years ago by his book of poems, *The Madman*. As I sat in his studio one day last April, on the occasion of Bojer's first visit to America, and saw him dip into the soul of the man who had written *The Great Hunger*, and produce in highlight and shadow this likeness upon his drawing board, I knew that Gibran's genius was two-fold — the poet and artist were inseparable.
>
> "This is an unusual face," declared Gibran.
> "So many hills and valleys!" replied Bojer.

Bojer was manifestly nervous. He folded and unfolded his hands as he talked — and his talk was mostly about fairy tales, tales of his own saga that declared his kinship with Hans Andersen. He told us stories as he sat and as Gibran drew. He was infinitely embarrassed and was difficult to pose. The sitting lasted more than an hour, and when it was over Bojer stood before the drawing with his hands behind his back, balancing himself upon his toes. Turning to

---

20 *New York Tribune*, March 21, 1920.
21 *New York Tribune*, October 10, 1920.
22 *New York Times*, January 9, 1921.
23 Carl Gad: *Johan Bojer, the man and his works*, Moffat, Yard and co., NY, 1920.

Fellow Artists and Writers

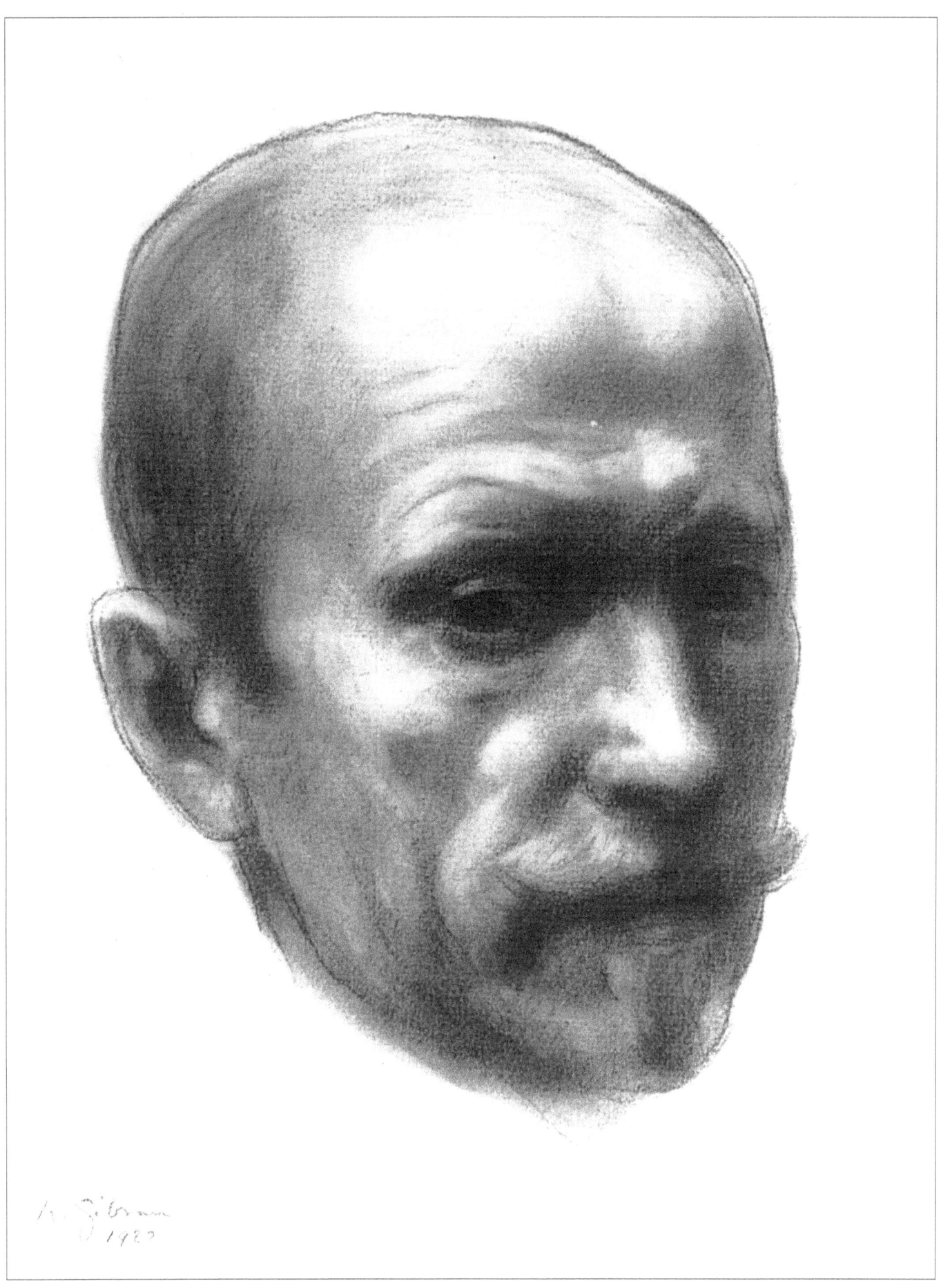

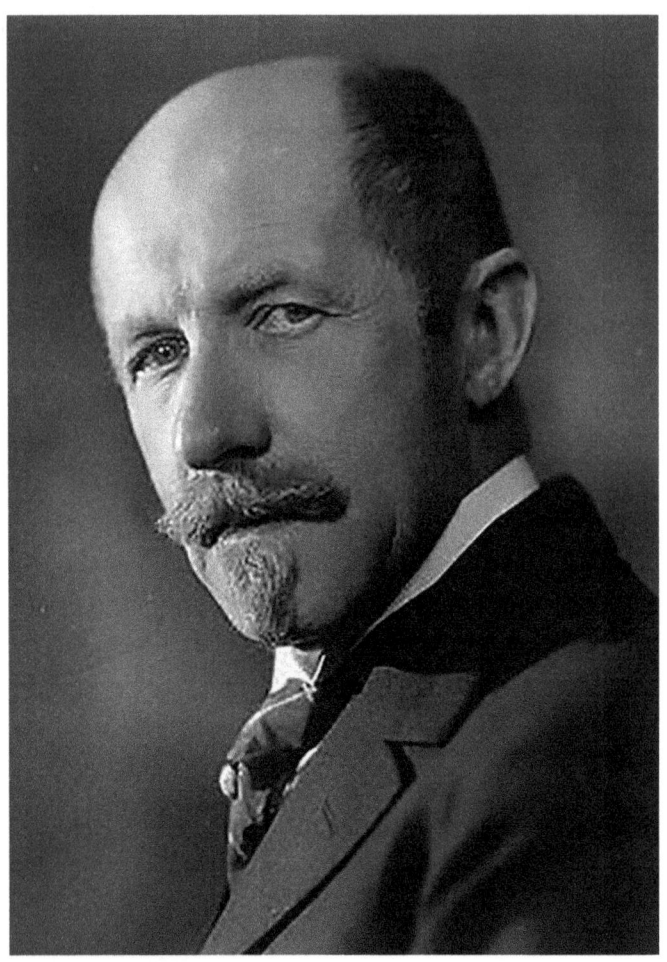

Studio Photograph of Johan Bojer

Gibran, he said: "You are a sculptor. Your work should be in marble! Your drawing resembles works by Michelangelo and Rodin."

Certainly those who know Bojer the man, who have felt the power of the restless, dynamic force that pervades his being, will find in this drawing a study of infinite power and penetrating character analysis. For those who love him as the writer who knows men's hearts, who understands life's ironies, and whose belief in Man makes possible the universal popularity of his translations, they too will see in the Gibran drawings these self-same things."

In discussions with Mary Haskell on April 20, Gibran commented on the portrait:

"One of the best heads I have drawn. Bojer says it is the first thing of himself he really likes. And it photographs very finely... It is a Rembrandt face and I liked doing it. A splendid head and a mind always busy and very restless." [24]

---

24 Mary Haskell Diary, April 20, 1920, University of North Carolina Library, Chapel Hill, NC, USA.

Fellow Artists and Writers

THE MAYA DEATH BELL - ALMA REED

The life of *Alma Reed* (1889–1966) was indelibly marked by her encounter with Mexico. In 1924, the young reporter joined an archeological mission to Chichen Itza sponsored by the Carnegie Foundation.[25] While in the Yucatan, she met the Governor of the Yucatan province, Felipe Carrilo, and they were to be married until he was captured by the *de la Huerta* rebels and executed just prior to their intended nuptials.[26] The tragic episode of her love and engagement made for sensational journalism. Newspapers reported the event with headings such as "Maya death bell tinkles near heart of Alma Reed,"[27] "Maya bell, a symbol of love and death, tinkles for beauty."[28]

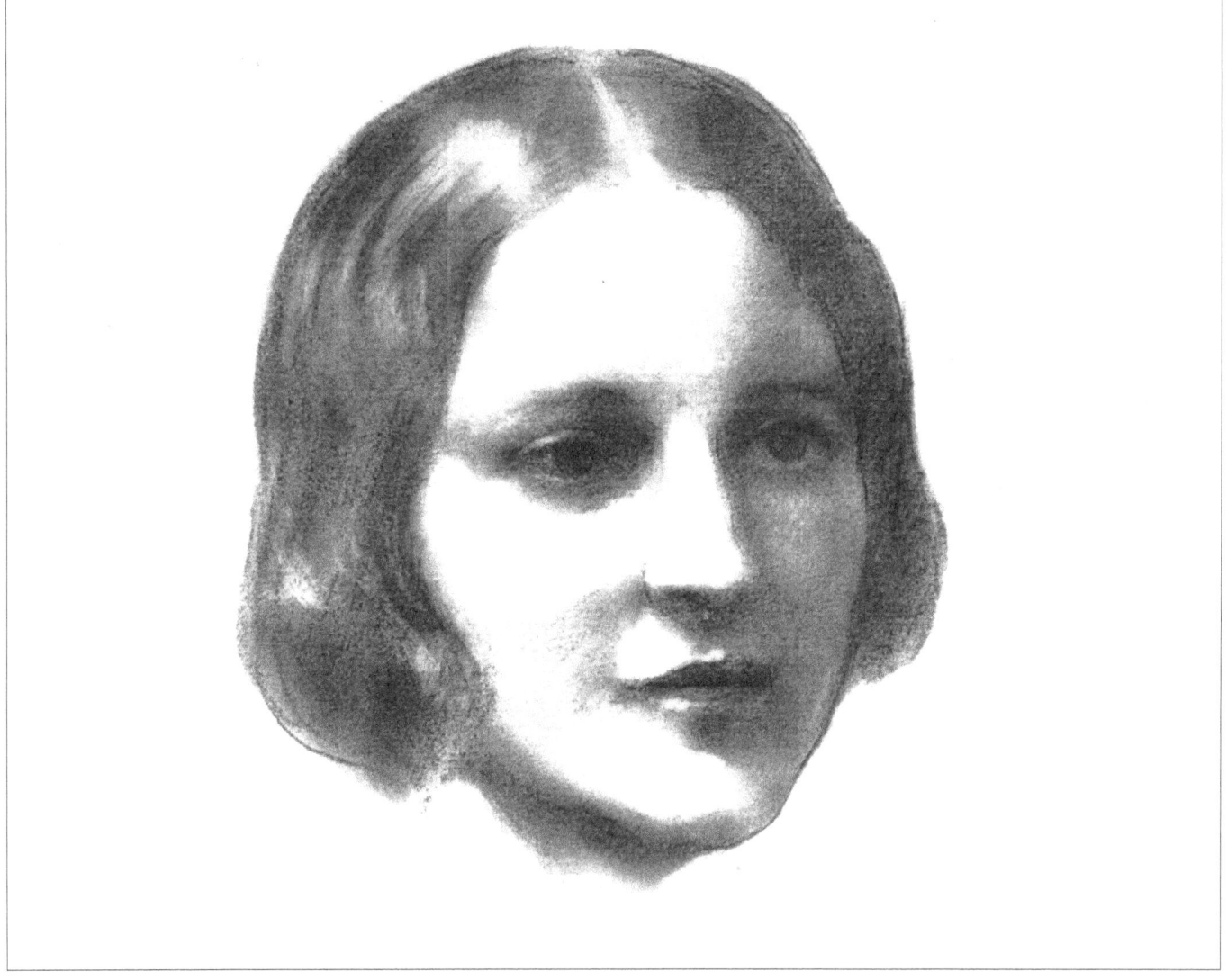

---

25 *The Escanaba Daily Press*, August 24, 1924.
26 Alma Reed, Michael Schluessleer: *Peregrina: love and death in Mexico*, University of Texas Press, 2007.
27 *The Buffalo Times*, April 27, 1924.
28 *The News – Herald*, April 29, 1924.

Alma's articles about the excavations in the Yucatan equally tickled the imaginations of American readers with reports of her personally descending into a pit dug in a Maya pyramid [29] "where an ancient people gave maidens to appease angry gods."[30] Alma played to the imagination of her readers describing the maiden sacrificed as being of "flawless beauty" wearing a "bridal wreath of white roses" on her way to the granite platform where she will be sacrificed accompanied by "sinister music." [31] After settling in New York, she took up translating world poetry, notably the Greek verses of Angelo Sikelianos.[32]

Her home in New York was a refuge for Latin American artists and others who cherished the dynamism of intercultural exchange. Reed was also instrumental in promoting the careers of such notable muralists as Jose Clemente Orozco whose biography she was to write.[33] Her sponsoring of the art of the dynamic Mexican artist was supplemented by publishing an illustrated book about him where she introduces his art and personality along with 247 plates of his frescoes, paintings, drawings and lithographs.[34] Orozco had decorated Alma's apartment with his work and Gibran chided her on being able to live surrounded by infernal visions.[35] This did not prevent Gibran and Orozco from becoming close friends and the Mexican was most understanding of Gibran's despondency at times because of the waning of his imaginative creativity.[36] Orozco painted Reed's portrait but soon destroyed it in a paroxysm, provoked by what he considered to be a far superior rendering by Gibran. The latter's admirable likeness includes the following dedication: "For Alma Reed: My dear and gracious friend, whose heart dwells in the world of truth and beauty. K. G. 1928."[37] Alma looks like a dreamer, a woman with a veil of sadness over her eyes and the setting of her mouth.

The friendship between Reed, Gibran, and Orozco deepened over the years despite the divergent views on art, with Orozco maintaining an "ominous silence" about Gibran's art except for the praise of his portrait of Reed. In January of 1929, Orozco and Reed celebrated Gibran's birthday in Orozco's studio, inviting an international gathering of artists and writers. During the festivities, readings of Gibran's works were done by noted artists and Gibran himself. Gibran was overtaken by an emotional sense of desperation at the end of the readings and confided in Reed that he had lost his creative power manifest in his early works.

---

29 *Times Colonist*, September 24, 1924.
30 *The Missoulian*, September 21, 1924.
31 *The Ogden Standard Examiner*, September 21, 1924.
32 *The San Francisco Examiner*, June 17, 1928.
33 Alma Reed: *Orozco*, Oxford University Press, 1956.
34 *The Cincinnati Inquirer*, December 18, 1932.
35 Jean Gibran and Kahlil Gibran: *Kahlil Gibran: His Life and World*, page 392.
36 Jean Gibran and Kahlil Gibran: *Kahlil Gibran: His Life and World*, page 393.
37 Alma M. Reed, Michael K. Schuessler: *Peregrina: Love and Death in Mexico*, University of Texas Press, 2007, page 18.

Fellow Artists and Writers

BETWEEN FAUST AND THE PROPHET - ALICE RAPHAEL

In March of 1917, *Alice Raphael* (1887-1975) published a review on Gibran's art in *The Seven Arts* journal soon after Gibran's second exhibition in New York.[38] In her article, she christened Gibran as a symbolist and tackled his artistic approach in very effusive praise.

Raphael's name had first appeared on the literary scene with a novel published in 1910 dealing with the struggles of personal fulfillment and social constraints.[39] The events of the novel take place against the exotic background of aristocratic St Petersburg and artistic Paris. Despite wide advertisement, the book found little sympathy from the serious critics who found "little personality in the book", and tepid dramatic content despite its "fine literary quality."[40] Raphael had planned a second novel, but apparently abandoned it.[41] She seemed to take to heart the advice of a critic of her first novel who thought that it would have been more absorbing if it had been condensed into a short story.[42] Hence, her next literary foray was into play writing and in 1917, she produced three one act plays.[43] She also delved into literary criticism,[44] and published a few poems in various journals.[45]

Alice Pearl Raphael was born on June 22, 1887 in Brownsville, Texas. She attended Barnard College in New York City and studied music in Germany. She later lived in Zurich, studied with Carl Gustav Jung, and was a lay analyst for several years, which explains the length of the psychological analysis that weighted her first novel. Her recent interest in paintings may have brought her in touch with Gibran and led to the publication of her laudatory review of his recent exhibition.

Raphael's essay in the journal the *Seven Arts* did much to elevate Gibran's stature in the artistic community and bolster his self-esteem. It also influenced reviews of Gibran's exhibitions in New York and Boston. In her review, Raphael is overly effusive in her evaluation of the place of Gibran's art:

It is at the dividing line of East and West, of symbolism and representation, of sculptor

---

38 Alice Raphael: The Art of Kahlil Gibran, *The Seven Arts*, March 1917, pp. 531-534.
39 Alice Raphael: *The Fulfillment*, Sturgis and Walton, NY, 1910.
40 *The Brooklyn Daily Eagle*, May 23, 1910; *New York Times*, April 2, 1910.
41 *The Baltimore Sun*, August 13, 1911.
42 *The Boston Globe*, April 2, 1910.
43 Dormer Windows, *The Drama*, volume 11, Nos 11-12, August September, 1921; An Interlude in the Life of St Francis, *The Drama*, volume 11, No. 2, November, 1920; and The Catcher.
44 The Jest, *The Drama*, volume 10, No. 4, January 1920.
45 *The Seven Arts*, June 1917, pp.188-89.

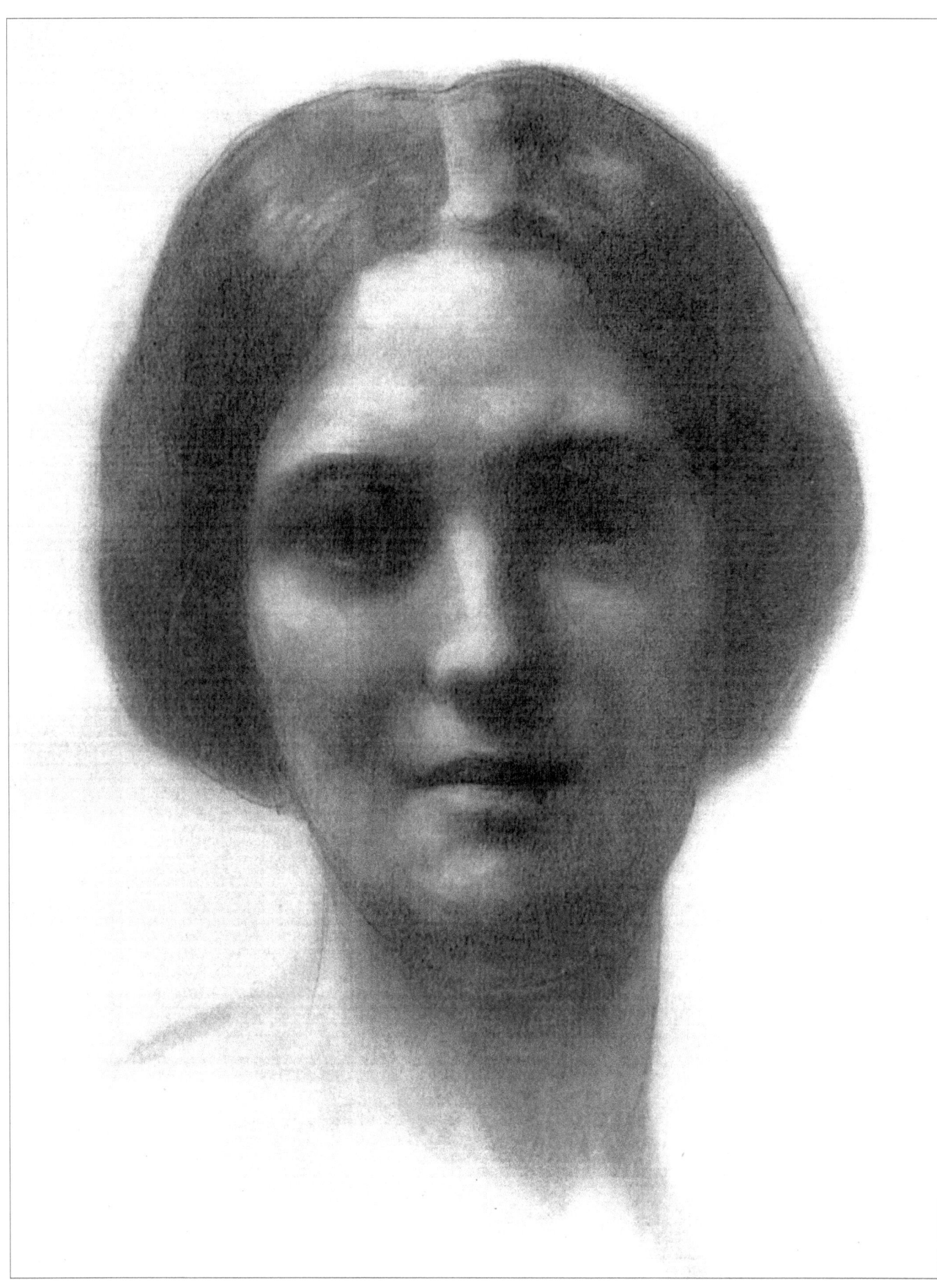

and painter, that the work of Mr. Kahlil Gibran (exhibited last month at Knoedler's) presents itself as an arresting force in our modern conception of painting.

When Mr. Sargent wishes to express himself symbolically, he has to have the vast walls of the Boston Library at his disposal. For to represent the Christos, let us say, it is essential for minds of his type to transcribe every incident in the birth and death of Christ or to portray the whole of religion.

Mr. Gibran needs only a small sheet of paper to give us the meaning of the human spirit and he says what he has to say as simply as possible.

Mr. Gibran's art is symbolic in the highest sense because its roots lie not in ideas but in those truths which are fundamental for all ages and all experiences.

Like Rodin, Mr. Gibran is a master not only in symbolism, but in the technical grasp of his material.

The head lying upon this luminous ground is so delicate that the throat veins seem to quiver and the pale lips to move. Actually, there is no drawing in the usual sense of the word; the painting is modelled in color; and this picture gave me an intense feeling of Mr. Gibran's sculptural power. That something flowing which alone makes marble other than a piece of stone lies in Mr. Gibran's paintings. It is the very soul of sculpture and he is expressing it in a kindred form. I cannot but feel that painting is not for him an adequate vehicle and that in sculpture he could again unite his many-sided nature and attain the fruition of the symbolic root which lies at the basis of his work.

Raphael's positive essay was contested by some reviewers. Glen Mullin wrote in *The Nation*: "This essay plucks out the heart of Gibran's mystery with a professional flourish. It burns incense to Gibran's art mainly upon its symbolic side – where it is weakest. It finds all manner of remote and subtle implications in the artist's work, which make rather persuasive reading until we carefully examine the drawings themselves. We will probably reject first of all the fantastic notion that Gibran's symbolism is a peculiar heritage of the Arabic race mind which has been grafted upon the traditions of the West as a novel contribution to a present era weary of ante-bellum realism; for it is difficult to see how the most adept of those who distil sublimations can recognize in Gibran's art any essence which countless Occidental artists might not equally claim."[46]

---

46   Glen Mullin: Blake and Gibran. *The Nation*, April 10, 1920, volume 110, Spring Book Supplement, pp. 485-486.

Raphael expanded her essay significantly when it appeared as an introduction to Gibran's book *Twenty Drawings*. The book was billed as a collection of drawings "representing the human form in attitudes expressing the eternal verities."[47] In this introduction, she goes beyond the focus of her original essay and explores Gibran's concepts of life and dialogue among civilizations. Raphael later produced a celebrated English translation of Goethe's Faust that was deemed among the best.[48] A Goethe scholar commented on her translation:

> Alice Raphael has the mark of Faust upon her, for she felt her way into the spirit of the immortal poem, before she resorted to scholarship to convince herself that what she had felt was not her creation, but a faithful reproduction of the original.[49]

Gibran drew Raphael's portrait in 1928 and dedicated it to her two daughters. In the portrait, the mature Raphael has an intelligent bright look and a scholarly gravitas, commensurate with her stature as a Goethe scholar.

THE CHRONICLER OF POETRY - HOWARD WILLARD COOK

In 1918, Howard Willard Cook (1890–1959) published the first edition of his book *Our Poets of Today* that presented to the public brief essays about 68 American poets. Gibran was not among them, but the author had dedicated his book "For all friends—who have made me know the beauty of poetry in friendship—and especially for my friends Julia Ellsworth Ford, Witter Bynner, Kahlil Gibran, Percy Mackaye." The dedication was there again in the revised edition of 1922 that had an expanded repertoire of 122 poets, and again in the 1926 edition. Ford, Bynner, and Mackaye appeared not only in the dedication, but also in essays presenting their work. The exclusion of Gibran was understandable; he was not an "American Poet", but a "Syrian poet." The list of poets in the book contains many of the poets that Gibran himself had drawn, or was associated with including Witter Bynner, Percy Mackaye, Vachel Lindsay, Edwin Markham, Josephine Preston Peabody, Corinne Roosevelt Robinson, James Oppenheim, Elinor Wylie, Orrick Johns, Mercedes de Acosta, and Leonora Speyer.[50] When the first edition was reviewed in *The New York Herald*, Cook's portrait by Gibran was featured prominently above the article.[51]

---

47 *New York Times*, January 11, 1920.
48 *Faust; a tragedy: in a modern translation*, Johann Wolfgang von Goethe; Alice Raphael. New York, The Heritage club, 1928.
49 Carl Schreiber: *A Note on Faust Translations*. Jonathan Cape and Harrison Smith, NY, 1930.
50 Howard Willard Cook, *Our poets of today*, New York, Moffat, Yard & company, 1923.
51 *The New York Herald*, New York, December 22, 1918.

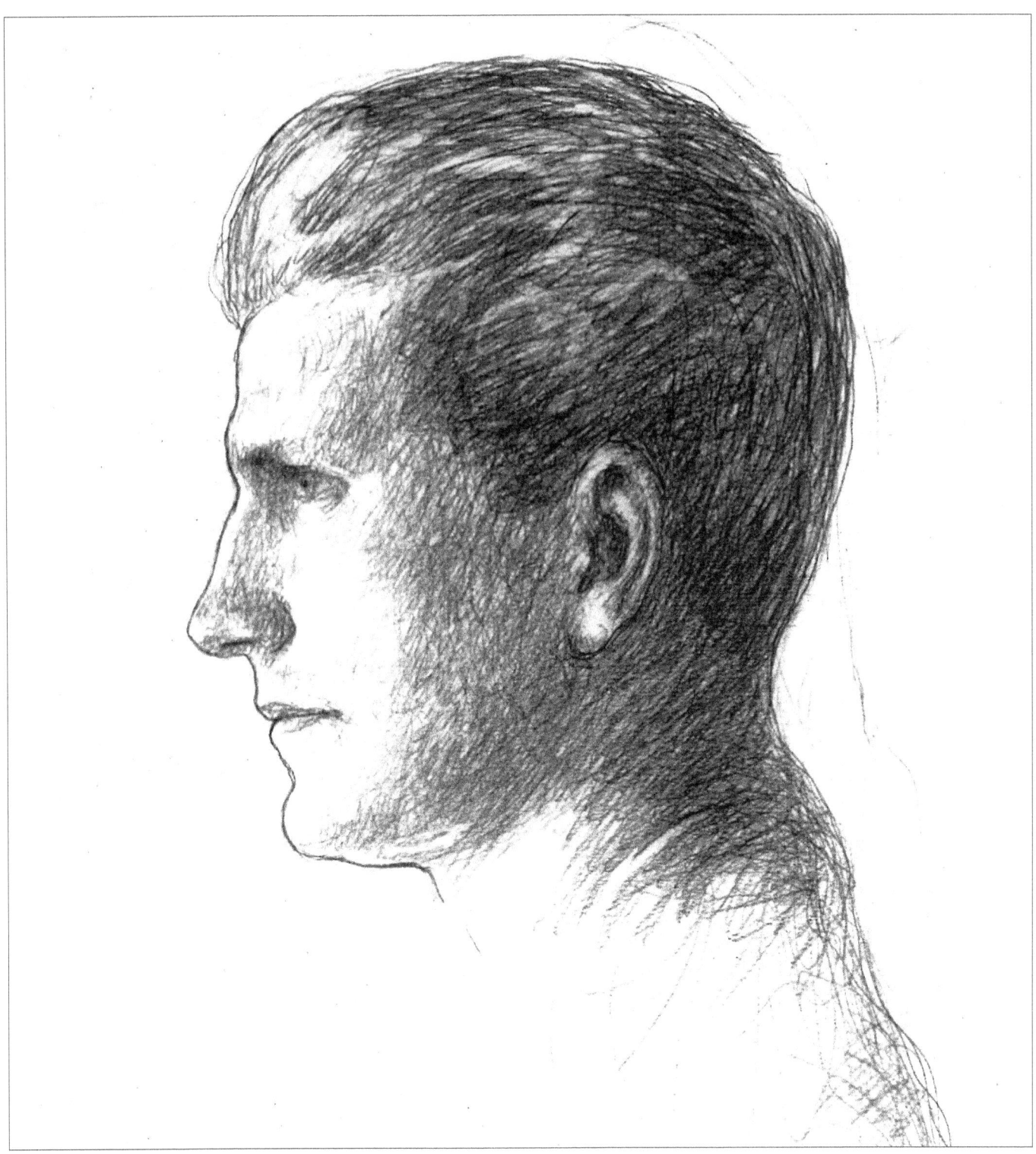

Gibran's portrait of Cook appeared in newspapers in conjunction with either publicity for the book, or in association with a review that Cook wrote of Gibran's work. *The Sun* also published that same month a review of *The Madman* by Cook[52] in which he extolled the twofold genius of Gibran for drawings "of rare beauty" and prose poems filled "with poetic life as the psalms

---

52 Howard Willard Cook: Kahlil Gibran, Poet of the East, *The Sun*, December 15, 1918, Section 5, Books and the Book World, page 4.

of David." A friendly orientalism also laced the review: "It is proper that out of Lebanon in Syria should come a new psalmist and writer of fables, who gives to us of the western world a note too seldom found in the writings of our own poets." Diffidently quoting the publisher claims of praise by Rodin and comparison to Tagore, Cook asserts "But Gibran is first himself. His talents are the offspring of an original being who is distinctive in his own originality. His work it that of an internationalist who writes not for one race of people, but for all."

Of the illustrations in the book, Cook has this to say: "In the three illustrations … there is the well-nigh perfect contour of figure that distinguishes his nudes, done with a sweeping grace. But their greatest charm lies in their life - Gibran's figures radiate life - and that same essence of human understanding dominating his poems is found again in them."

A Constellation of Luminaries

THE DIVINE SARAH - SARAH BERNHARDT

Sarah Bernhardt (1844-1923) arrived in New York on May 4, 1913 after spending five months on the West Coast.[1] Her planned engagement in New York was for 2 weeks at the *Palace Theater* where she was to perform in a new one act play and selection of acts from her famous repertoire, all naturally in French.[2] The other plays she was to perform during her New York stay were typically short selections, like the second act of Victor Hugo's Lucrece Borgia,[3] or the third act of Victorien Sardou's Theodora.[4]

Gibran attended her performance of the one act play *Une nuit de Noel sous la Terreur* written for her by her son Maurice Bernhardt in which she plays the role of a young *vivandière* named Marion. It tells the story of a young circus girl who joins the revolutionary army in 1793 as a *vivandière*, while still harboring some sympathy for the waning French aristocracy. She manages to save the lives of the Comte and Comtesse de Kersahrt and their little daughter.[5] The seventy-year-old actress in the role of the youthful *vivandière* must have required many adjustments. As a reviewer for the *Evening World* put it: "The voice that once rose from the depth of woe to the heights of passion now sounds like an echo; the long catlike step that used to carry Bernhardt across the stage halts at the first table or chair… For the first time in her glorious career, she finds it hard to hide her age."[6] The setting of the play was arranged to meet the needs of the aging actress: "It was a sight never to be forgotten to see the illustrious Sarah brought on in a cart as a *vivandière* who saves the aristocratic refugees in the barn of peasants still stupid enough in 1793 to be true to royalty. Fortunately, the furniture in the barn was placed so that the skilled actress could grasp it as easily as she did the play."

Gibran approached her after the performance and she was intrigued by his background, even telling him that her mother spoke Arabic! She initially demurred stating a busy schedule and fatigue, but she later granted him a sitting on May 26, 1913.

---

1   *New York Times*, May 5, 1913; *The Brooklyn Daily Eagle*, May 4, 1913.
2   Joanna Richardson: *Sarah Bernhardt and her world*, page 204.
3   *Brooklyn Daily Eagle*, May 20, 1913.
4   *Brooklyn Daily Eagle*, May 12, 1913.
5   *Brooklyn Daily Eagle*, May 6, 1913.
6   *Evening World*, May 6, 1913.

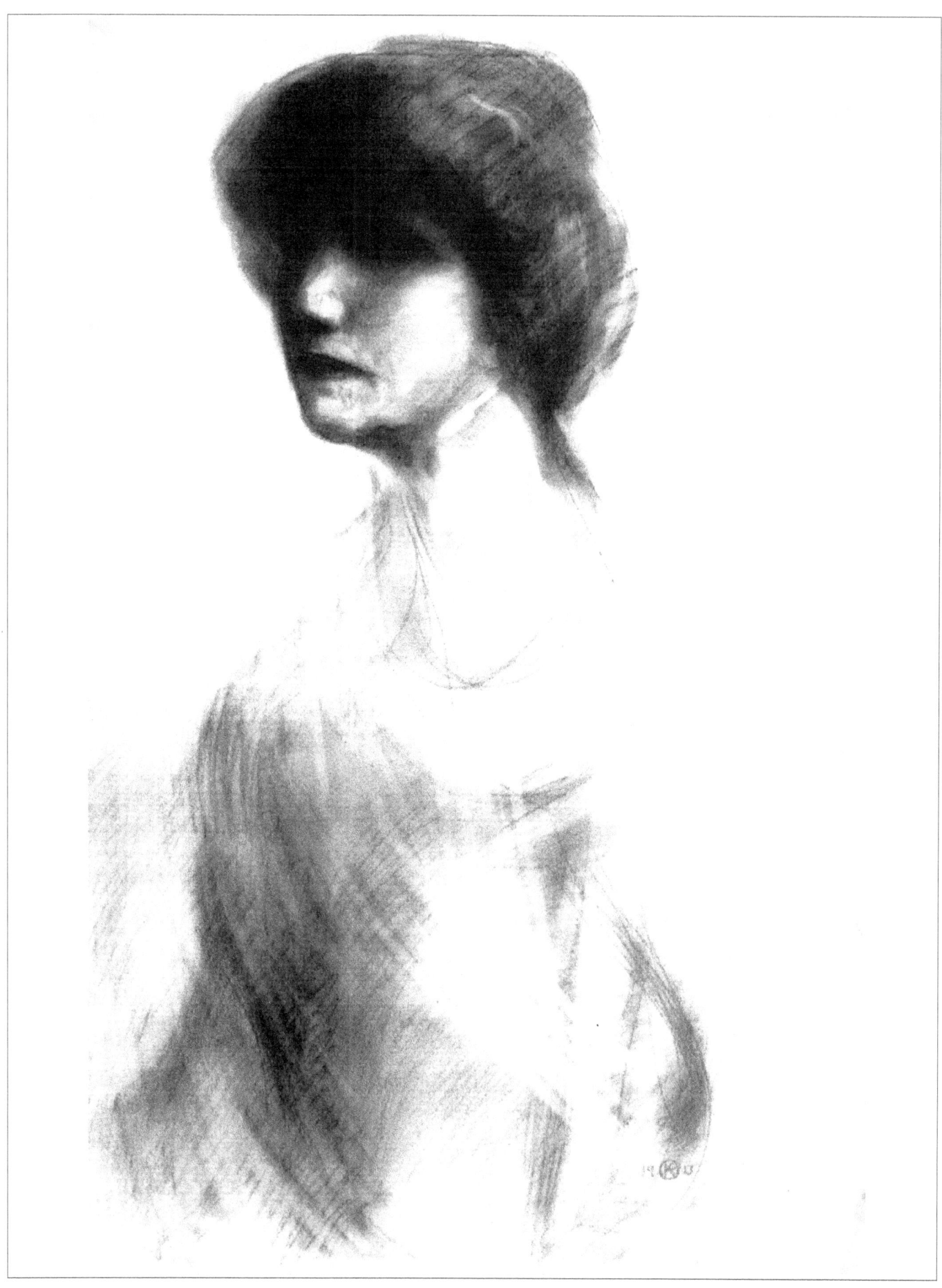

A Constellation of Luminaries

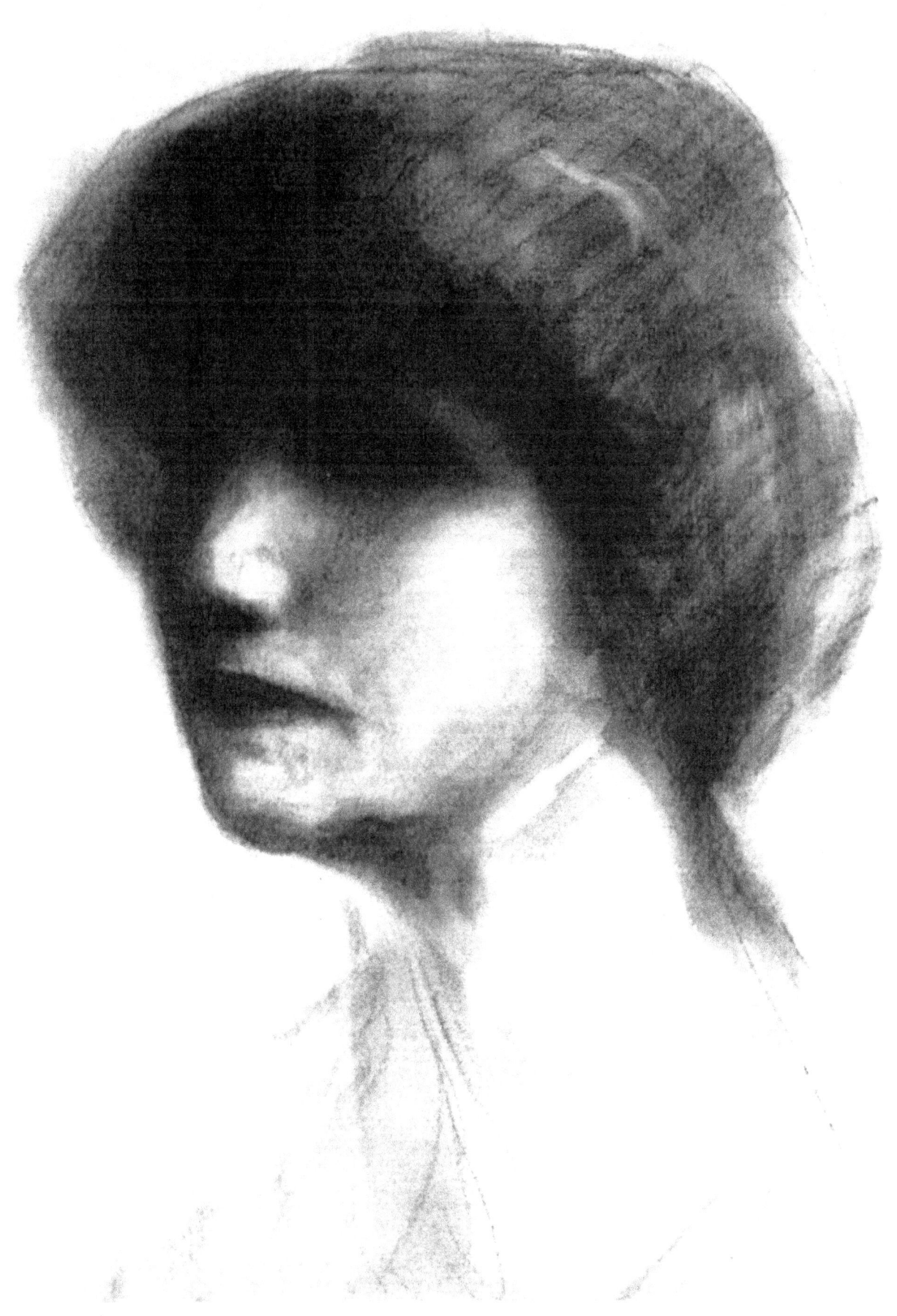

The Divine Sarah Bernhardt is here. I was given the great pleasure of seeing her off the stage last Tuesday. She was most gracious – gracious is the only word. She spoke with more than delight of her visits to Syria and Egypt. She also said that her mother spoke Arabic and that the music of that language lived and is still living in her soul. But when it came to posing for a drawing she smiled and said, "How can I do that now? I am so tired. I am giving two performances a day – even Sunday." After that she said, "I will try. Come and see me again next week." [7]

Sarah treated Gibran to a heavy dose of her famous lies and deceptions.[8] She is known to have offered so many different versions of her family origin and connections that biographers are bewildered and confused. Sarah's mother was a rather successful courtesan of Dutch Jewish ancestry. Youle van Hard-Bernard, Sarah's mother, was born in Amsterdam and spent all her life on the Continent. The claim of speaking Arabic is laughable at best. The invented affection and closeness to her mother is a mirage that Sarah used to cover the fact that her courtesan mother had no time for her and had placed her in multiple homes, even a convent, and always away from her.[9] While Sarah's story about her mother speaking Arabic is clearly contrived, her own association with the Arab world may have merit. Sarah had been to Egypt in 1888 visiting Alexandria and possibly giving a performance in its famed opera house.[10]

Sarah's age during this tour was subject to many remarks by the reviewers. The *New York Tribune* critic observed: "the years are at last beginning to conquer even her. There is still… the old fire in her climaxes; she retains to an almost incredible degree her control of facial expression… The French actress conceals these limitations imposed upon her so ingeniously, so naturally, that only close observation reveals them. It is a remarkable exhibition of the economy of effort, the husbanding of strength. She moves but little, whenever possible she supports herself, by a well calculated gesture, on the shoulder or arm of one of her associates."[11]

At last the divine Sarah is caught! The drawing which I made yesterday [May 26, 1913], though it does not show her real age, is a great success. But if I am to go through the same process with other great men and women, I might as well give up art and become a diplomat! She wanted me to sit at a distance so I may not see the details of her face. But I did see them. She made me take off some of the wrinkles. She even asked me to change the shape of her huge mouth! Sarah Bernhardt is hard to please, to understand, and to be

---

7   *Beloved Prophet*, page 126. *Letters of Kahlil Gibran*, page 261.
8   Robert Gottlieb: Sarah: *The life of Sarah Bernhardt*, Yale University Press, New Haven, 2010.
9   Arthur Gold and Robert Fizdale: *The Divine Sarah: a life of Sarah Bernhardt*, Alfred A. Knopf, NY, 1991, pages 10-13.
10 Arthur Gold and Robert Fizdale: *The Divine Sarah*, page 239.
11 *New York Tribune*, May 11, 1913.

with. She has a temper. She must be treated as a mighty queen, and if you do not treat her as such, you are done for! I think I understood her yesterday, and I behaved accordingly; and perhaps that is the reason she liked me a little, for when I wanted to leave her she gave me her left hand to kiss. [12]

The viewer would be hard pressed to identify the person in the portrait as Sarah Bernhardt. The cheek, lips and chin suggest a much younger woman and Sarah's famous piercing gaze is obscured in shadow to avoid drawing the wrinkles surrounding her eyes Only her hair appears to have a semblance of realism to the way the actress looked at the time.

Gibran echoes the above narrative in an interview he gave in 1914: "He showed me a tall sinuous-looking drawing of Bernhardt. "The most great artificial artist of the nineteenth century' he commented. 'Every feature, every limb, every gesture has been worked over to produce the effect of youth. Not one natural tone or movement.' He recalled with horror the afternoon 'the woman who tries to be young' posed for him. She insisted on keeping at the far end of the room so that he might not see her wrinkles. She covered her neck with veils in a vain attempt to give the illusion of youth with which she can deceive her audiences only by the aid of cunning stage appliances. Mr. Gibran's study of her gives the impression of a woman whose youth and beauty is veiled, lost in shadow.[13]

Gibran's views echo those of other perceptive writers like Anton Chekov and Bernard Shaw who did not particularly like the actress although admired her skill at her craft.[14]

---

12 *Beloved Prophet*, pp 126-127. *Letters of Kahlil Gibran*, pp 261-262.
13 Ruth Danenhower: Artist puts Roosevelt, Wilson and Edison in his Temple of Fame. *The New York Press*, June 7, 1914.
14 Robert Gottlieb: *Sarah: The life of Sarah Bernhardt*, page 112.

THE DANCE OF FLAMES - RUTH ST DENIS

Ruth St Denis (1879-1968) was a recurrent visitor to the Ford household. Gibran had attended one of her Egyptian shows in Boston in December of 1910.[15] He met her in person when he attended the premiere of a play by Percy MacKaye in January of 1914 as a guest of the Fords.[16] The two artists found their interests in mystical subjects and the Orient as a common ground for a lasting friendship. Gibran was soon visiting the dancer in her elegant studio and making rapid flowing sketches of her dancing almost nude[17].

> Ruth St Denis danced for me yesterday afternoon [January 20, 1914] almost nude. I made a few little drawings of her while she was moving and whirling in her fine large studio.[18]

On seeing the sketches, Mary Haskell commented:

> April 26, 1914. The small sketches of Ruth St Denis are beautiful – full of nebulae curves. 'She is very remarkable. She couldn't dance as she does if she were not. She wants to come here and dance for me but I do not want to see her.' The sketches are almost all nude. "She wore some gauze but I just didn't see the gauze. She was delighted with the sketches and wants them but I told her I'd make some more for her. I won't let her have these."[19]

Ruth's nakedness was a matter of artistic expression, not seduction.[20] She is known to have been averse to sexual advances as in her famous confrontation with Rodin who after drawing her dancing in flimsy veils attempted to molest her sexually.[21] The French sculptor was famous for such behavior with his models and with other artists like Isadora Duncan.[22]

By early February, Gibran had produced a unique portrait of the dancer in Oriental garb. He wrote effusively about her to Mary[23], and it is possible that a parable in his book *The Wanderer* entitled *The Dancer* was inspired by their friendship[24].

---

15 Jean Gibran and Kahlil Gibran: *Kahlil Gibran: His Life and World*, page 200.
16 *Letters of Kahlil Gibran*, page 297.
17 *Beloved Prophet*, page 172. *Letters of Kahlil Gibran*, page 302.
18 *Beloved Prophet*, page 172. *Letters of Kahlil Gibran*, page 302.
19 *Beloved Prophet*, pp 186-7.
20 Jack Anderson: *Art without boundaries*, University of Iowa Press, Iowa City, 1997, page 36.
21 Ruth Butler: *Rodin: The Shape of Genius*, Yale University Press, New haven, 1993, page 442. Frederic Grunfeld: *Rodin: a Biography*, Henry Holt and Company, NY, 1987, pp 513-514.
22 Frederic Grunfeld: *Rodin: a Biography*, Henry Holt and Company, NY, 1987, pages 413-414.
23 Jean Gibran and Kahlil Gibran: *Kahlil Gibran: His Life and World*, pp 264-265. *Letters of Kahlil Gibran*, page 308
24 Ruth St Denis: The Independent Art of the Dance. In *Theatre: Essays on the Arts of the Theatre*, edited by Juliet Rich Isaacs, pp 218-219.

A Constellation of Luminaries

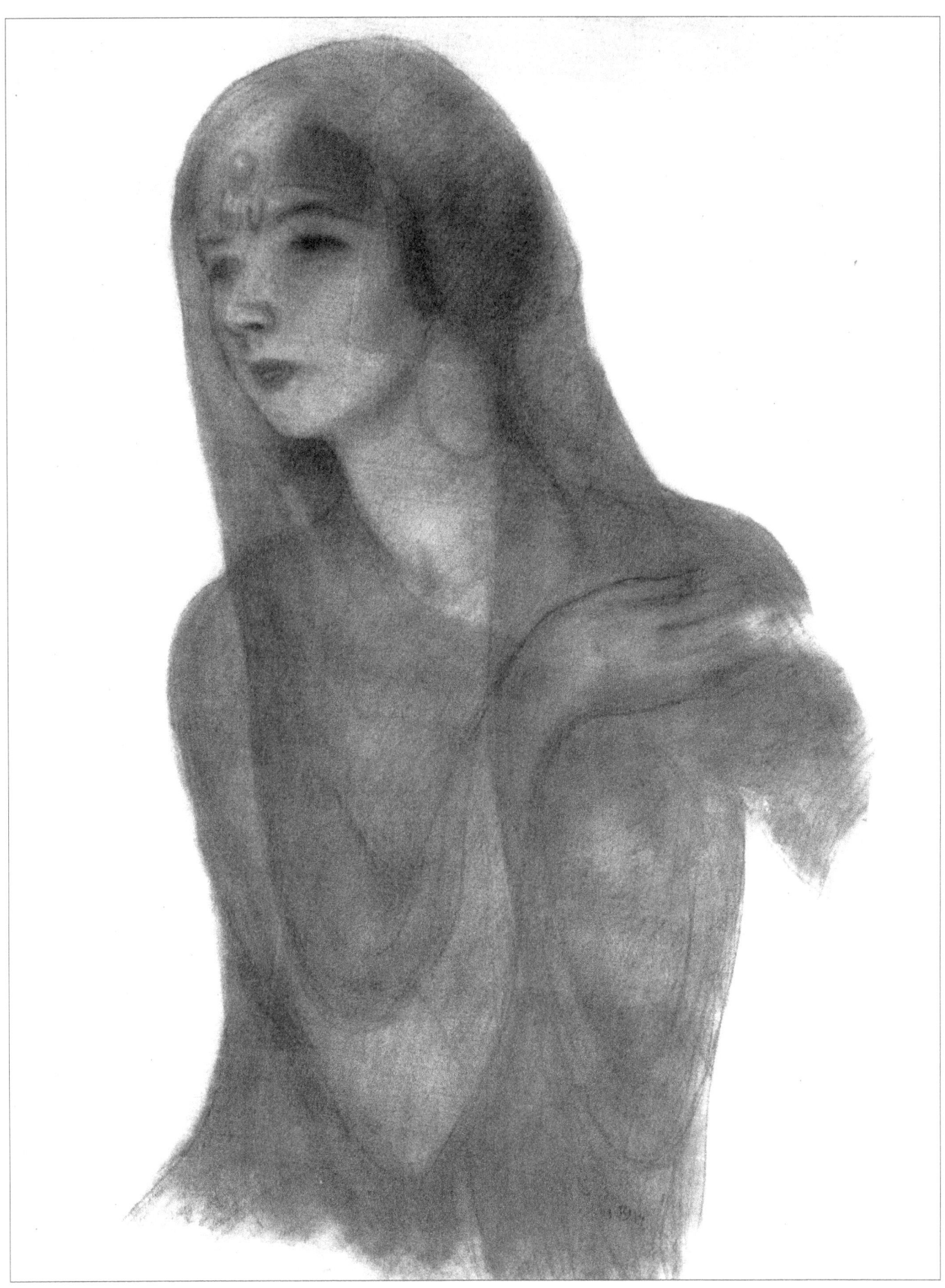

Exoticism is the hallmark of Gibran's drawing of Ruth. The delicate features of the dancer are clothed in veils and gestures suggesting mystery and an oriental spirituality. We can almost discern a fashioned jewel on her forehead and her folded arm and hand gesture and sinuous silhouette suggest the beginning of a dance. A sensuality is suggested by the treatment of the eyes and slightly parted lips.

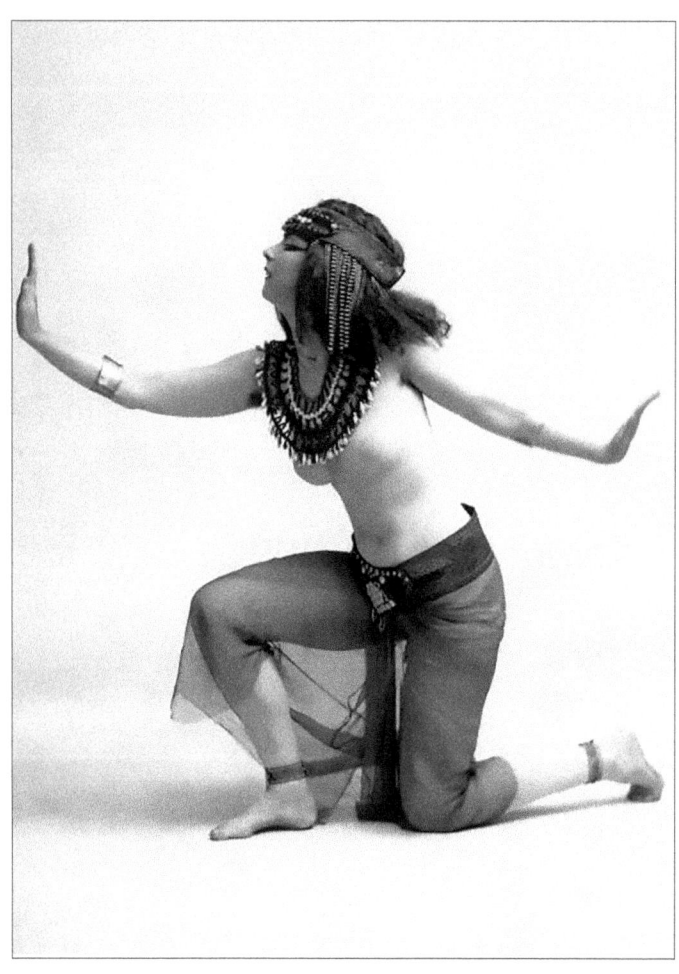

THE DANCER

"Once there came to the court of the Prince of Birkasha a dancer with her musicians. And she was admitted to the court, and she danced before the prince to the music the lute and the flute and the zither.

She danced the dance of flames, and the dance of swords and spears; she danced the dance of stars and the dance of space. And then she danced the dance of flowers in the wind.

After this she stood before the throne of the prince and bowed her body before him. And the prince bade her to come nearer, and he said unto her, "Beautiful woman, daughter of grace and delight, whence comes your art? And how is it that you command all the elements in your rhythms and your rhymes?"

And the dancer bowed again before the prince, and she answered, "Mighty and gracious Majesty, I know not the answer to your questionings. Only this I know: The philosopher's soul dwells in his head, the poet's soul is in the heart; the singer's soul lingers about his throat, but the soul of the dancer abides in all her body." (From Kahlil Gibran: The Wanderer).

In the parable, Gibran was expressing thoughts akin to Ruth's philosophy of her approach to dancing.[25]

---

25 Ruth St Denis: The Independent Art of the Dance. In *Theatre: Essays on the Arts of the Theatre*, edited by Juliet Rich Isaacs, pp 218-219.

A SOCIALIST IN THE MIX - CHARLES RUSSELL

Charlotte Teller was a very active and prominent member of the socialist movement and introduced Gibran to the leaders of the movement in the city. *Charles Russell* (1860-1941) was one of the political leaders Gibran drew. Gibran was sympathetic to some of the ideals of socialism.[26] After drawing the portrait, Gibran writes to Mary Haskell:

> And guess what I did this afternoon [May 30, 1911]. I made a drawing of a truly big man whom you admire very, very much - Mr. Charles Russell. It was a great joy to draw his remarkable face and to talk with him about art in general and about the eternal question of the Near East. Of all men I have met in New York Mr. Russell is the most appreciative -- His knowledge of drawings is like that of an artist. He has an eye for fine lines and he knows where to look for the poetry in things. After the drawing was finished, we had quite a long talk on Syria and the Syrians. Oh - what a good time it was!"[27]

Russell had joined the Socialist Party while a journalist and rapidly ascended in its ranks. In 1910 and 1912, he ran for governor of New York on the socialist ticket[28] and in 1914, he ran for the US Senate seat for the State of New York.[29]

The Socialist Party was against any involvement in the European war.[30] Charles Russell broke with the socialist pacifist views and became an ardent advocate of persecuting the war until Germany was "brought to her knees"! In February 1917, he declared his support of the US decision to join the war against Germany.[31]

He had opportunity to visit Russia as part of the Root mission, and initially he hailed the Russian Revolution as the harbinger of a free and democratic Russia.[32] The advent of the Bolsheviks changed his view and he became a fierce opponent of Bolshevism characterizing it as "Autocracy's twin brother" under the detestable dictatorship of Lenin.[33]

Mary Haskell was very perceptive and sensitive to Gibran's approach to portraiture. Of these early works, she wrote lovingly how they captured the essence of their subjects. She wrote

---

26 *Letters of Kahlil Gibran*, page 279.
27 *Beloved Prophet*, page 42. *Letters of Kahlil Gibran*, page 77.
28 *New York Tribune*, November 8, 1910.
29 *New York Times*, October 24, 1914.
30 *New York Times*, October 25, 1914.
31 *New York Times*, February 9, 1917; February 15, 1917; September 29, 1918.
32 *New York Times*, August 12, 1917; September 29, 1917.
33 *New York Times*, January 12, 1919; *New York Herald*, June 8, 1919 and August 10, 1919.

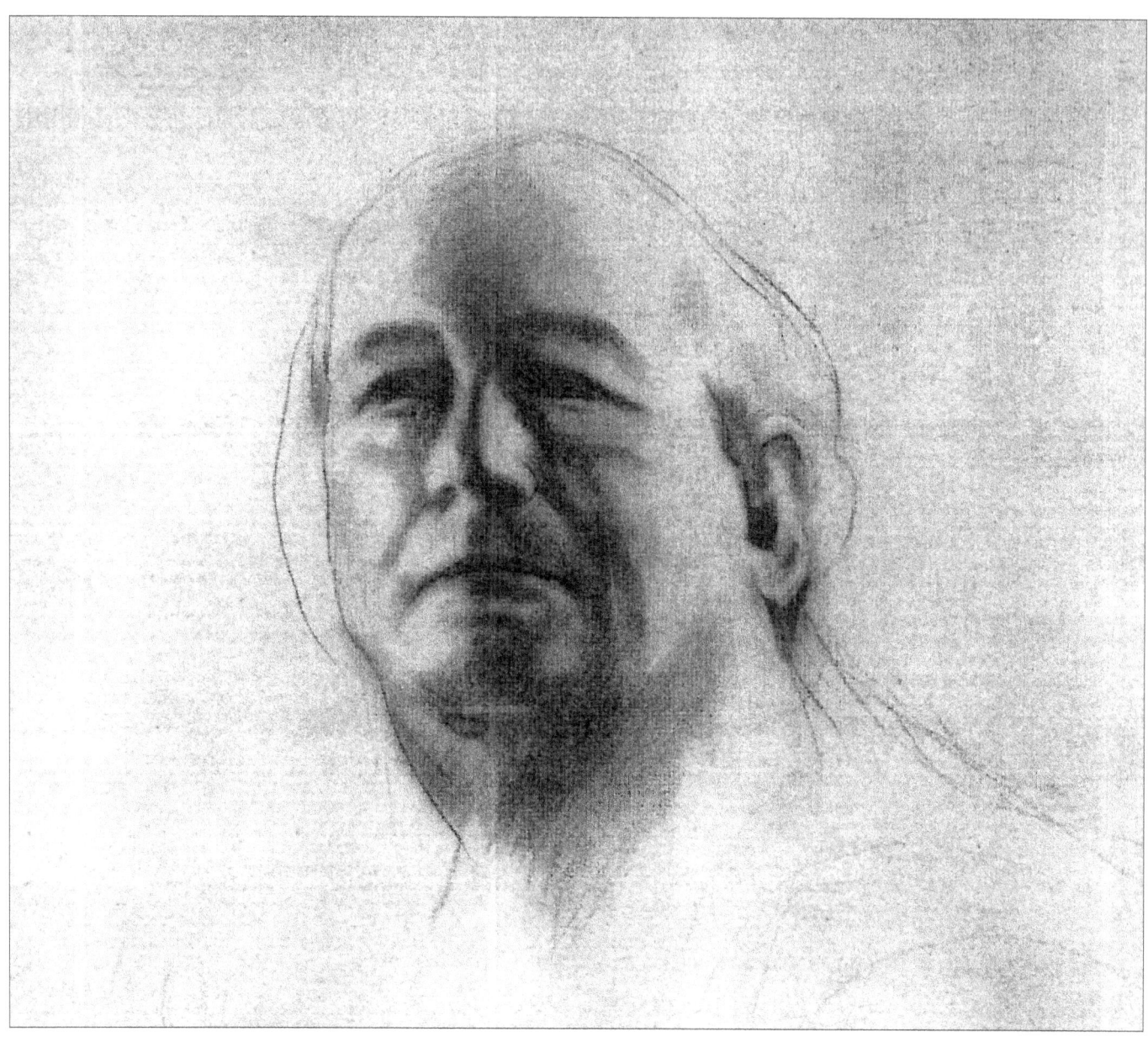

how the portrait of Russell portrayed the great dreamer and idealist who is also concerned for the small things in life, a composite of humanity, "the eternal child in it, the old man, the boy, the doer, the dreamer, the lover, the worker, the lonely man and the arch-comrade."[34]

---

34 Mary Haskell's diary, entry for June, 1911, University of North Carolina Library.

Rogue Grandson - Giuseppe Garibaldi II

In addition to various poets and writers, Gibran will meet at Mrs. Ford's evenings several politicians. He developed a special affinity to *Giuseppe Garibaldi II* (1879-1950), the grandson and namesake of the great Garibaldi. Not only did Gibran draw his portrait, but also he introduced him to fellow Syrians in New York and invited him to a special session of a Syrian club in New York to discuss the question of emancipation of oppressed nations.[35] Garibaldi had participated in multiple liberation movements around the Mediterranean and Latin America.

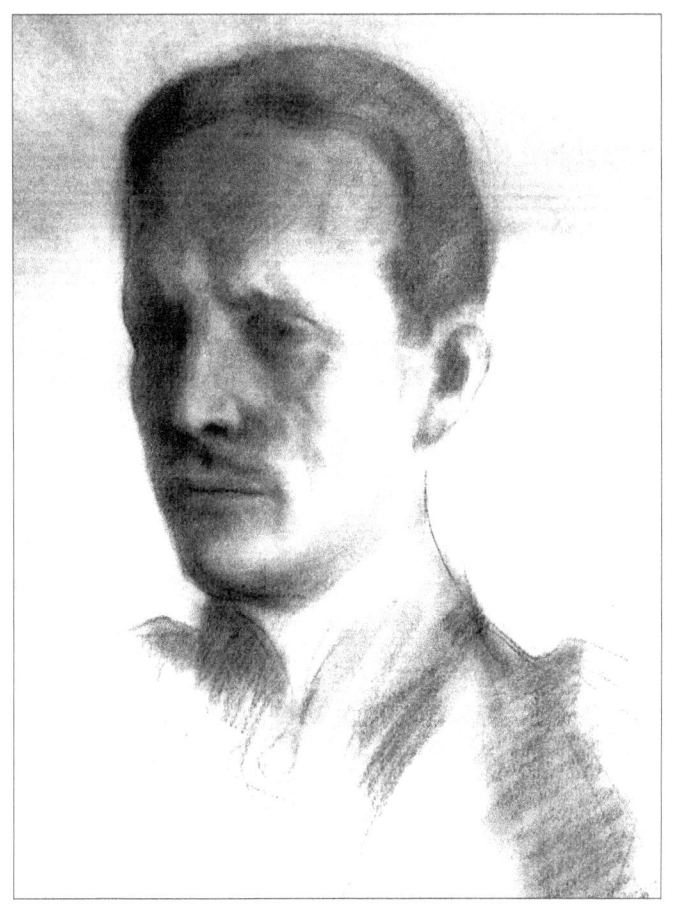

Gibran depicted the grandson of Garibaldi as a man full of life experience and an undaunted spirit. The slightly furrowed forehead and serious gaze reflect an iron determination and a readiness to engage in perilous pursuits. Garibaldi signed the portrait, an unusual occurrence in this series, and likely as a sign of satisfaction and friendship.

The meeting with Garibaldi coincided with a period of political effervescence among Syrian immigrants in preparation for the *Arab Congress* that was to be held in Paris and aimed at obtaining home rule for Syria and the other Arab provinces. Gibran told Mary that he was asked to participate as one of the representatives of the State of New York Syrians. He declined on the basis of disagreement with the policy of the Congress to seek redress through diplomatic means by appealing to the European Great Powers to pressure Turkey into granting the Arab provinces home rule. He believed such efforts are fruitless because Turkey can always renege on any understanding reached with the European powers. "Kahlil wants revolution. Arab military strength is enough for revolution… the worst that can happen is a protectorate by England or France, preferably England." [June 22, 1913] Having failed to go to France and regretting it, he was planning a follow up congress in New York. "General Garibaldi is here, to be sure he and Kahlil are twins in mind. Garibaldi can't take part in the conference, but he will be great in carrying out the revolution."

---

35 *Letters of Kahlil Gibran*, page 262.

THIRST FOR THE ABSOLUTE - THOMAS RAYMOND

Another politician he met and drew at the house of Mrs. Ford in the spring of 1914 was the judge *Thomas Raymond* (1875–1928).[36] This meeting was the beginning of a lasting friendship between the two men. Raymond was very helpful during the First World War in finding for Gibran a forum to appeal to American support for the suffering and starving Syrians[37]. After Gibran's death, the curator of the Newark Museum appealed to Mary Haskell to obtain the portrait for the museum's collection and Mary facilitated the transfer.

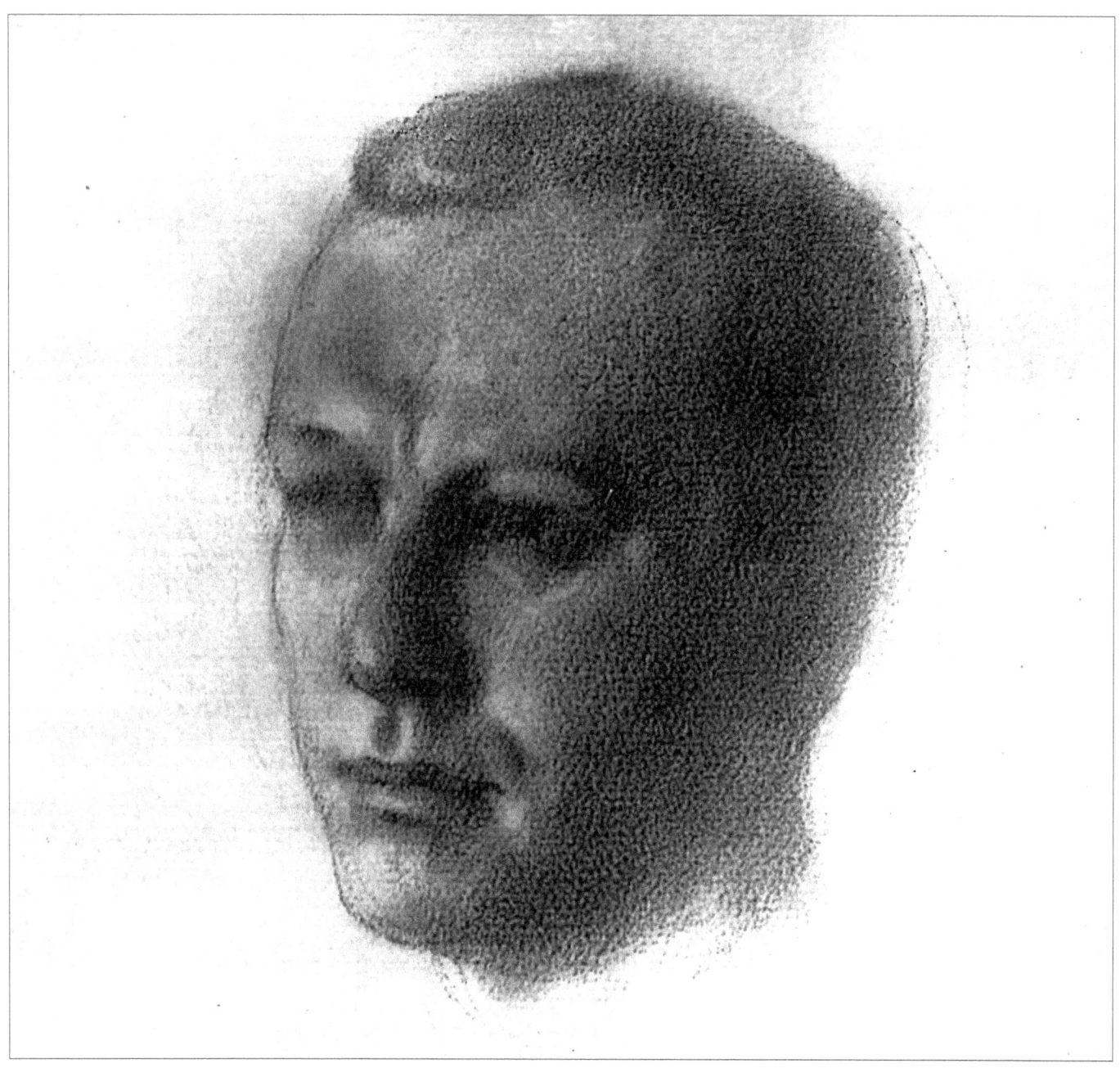

---

36 *Letters of Kahlil Gibran*, page 262.
37 *Letters of Kahlil Gibran*, page 555.

A Constellation of Luminaries

The Blind Baritone - Vladimir Resnikoff

When Russian baritone *Vladimir Resnikoff* (1890-1920) died of pneumonia on February 5th, 1920,[38] he left his affairs in the hands of his friend and sponsor Rose Parks Stokes, the socialist writer and activist. Among his books was a handsomely bound copy of *The Madman* by Gibran that Stokes forwarded to the author as a remembrance of their common friend.[39] Resnikoff was very fond of the book and had expressed his intent to translate it into Russian. A review of the book had quoted Resnikoff as saying: "No one can have any idea as to how much Gibran means to me, his work, his spirit, his beautiful measures of song."[40]

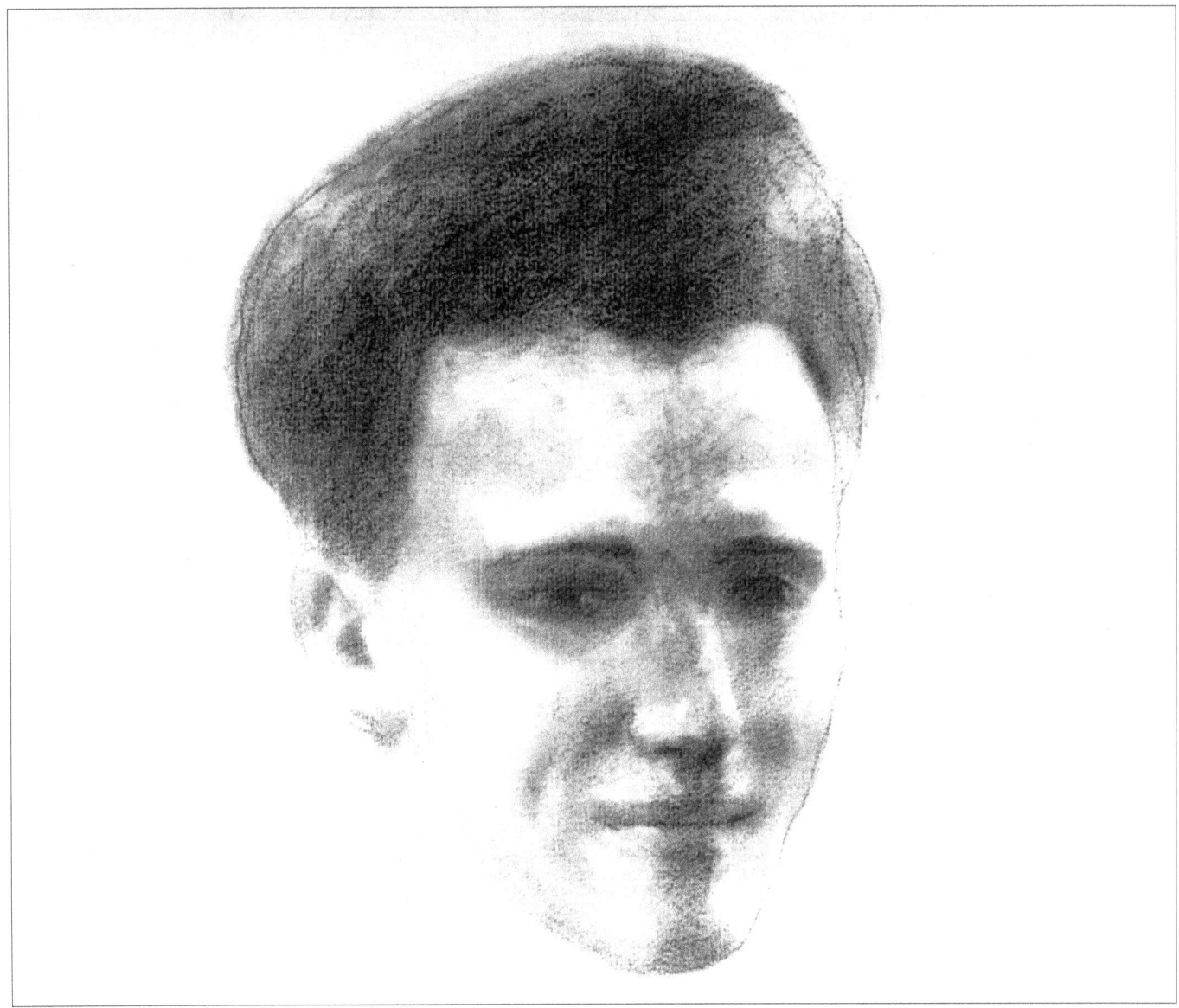

---

38 *New-York Tribune*, February 7, 1920.

39 Diary of Mary Haskell, April 17, 1920.

40 James Waldo Fawcett: The Madman (book review), *Unity*, March 6, 1919, volume 83, number 1, page 10.

Resnikoff, Stokes, and Gibran had known each other for a few years and cooperated in a few activities. Rose Park Stokes set up in 1917 and 1918 a series of concerts for Resnikoff, the proceeds of which were to benefit the singer and likely the socialist cause.[41] The flyer advertising the event carried a testimonial by Gibran who wrote that Resnikoff's "art is not an expression but a longing for the Unknown."[42]

Neither Gibran nor Resnikoff were adherents to the socialist cause, but both were close to Rose Park Stokes. There is an oft-quoted anecdote that when Gibran was reading from his book *The Forerunner* at the MacDowell Club in April 1920, Stokes was the only one that applauded when he finished reading the piece titled "The Capitalist", later renamed "The Plutocrat". In that piece, Gibran represents the capitalist as "a man-headed, iron-hoofed monster who ate of the earth and drank of the sea incessantly," a description clearly consonant with Stokes socialist convictions. In a letter to Stokes on December 11, 1918, Gibran responds to a note she sent him about his book *The Madman*:

"How gracious and generous you are to write me so wonderfully about my little book. And though your letter reveals a world of truth and beauty far beyond my reach, yet I cannot but be moved and strengthened by it. We children of hunger and thirst are always sustained by the very thing that intensifies our thirst and deepens our hunger. It is the unattainable that comforts us. And how well you have expressed the unattainable by likening my little book to Olive Schreiner's[43] *Dreams*, and how much you have comforted me."[44]

Resnikoff was born in Russia and lost his sight at the age of three after an illness. He grew up in a rural setting avidly learning and singing Russian folksongs. It is reported that by the time he reached the US, he had more than hundred such songs in his repertoire. His family immigrated to the USA when he was 15 years old and were on the verge of being deported from Ellis Island because of Resnikoff's blindness and were held up a fortnight there until the matter was resolved.[45]

He enrolled in the New York Institute for the Education of the Blind[46] where his unusual

---

41 "Blind Russian tenor gains the friendship of Caruso," *Musical America*, March 10, 1917, volume 25, No.19, page 40.
42 Robin Waterfield: *Prophet: The Life and Times of Kahlil Gibran*, page 205.
43 Olive Schreiner (1855 – 1920) was a South African progressive writer and champion of socialism and gender equality. Her book Dreams was published in 1890.
44 Letter from Gibran to Rose Pastor Stokes, December 11, 1918. Rose Pastor Stokes Papers, General Correspondence, Manuscripts and Archives, Yale University Library, New Haven, CT, USA.
45 *Chicago Tribune*, October 21, 1917.
46 *Seventy Fourth Annual Report of the New York Institution for the Blind*, Year Ending September 30, 1909. New York.

musical gifts soon attracted attention, and he came under the care of Dr. Floyd S. Muckey, author of the book *The Natural Method of Voice Production*,[47] who contributed to his vocal training.[48] His recitals alternated between programs of Mussorgsky songs[49] or folk songs, or a combination thereof.[50] Some of these concerts were for the benefit of social causes such as the aforementioned concert organized by Stokes, for the American Red Cross (in Chicago in October-November 1919), or for the New York Association for the Blind.[51] He also performed in other standard venues in the New York area either as a solo performer or with other artists.[52]

Resnikoff like Gibran lived near Washington Square in a neighborhood "infested with artists" and it was inevitable that the two should meet. Gibran described to Mary Haskell the special character of their relationship: "You know the Russian singer I was so fond of, Resnikoff, he died. I went to see him in the hospital. And he tried to sing at the end. Oh! It was so touching! Mary, he loved me, he loved me in a way that was so wonderful to me. I never knew anything like it."[53]

A friend of Resnikoff describes him thus: "Strikingly handsome, beaming with vitality, his sensitive mouth wreathed with generous smiles, his calm brown eyes – that no one ever thought sightless – gazing bravely into the dark." [54] In the portrait, Gibran hints at Resnikoff's blindness in the subtle treatment of his subject's eyes. The portrait is executed with an ethereal tenderness that conveys a graceful appreciation of the talent of the singer.

---

47 Scribner, New York, 1916.

48 *The New music review and church music review*, volume 15, June 1916, page 296.

49 *Chicago Tribune*, October 21, 1917.

50 The *New York Times*, March 4, 1917. *New York Tribune*, December 23, 1918. *New York Tribune*, March 2, 1919. *Musical America*, December 28, 1918, March 8, 1919.

51 *Chicago Tribune*, October 21, 1917. *New York Association for the Blind Annual Report*, volume 10, 1916.

52 *New York Tribune*, December 23, 1918; March 2, 1919.

53 Diary of Mary Haskell, April 17, 1920.

54 James Waldo Fawcett: Vladimir Resnikoff. *Unity*, February 23, 1922, page 380.

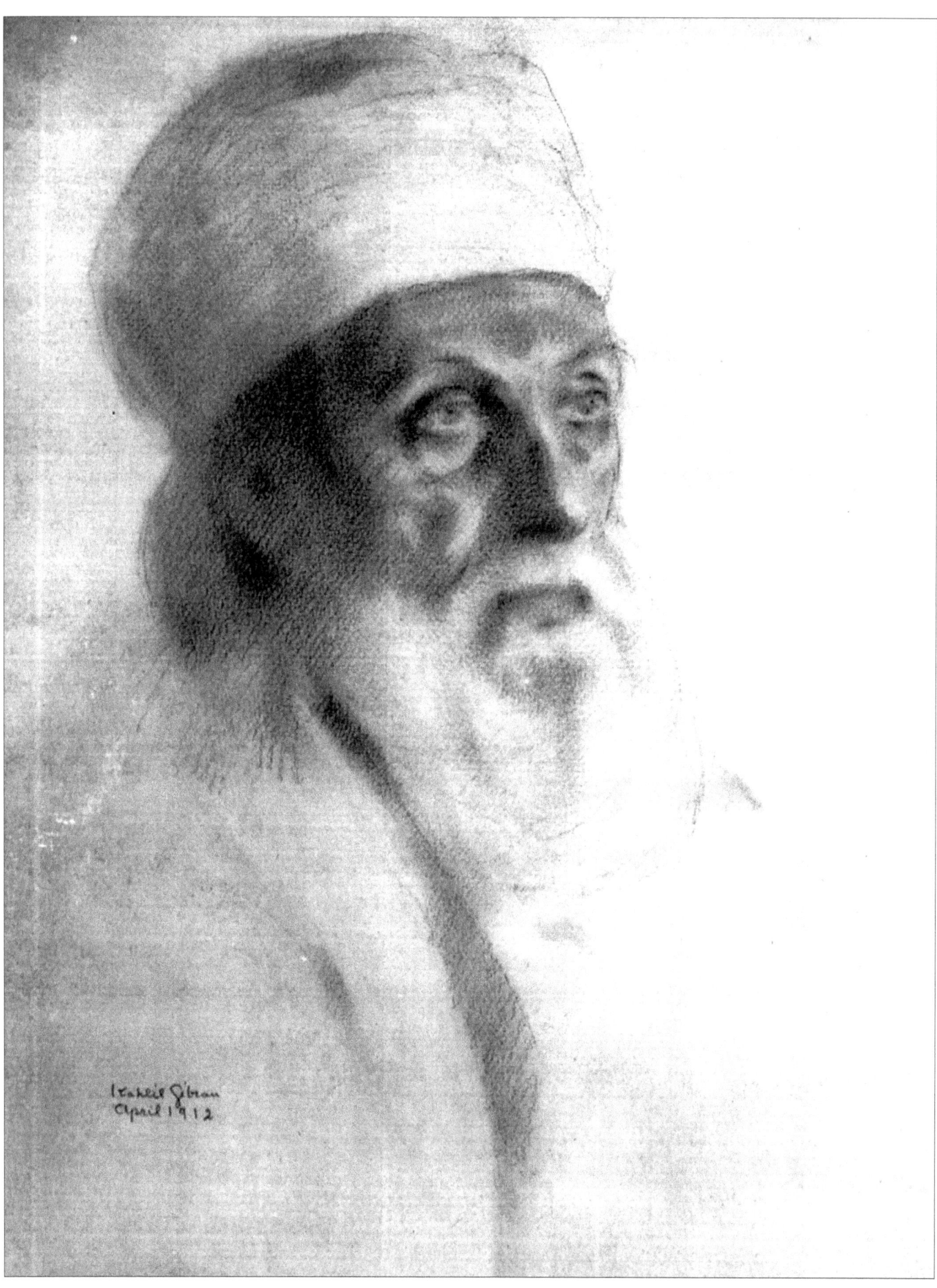

A Constellation of Luminaries

The Splendor of God - Abdul Baha

Syrians at home and abroad were familiar with the Baha'i faith that had chosen the city of Haifa on the Syrian coast as its world base. Syrian periodicals in Beirut, Egypt, and New York carried commentaries about the faith, its origins, teachings and recent political strife. Indeed, the earliest advocate of the Baha'i faith in America was a Syrian named Ibrahim George Khairallah who nurtured the first chapter of the faith in Chicago and subsequently on the East Coast. Khairallah had a fall out with the dominant branch of the Baha'i dynasty over questions of the tenets of the faith and control over financial assets, but the movement had grown to withstand such conflicts and had garnered a significant following in the US.[55] Gibran would have been very familiar with the faith, and his mystic tendencies have encouraged some biographers to overplay the role of Baha'i religious figures in his intellectual development[56].

Gibran met *Abdul Baha* (1844-1921) in the spring of 1912 during the latter's visit to America[57] through the intercession of his artist friend and neighbor Juliette Thompson who was a devout follower of the sect. Juliette was to later claim that Gibran told her that the image of Abdul Baha was foremost on his mind when he was writing *Jesus the Son of Man* in 1928! What is certain is that Gibran was eager to have Abdul Baha included in his series and that he pressed Ms. Thompson to secure an appointment for him.[58] Gibran met Abdul Baha three times in April and on one occasion claims to have acted as a translator for the cleric,[59] which is likely an exaggeration as Abdul Baha was accompanied by several translators on his trip. He was fascinated by the face of the Baha'i master and secured an appointment for the portrait that he executed on April 18.[60] Gibran had to start early in the morning at 7:30 am and was finished by 9 am. Abdul Baha had a very busy schedule in New York and was leaving to Washington on April 20.

The portrait was an evident success that pleased the Baha'i master and his followers. Gibran himself considered his portrait to be more poetic than his portrait of Rodin.[61] The portrait does indeed reflect the calm countenance of the religious figure and an ethereal gentleness. Baha'i master is gazing at a far away object from the observer as if he was contemplating the spiritual realm beyond reality.

---

55 William McElwee Miller: *The Baha'i Faith: Its History and Teachings*, pp 193-202.
56 Suheil Bushrui and Joe Jenkins: *Kahlil Gibran: Man and Poet*, page 126.
57 *The Sun*, March 7, 1912; *Brooklyn Daily Eagle*, April 7, 1912; *New York Times*, April 21, 1912.
58 *Letters of Kahlil Gibran*, page 160.
59 *Letters of Kahlil Gibran*, page 163.
60 *Letters of Kahlil Gibran*, page 165.
61 *Letters of Kahlil Gibran*, page 174.

Kahlil Gibran - Portraits

The success of the portrait and Gibran's praise of the beauty of Abdul Baha's face should not be construed as Gibran's full endorsement of the Baha'i faith or a lifelong admiration of the Baha'i master. Indeed, Gibran levels some very harsh criticism to the message of peace and harmony that Abdul Baha seemed to dispense liberally during his American sojourn[62]. When the fog of naïve adulation cleared, Gibran returned to a position more consonant with the views he was expressing in his writings in the Syrian periodicals of New York and Egypt, an exhortation to dynamic renewal and rebirth rather than the platitudes of simplistic pacifism. On May 16, 1912, barely a month after obtaining the portrait, he writes to Haskell:

> Abdul Baha came back to New York[63] a few days ago and the Women's Committee of the New York Peace Society gave him a great reception at the Hotel Astor Monday afternoon. There were many speakers beside Abdul Baha, and "Peace" was the only subject![64] Peace! Peace! Peace! International Peace! Universal Peace! It was tiresome, illogical, flat and insipid. Peace is the desire of old age, and the world is too young to have such a desire. I say let there be wars among nations; let the children of the Earth fight one another until the very last drop of impure animal blood is shed. Why should man speak of Peace when there is so much of ill-at-easeness in his system that must go out one way or another? And was it not the Peace disease that crept into the Oriental nations and caused their downfall? I believe that because we do not understand Life we fear Death, and the fear of Death make us dread strife and war.[65]

Gibran's words to Mary are a direct refutation of Abdul Baha's speech in which he said: "Today there is no greater glory for man than that of service in the cause of the Most Great Peace. Peace is light, whereas war is darkness. Peace is life; war is death. Peace is guidance; war is error. Peace is the foundation of God; war is a satanic institution. Peace is the illumination of the world of humanity; war is the destroyer of human foundations. When we consider outcomes in the world of existence, we find that peace and fellowship are factors of upbuilding and betterment, whereas war and strife are the causes of destruction and disintegration."

Gibran reiterated his criticism of Abdul Baha in later years in a conversation with Mary Haskell when on recalling Abdul Baha he tells Mary of the discordance between what Abdul Baha shared in private and his public discourses. While he believed in the sincerity of Abdul Baha, he observed that his lack of appreciation of the task before him in America and his lack of dynamism were the main reasons for his failure.[66]

---

62 *Beloved Prophet*, page 77. *Letters of Kahlil Gibran*, page 176.
63 In the interim, Abdul Baha had visited Washington DC and Chicago where he was present at laying the foundation stone of the famous Baha'i Temple.
64 For the text of Abdul Baha speech at the reception see Elaine Lacroix Hopson: *Abdul Baha' in New York: The City of the Covenant*, New Vista Design, NY, 1999.
65 *Beloved Prophet*, page 77. *Letters of Kahlil Gibran*, page 176.
66 Mary Haskell Diary, August 20, 1920.

UNDERGROUND OF THE SOUL - CARL JUNG

It was inevitable that Gibran would meet *Carl Jung* (1875–1961) in New York. Charlotte Teller had introduced Gibran to the circle of Jungians in the city including the famous Dr Hinkle. The poet James Oppenheim, who involved Gibran in his *Seven Arts* magazine, was a devotee of the Austrian thinker. Gibran apparently met Jung several times and drew his portrait around April of 1913. In the portrait, Jung appears as if he is gazing into the archetypal soul of the observer.

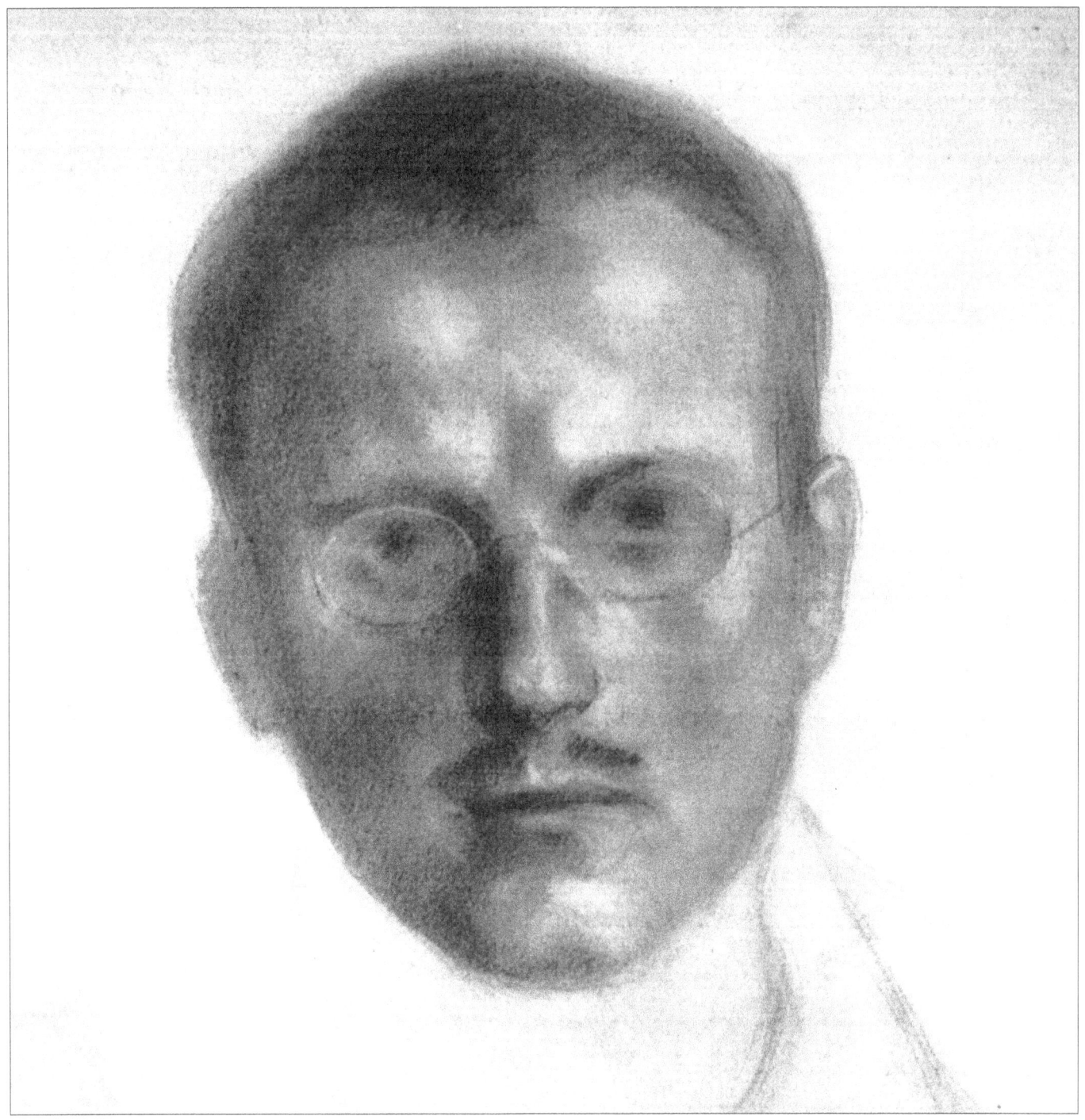

Gibran told Mary that Jung invited him to visit him in Zurich on his next trip to Europe[67]. Gibran and Mary maintained an interest in the psychoanalytic school and traded the books of Jung and Freud between them.[68] Gibran's use of historical-cultural archetypes in his writings may have stemmed from his exposure to this school of thought.

Gibran's interest in psychoanalysis in its various Freudian and Jungian disciplines appears to have been reciprocated. We find mention repeatedly in his correspondence with Mary Haskell of his encounters with Dr. Hinkle, a psychoanalyst friend of Charlotte Teller. Gibran's writings also appear to have been examined in the psychoanalytic literature of the time. His text from *The Madman* titled 'The Sleepwalkers' was considered by Charles Odier "as an exceptionally clear and poetic representation of the ambivalency characteristics of the Oedipus complex." The author, writing on the pages of the International Journal of Psychoanalysis, the official organ of the International Psychoanalytical Association, and under the direction of Sigmund Freud, reports having corresponded with Gibran on the circumstances of the writing and his experience with psychoanalysis.[69]

---

67 *Beloved Prophet*, page 120.
68 *Beloved Prophet*, page 278.
69 Charles Odier: A Literary Portrayal of Ambivalency. *The International Journal of Psychoanalysis*, Volume 4, July 1923, pp. 321-322.

New York Elite, Friends and Companions

Among Gibran's extant portraits, we find representations of friends and associates that may not have figured in his original concept of the *Temple of Art* series, but who played an important part in the intellectual environment he lived in such as Mrs. Ford, and Blanche Knopf, and his Syrian colleagues Ameen Rihani, Mikhail Naimy, and Nassib Arida. We also find portraits of the 'beautiful people' of New York, the rich and famous who either commissioned works from Gibran or offered their hospitality.

Matron of Songs - Julia Ellsworth Ford

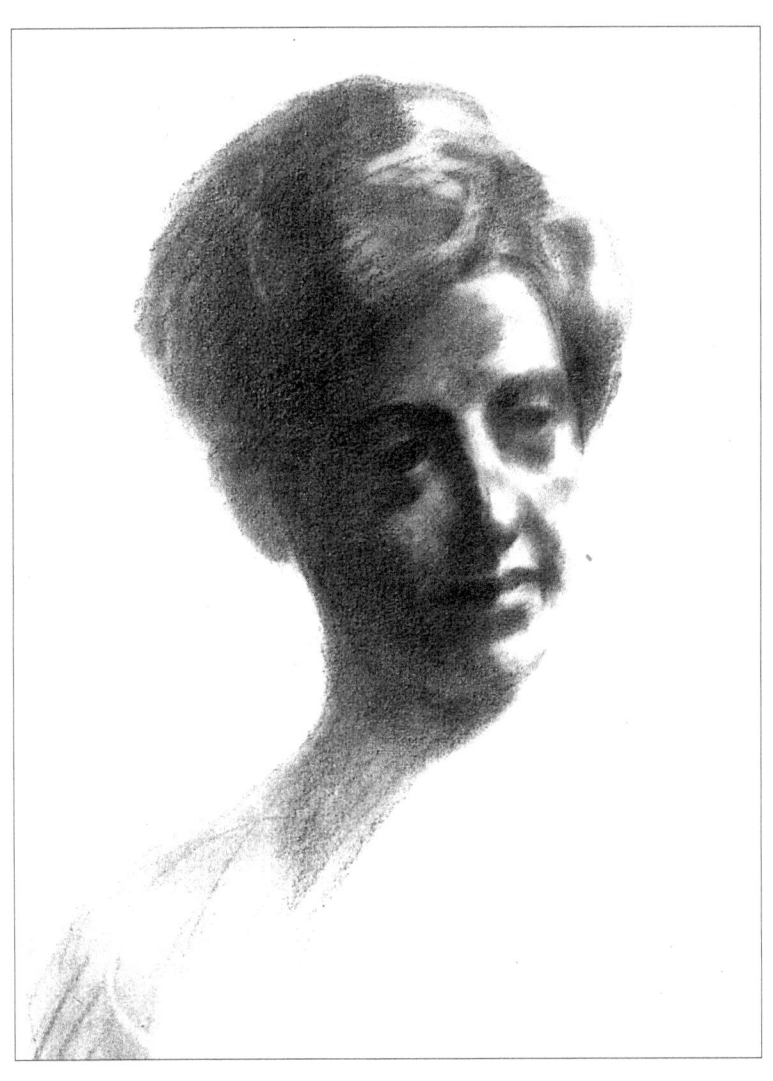

Julia Ellsworth Ford (1859-1950) was a New York socialite, philanthropist, art collector, fervent patron of the arts, as well as an author of children's books, plays and art criticism. Her husband Simeon Ford was a financier and real estate developer. Like many women of wealth and talent in New York, Mrs. Ford presided over a twice-weekly salon at her New York town house to which she invited established and emerging talent in the various arts. Poets, artists, actors, dancers, novelists of various nationalities and interests flocked to her salon and enjoyed her hospitality. As alluded to in the course of this book, Gibran met many of the subjects of his portraits at her salon who, in the words of Mercedes de Acosta, "had to sing for their dinner." Gibran was not only a habitué of her Salon, but also a frequent guest at her estate outside the city.

BEAUTIFUL PEOPLE - THE ERDMAN FAMILY

Gibran's portraits of Dr. Erdman and members of his family is likely a commissioned work as by the time of their execution Gibran was no longer pursuing the *Temple of Art* series and the subjects of the portraits would not qualify for inclusion in the series. Indeed, most of the portraits that Gibran executed during the 1920s appear independent of his earlier project.

Dr. John F. Erdman was an internationally renowned surgeon who counted among his patients the luminaries and elites of New York, its politicians, celebrated financiers, and captains of industry. He was president of the Interstate Postgraduate Medical Association of America.

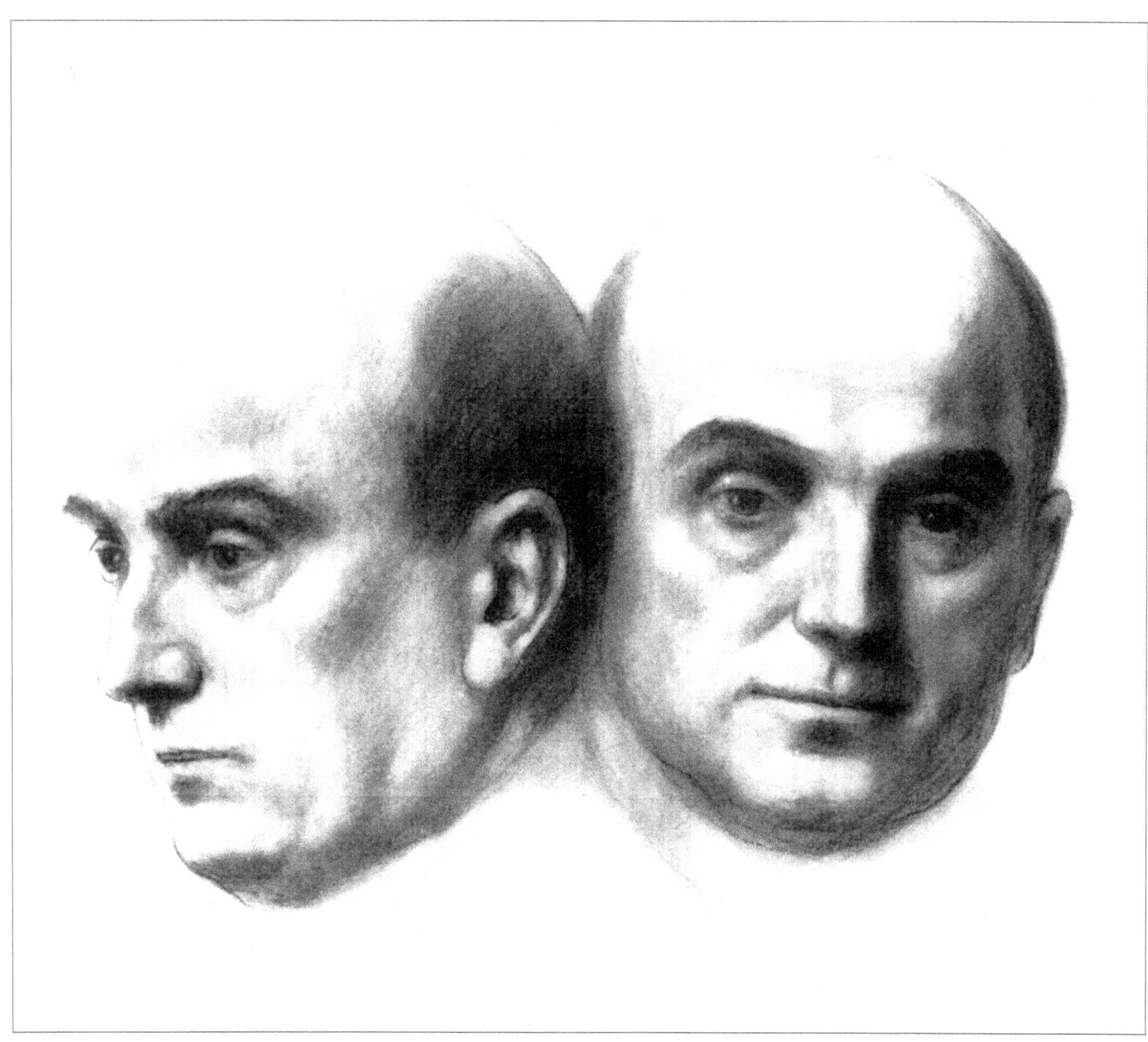

New York Elite, Friends and Companions

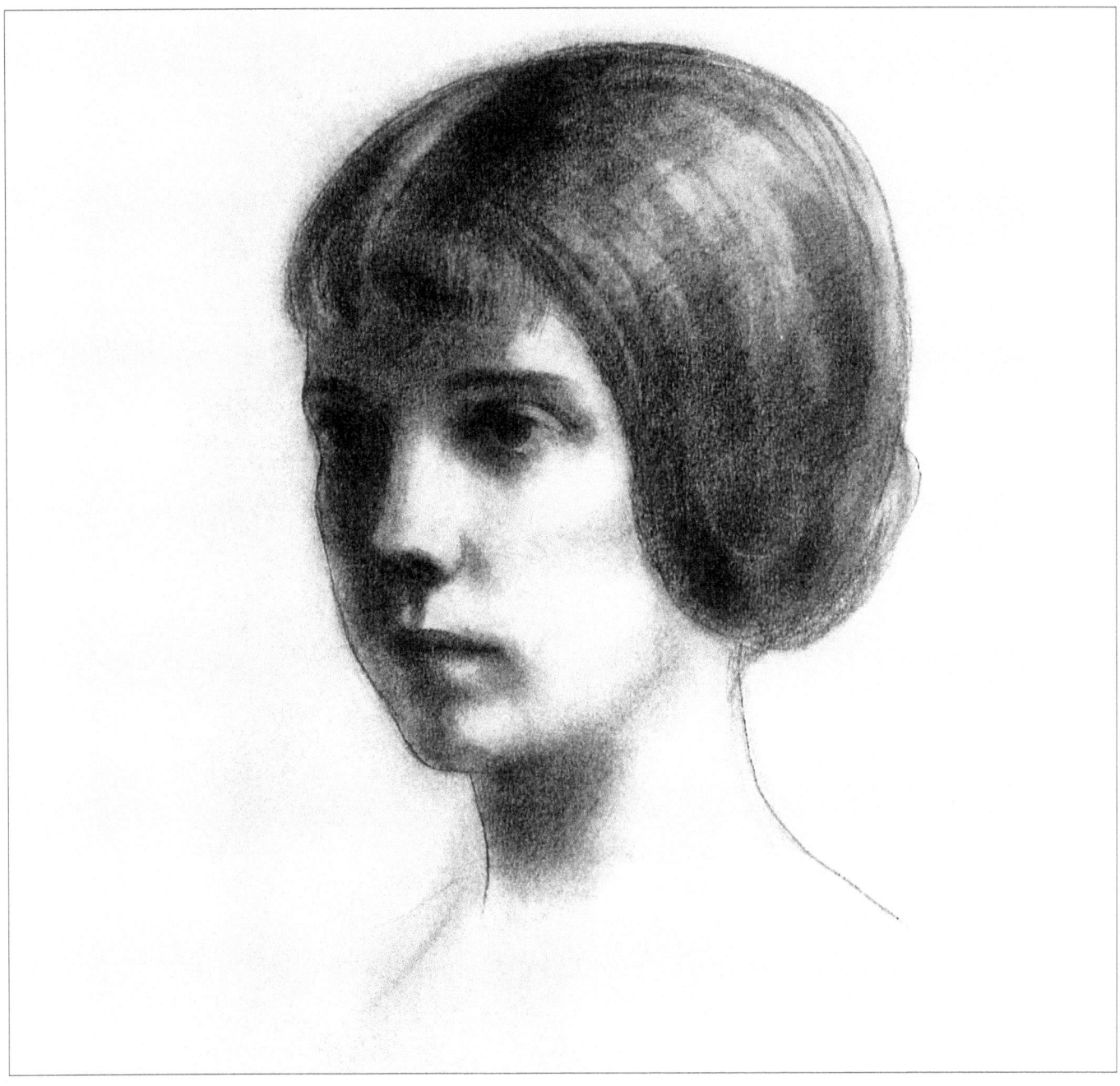

The portrait of the youngest daughter, Jane Erdman, depicts a lovely teenage girl as indeed she was at the time Gibran drew her as she did not have her debutantes premier until Christmas of 1928.[1] Gibran did not need to 'beautify' the portrait in the least as Jane was indeed a very beautiful and fashionable woman whose photographs frequently graced the social pages of major newspapers in New York,[2] and her beauty and elegance were celebrated on their fashion pages.[3] She was frequently asked to model high end fashion at charity events. In short, she was the prototype of a supermodel among the elites of New York.

---

1   *Daily News*, December 24, 1928.
2   *The Brooklyn Daily Eagle*: September 1, 1930; August 23, 1931; August 28, 1932; March 25, 1934.
3   *Daily News*: August 2, 1931; March 30, 1934; May 26, 1940.

The triple portrait below showing Mrs. Erdman, Mrs. Whitney, and Mrs. Kusar is also a family portrait of sorts. Mrs. Kusar is Jane's older sister, Olivia Erdman Kusar, who had wed John Kusar in 1922, and was equally elegant and beautiful, but less a darling of the news outlets as her sister.[4] Mrs. Erdman in the portrait is their mother, the wife of Dr. Erdman. Mrs. Whitney belongs to the notable family into which Jane would later marry, so the depicted lady may well be her future mother-in-law.

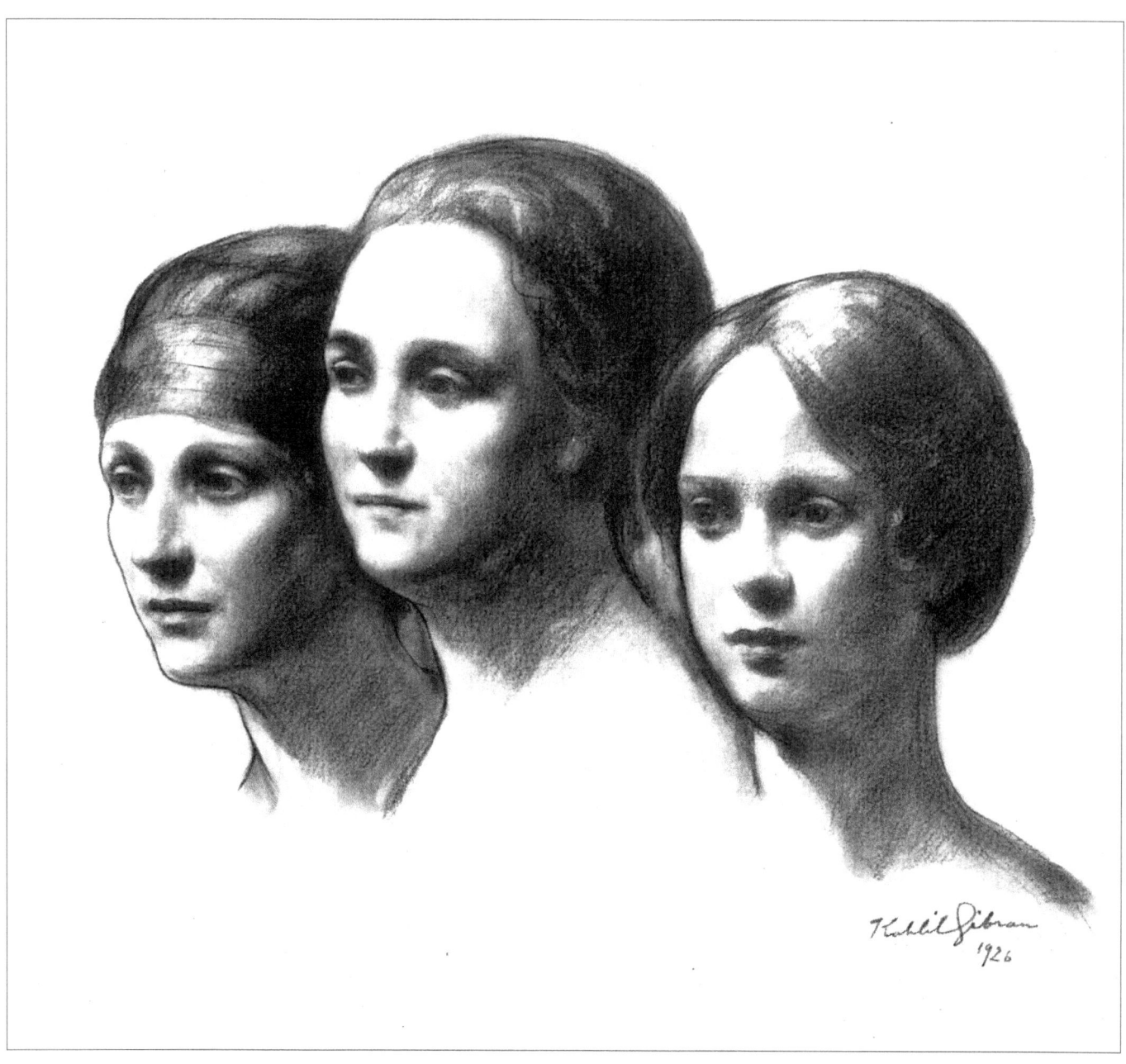

[4] *The New York Times*, January 8, 1922.

New York Elite, Friends and Companions

SHE HERSELF IS ART! - RITA DE ACOSTA

Rita Hernandez de Alba de Acosta Stokes Lydig (1875 – 1929) was a woman of "nearly perfect beauty" and known as "the most picturesque woman in America." The most famous portrait painters of the period vied to capture her beauty and allure on their canvases.[5] However, she was more than a pretty face and a paragon of elegance and style. She was well versed in literature and art. Her collections of books and art objects contained unique elements, a testament to her understanding and discriminating taste.[6] She claimed many intellectuals in France and the US as her friends. She was a creative force herself, and had a tremendous influence on art and fashion of the day. She was a leading figure in the suffrage movement and Chairman of the Social Welfare Committee during the Great War. When the American painter John Singer Sargent was asked why de Acosta never created art herself, the artist replied, "Why should she? She herself is art."

Rita de Acosta was the eldest of five de Acosta sisters who were the talk of New York during the early part of the twentieth century for their beauty, talents and complex matrimonial entanglements![7] Gibran's early association with the family was with Mercedes de Acosta, an author, a scriptwriter, social critic, and a lover of Eva LeGallienne the daughter of his friend,[8] and movie star Greta Garbo,[9]. Another sister, Aida de Acosta, became the first female to fly a powered aircraft solo and was the second wife of United States Assistant Secretary of War Henry Skillman Breckinridge, Maria, the third sister, was the wife of composer Theodore Ward Chanler.

The first meeting of Gibran and Mercedes de Acosta was serendipitous. John Barrymore (1882–1942) was asked by his publicist to have Gibran draw his portrait. He asked Mercedes, a close friend, to accompany him to Gibran's studio. The encounter was to be for Barrymore the beginning of a special friendship with Gibran and for Mercedes a dramatic introduction to spiritualism.

> We went down to Kahlil Gibran's studio on West Tenth Street. I am ashamed to say that at this time I was as ignorant about Gibran as Jack was which is enough to have crossed us both off as a pair of idiots.

---

5   *St Louis Dispatch*, April 24, 1927.
6   *The Philadelphia Enquirer*, April 5, 1913.
7   *The Birmingham News*, December 27, 1925.
8   *St Louis Dispatch*, March 27, 1923.
9   *Daily News*, July 25, 1932.

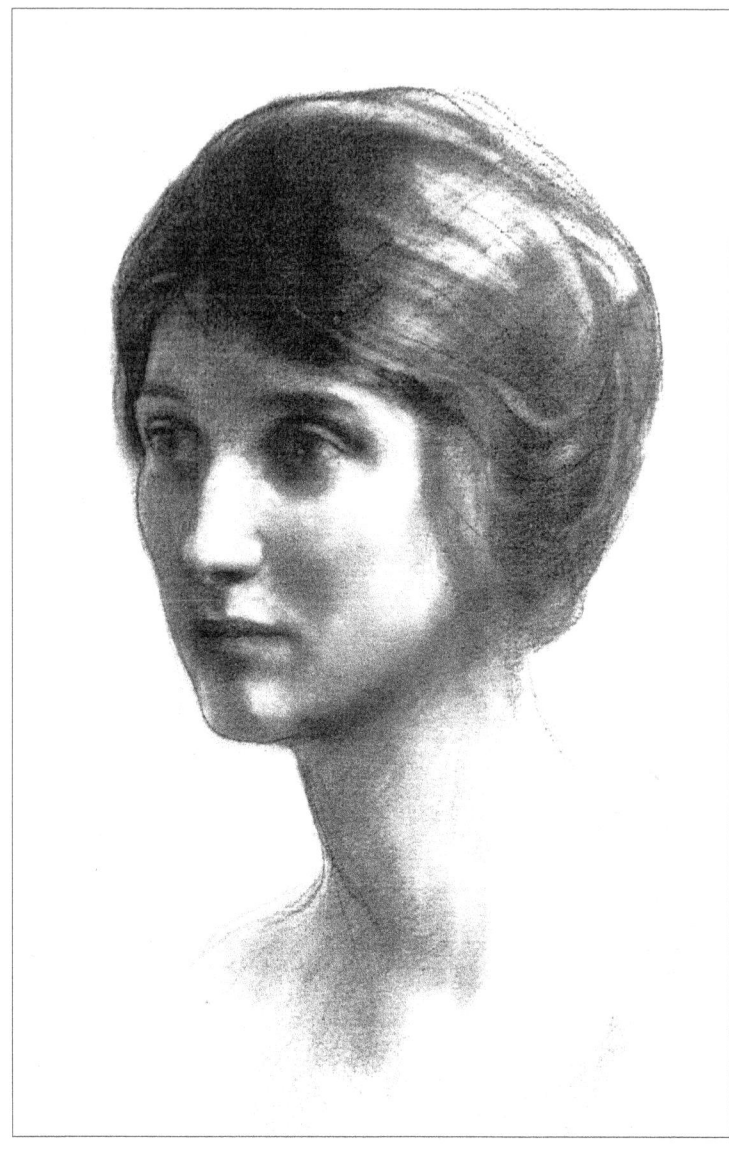

Kahlil Gibran received Jack and me quietly and graciously in his studio. I apologized for having come uninvited, but he put me at ease at once and made me feel it was the most natural thing in the world that I should be there. To prove this he expressed a wish to do a drawing of me, too. I was deeply impressed by his looks and by his personality.

In stature, he was a small man, but as his head was massive and remarkably shaped, he looked taller than he actually was. I never saw a nobler brow than his. The most impressive thing about him was his eyes. He seemed to look at you with a gaze that came from some deeper region than the physical. When later I came to understand certain things better I felt that — like Buddha — he must have had a third eye. He was a poet, artist, musician, philosopher, mystic, and beyond all these — a great spiritual teacher. He was an initiate who came at a certain moment to bring a spiritual message to the Western world...

This particular morning, when he began to work, he had not drawn ten lines before Jack and I knew he was a master artist. Jack himself could draw well and was a gifted artist. I saw him relax as Gibran continued the portrait, and at the end, after several hours, a strong and fine head of Jack was on the paper. During these hours Gibran had only spoken once or twice, yet his silence seemed light and not at all awkward. Jack said afterwards, "Actors could learn the force of silence from this man."

As we left the studio, almost as though it was an afterthought, Kahlil Gibran handed me a book. He said, "Read this . . . and when you have finished it call me and tell me what you think of it.[10]

---

10 Mercedes de Acosta: *Here Lies the Heart: a Tale of my Life*, Reynal, NY, 1960, pp. 91-93.

New York Elite, Friends and Companions

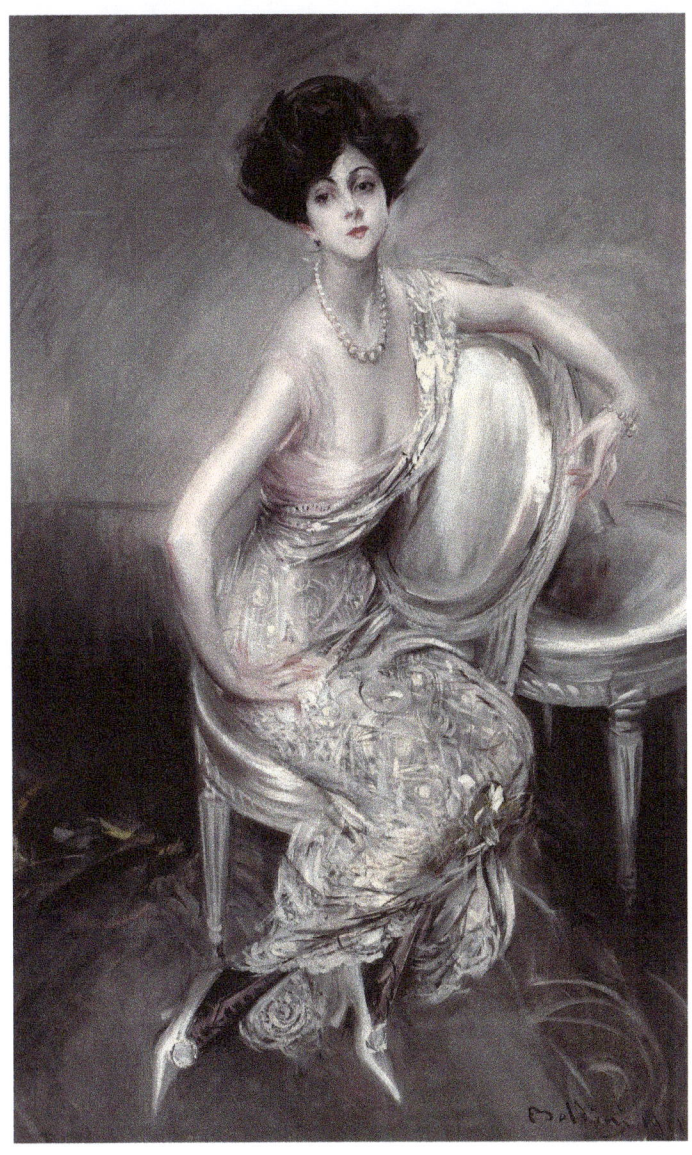

Portrait of Rita de Acosta by Giovanni Boldini

Then ensued a friendship between Mercedes and Gibran amply documented in her writings, and it would have been natural that he would meet her sister particularly since the latter would have a close association with another Gibran acquaintance, Dr Percy Grant. Indeed, Rita de Acosta's fated romance with Dr Percy Grant would have been very familiar to Gibran.

In 1921, Rita announced her engagement to Reverend Percy Stickney Grant (1860–1927), rector of the Church of the Ascension.[11] Their wedding plans were broken off in 1924 when Bishop William Manning refused to authorize the marriage, citing de Acosta being a divorcée with two living former husbands.[12] She had been married to W. Stokes in 1895 and Phillip Lydig in 1902. Percy Grant was a progressive pastor, unorthodox in his ways and activities. He had invited AbdulBaha' to preach at his church, and Gibran to read from his works, particularly *The Prophet*. It would not be farfetched to imagine an encounter between the beauty and the Syrian artist happening either via the medium of her sister or via her friendship with Dr. Grant. The date of the portrait allows for both possibilities.

---

11 *Chicago Tribune*, August 6, 1921. *Boston Globe*, August 6, 1921.
12 *Chicago Tribune*, December 12, 1922. *Indianapolis Star*, May 4, 1923.

GODMOTHER TO BOOKS - BLANCHE KNOPF

Blanche Wolf-Knopf (1894-1966) was Alfred Knopf's most dynamic associate in building their publishing firm that was home to all of Gibran's English books. A lover of fiction and poetry, she brought passion and intellectual fierceness to the company, facilitating the recruitment of many non-US authors from Europe (Gide, Camus and Sartre) and South America. Like her husband, she fostered an image in both books and personal affairs. She lived in a stylish Manhattan apartment, wore Dior, Chanel and Schiaparelli, and had a string of lovers. Gibran's portrait captures her vanity by 'beautifying' her. While traditional Gibran biographers credit Witter Bynner with facilitating the introduction of Gibran to Knopf, modern biographers of Blanche claim she was the driving force behind the publication of *The Prophet*.[13]

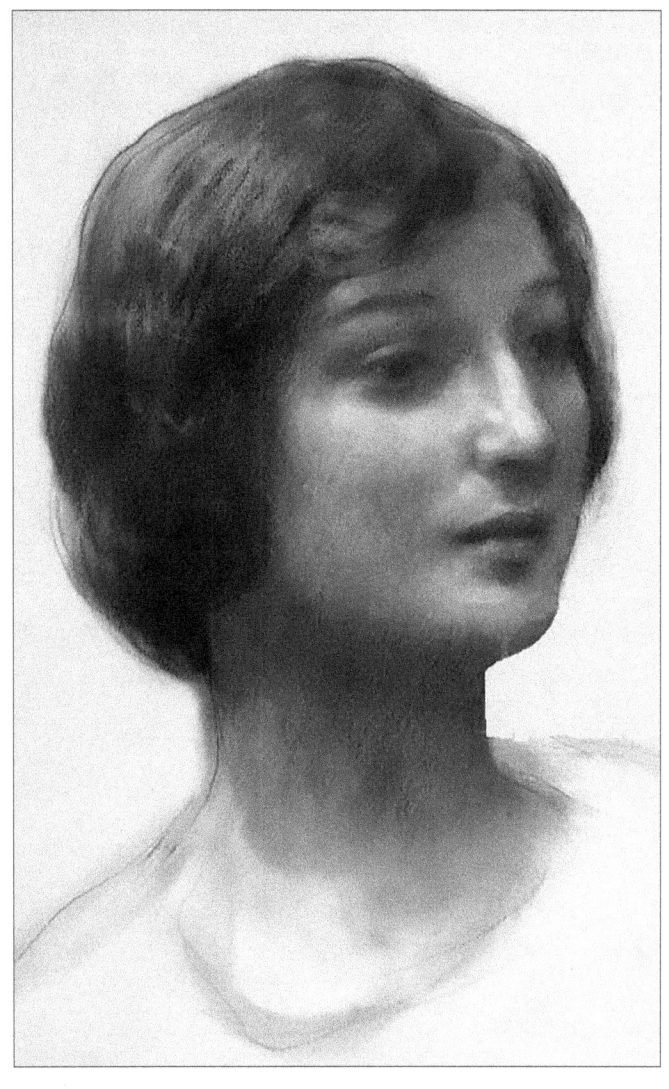 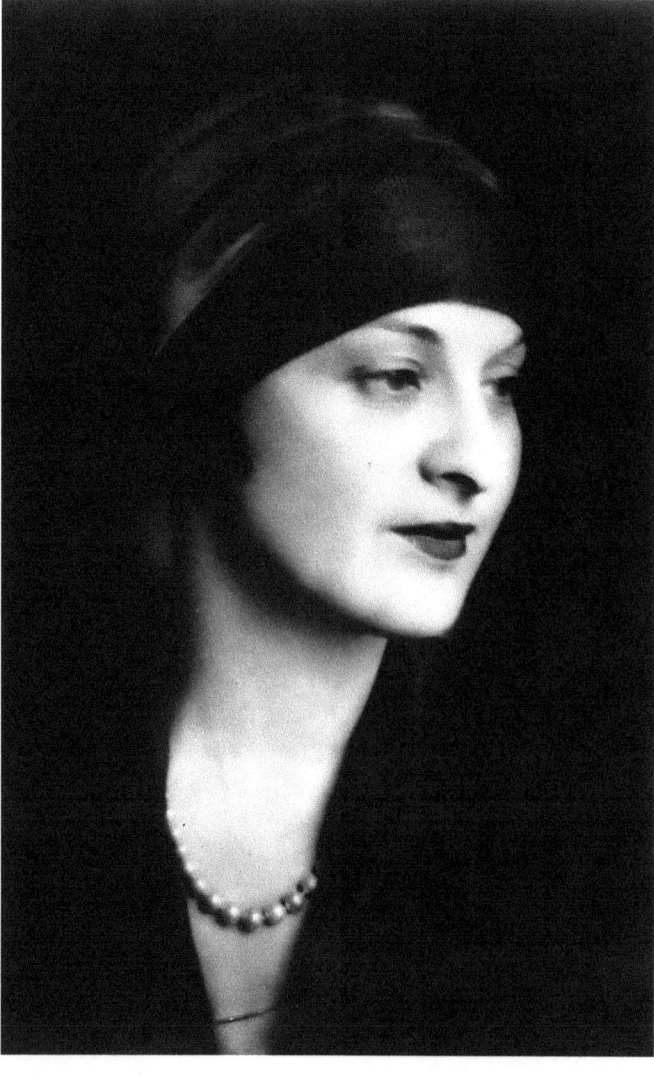

---
13 Laura Claridge: *The Lady with the Borzoi: Blanche Knopf.* Farrar, Straus and Giroux, NY, 2016.

Women Friends and Lovers - Margaret Lee Crofts

Margaret Lee Crofts was a philanthropist who befriended Gibran and offered him opportunities to escape from the city to spend time in the countryside. She is best remembered as a supporter of aspiring young musicians through a scholarship and fellowship system she established with a generous endowment. Gibran had met her before she married and in 1917 had given her a handwritten parable that would become part of *The Madman*.[14] On her wedding day, he sent her a congratulatory note wishing her "a life full of blessings and fulfillments." He produced two delicate portraits of Mrs. Crofts and corresponded with her on various topics in a casual and friendly vein. Crofts was a struggling writer prone to destroying her manuscripts if she felt them inadequate. In one letter, Gibran discourages her from this habit: "I must say that I do not agree with you about burning the things you write which for the moment you do not like. It seems to me that you should keep them as documents. I have often been sorry for destroying what I might have made better by going over it a year after." Many years later, Mrs. Crofts would publish a single work entitled *Armed with Light*.[15]

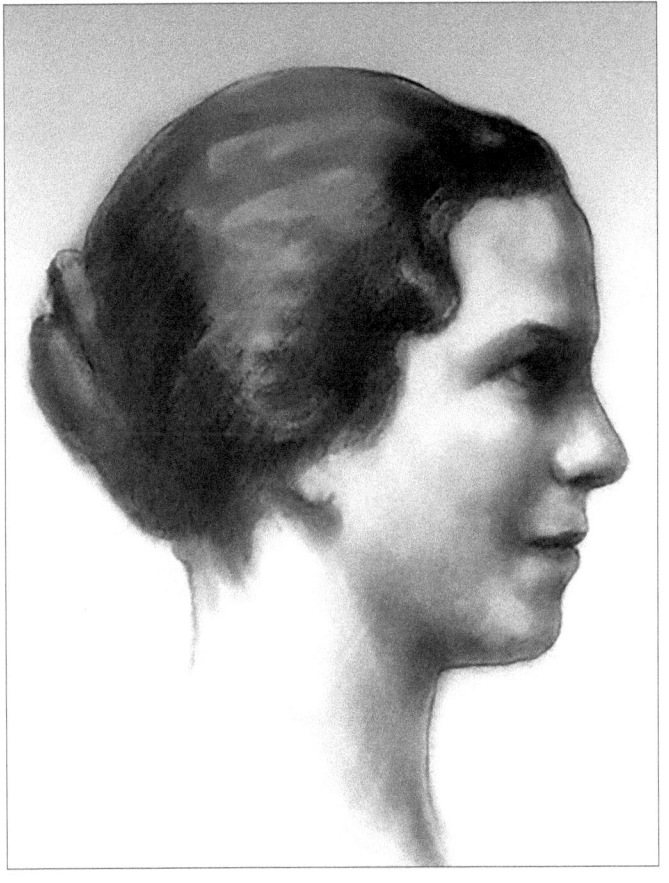
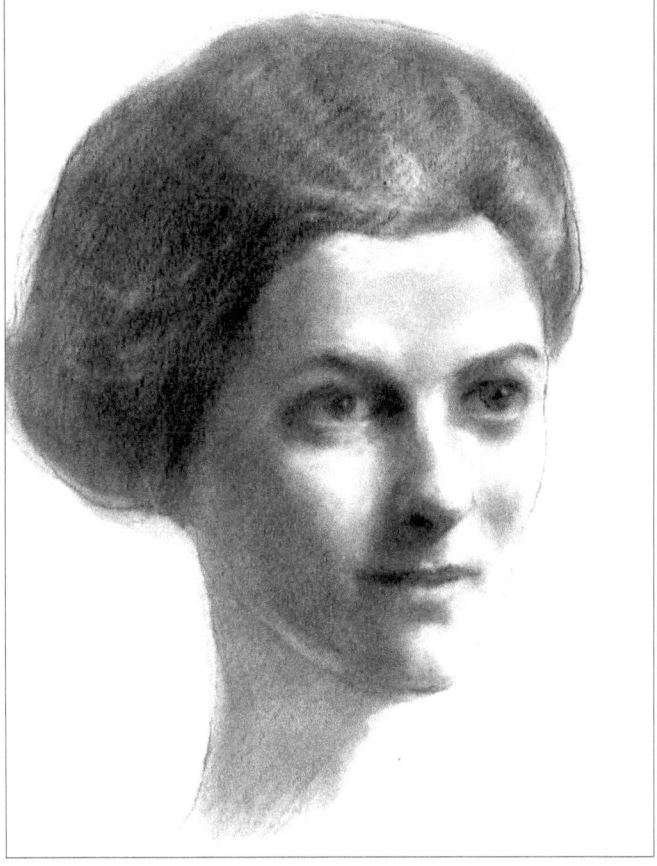

---

[14] Margaret Lee Crofts correspondence, Library of Congress Manuscript Division, Washington, DC.
[15] Margaret Lee Crofts: *Armed with Light*. Garden City, N.Y. Doubleday, Doran and Co., 1937.

Marie-Luise Schloss

Little is known about *Marie-Luise Schloss* of whom Gibran drew a richly textured portrait. The warm inscription he penned on copies of his books that he offered her suggests a closeness that is otherwise undocumented. In the inscription on *The Prophet* he quotes himself "Love is winging the day through work and work is love made visible." He is ever complementing her, and in one letter, he says humorously, "your tresses, like molten gold, falling from the heaven to earth will bring pleasure to the gods of this world – and the gods of other worlds!" In the inscription on *Jesus, the Son of Man*, he credits her for being there when the book was first thought of and of being supportive and helpful.

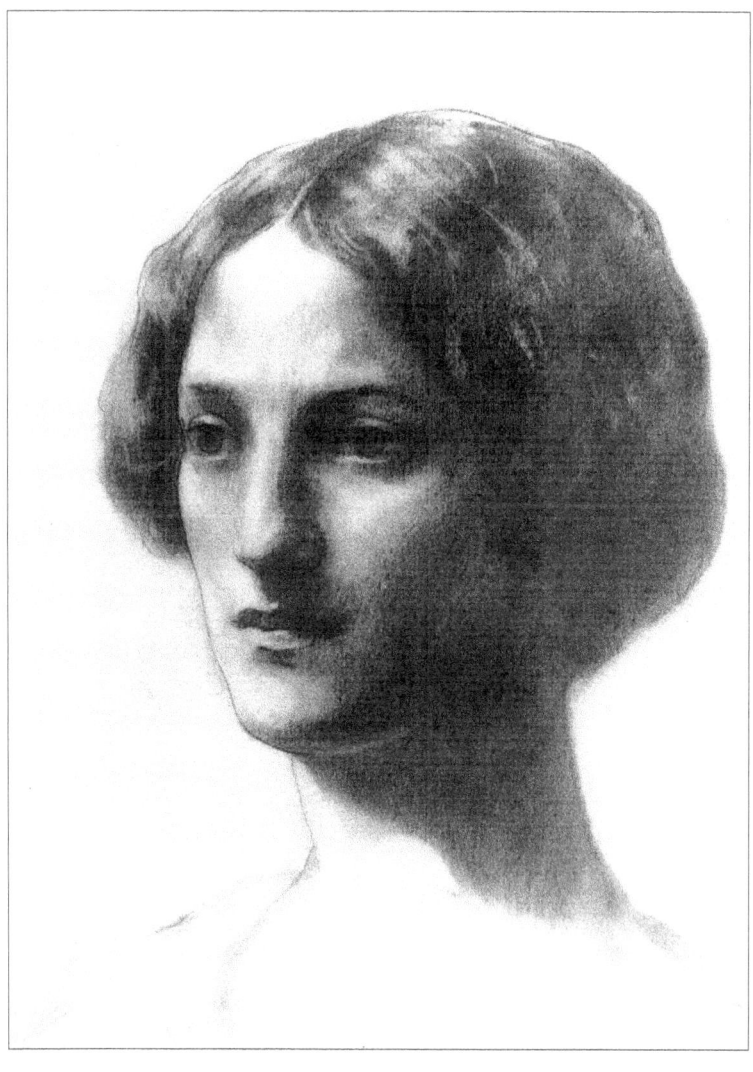

Gibran produced many portraits of the women he loved and his portraits of Mary Haskell, Emily Michel (Micheline) and Charlotte Teller are too many to reproduce in the current work. Similarly, he has many self-portraits that he continued to create from his early youth until late in life. It could even be argued that the face of *The Prophet*, and the face of the Beloved Apostle in *Jesus, The Son of Man*, bear sufficient resemblance to Gibran to be considered in that group.

New York Elite, Friends and Companions

Fellow Syrians - Ameen Rihani

The relationship between Gibran and *Ameen Rihani* (1876-1940) is a complex matter that cannot be dealt with within the scope of this work.[16] Rihani had preceded Gibran as the most vocal and controversial social and literary reformer among Syrian Americans. His facility in English exceeded anything Gibran could aspire to, and his erudition was clearly superior. This did not prevent the two Syrian writers from becoming friends. Rihani visited Gibran in Paris and the two travelled together to London on a cultural pilgrimage.

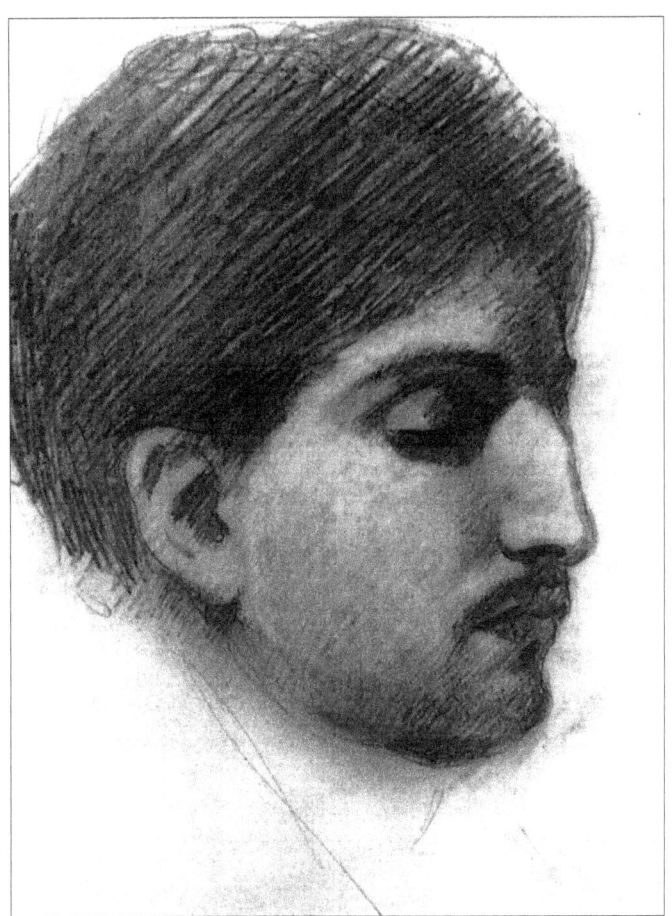
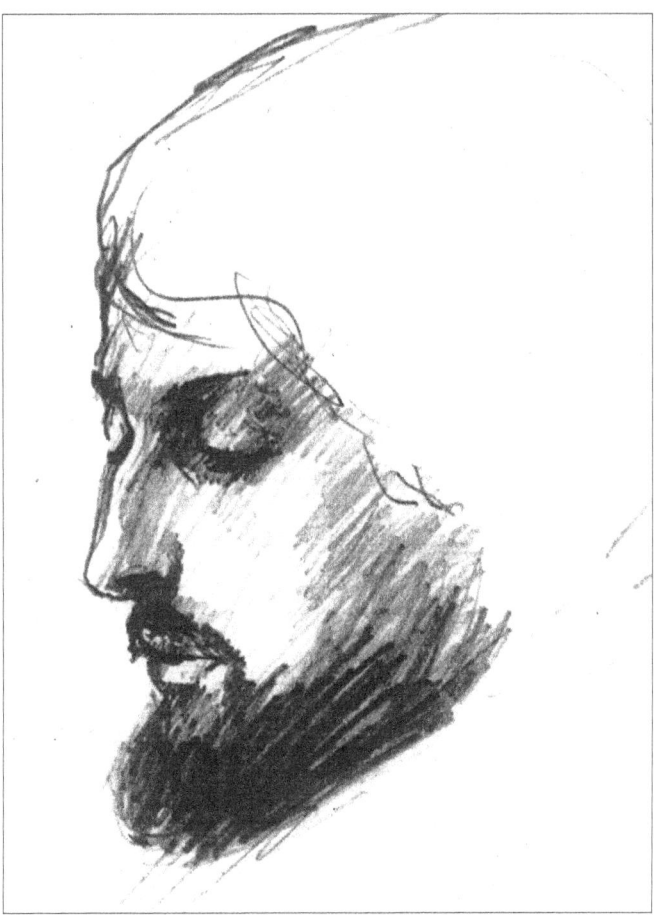

When Gibran moved to New York, he rented a room in the house where Rihani lived and for many years, the two were inseparable.[17] Rihani introduced Gibran to the circle of poets in New York[18] and facilitated many of his projects for obtaining portraits of the New York literary elite.[19] Gibran introduced Rihani to Charlotte Teller with whom Rihani had a heated romance that ended acrimoniously. During the First World War, Gibran and Rihani participated in the

---

16 *Letters of Kahlil Gibran*, pp 70.
17 *Letters of Kahlil Gibran*, pp 73.
18 *Letters of Kahlil Gibran*, page 75.
19 *Letters of Kahlil Gibran*, page 74.

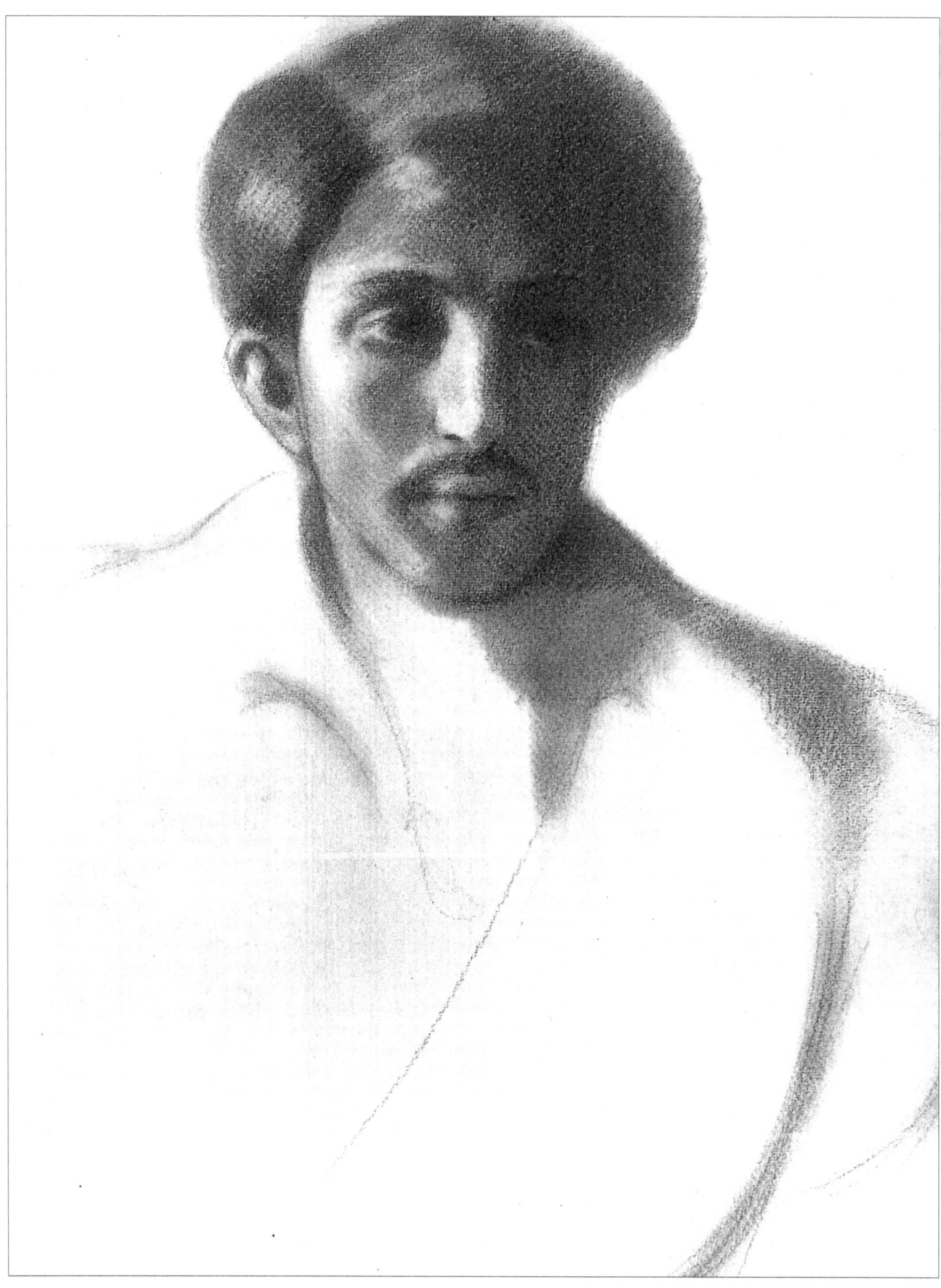

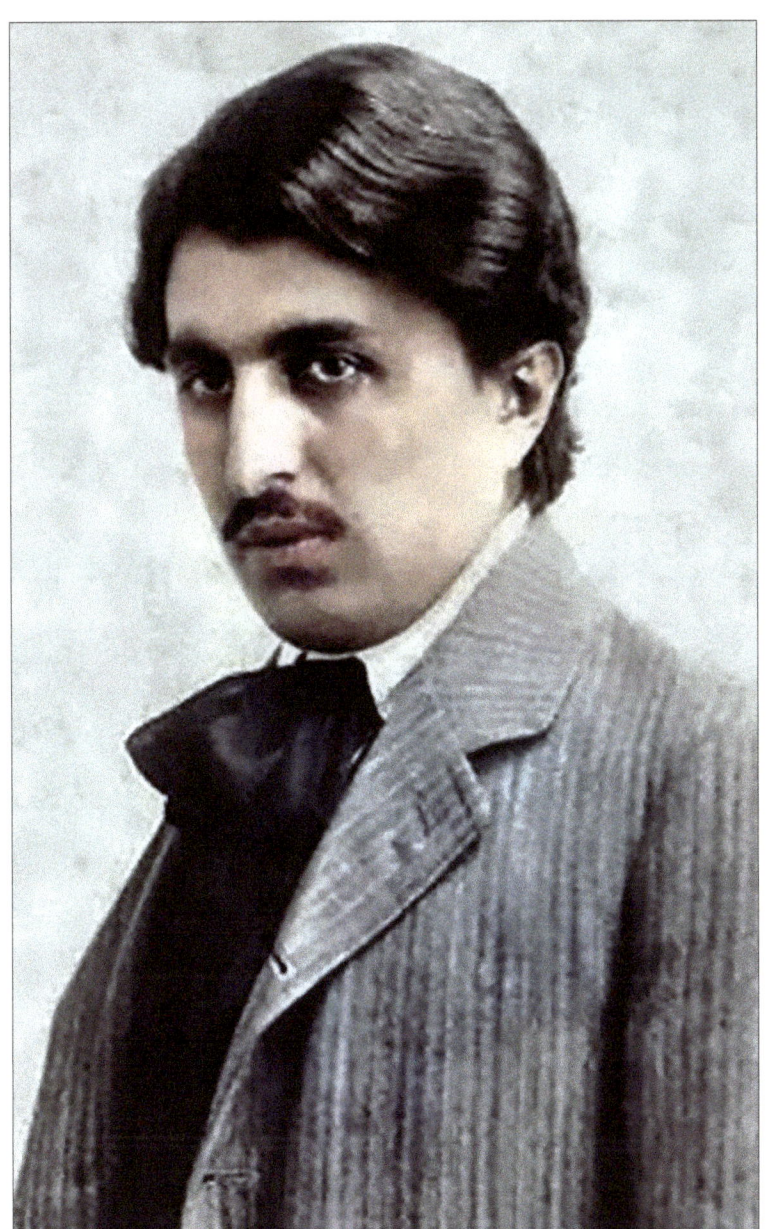

various committees that were active among Syrian immigrants in support of their motherland. It is at this juncture that the two seem to have developed some irreconcilable differences that may have emanated from differences in political tendencies Gibran being a francophone Syrian and Rihani with Arab sympathies, although it is likely that the reasons for the breach in the friendship are more complex. Rihani, however, remained true, albeit silent, to the spirit of their friendship. His eulogy of Gibran attests to the genuineness of his feeling. When Naimy published a rather caustic posthumous biography of Gibran, Rihani led the campaign to rectify the slight.

Gibran drew a few sketches and a major portrait of Rihani. In the main portrait, the sweeping lines in lieu of Rihani's torso suggest that the man with delicate features has great power hidden in him. It also conveys the impression of the loose robes of Syrian mountain elders.

MIKHAIL NAIMY

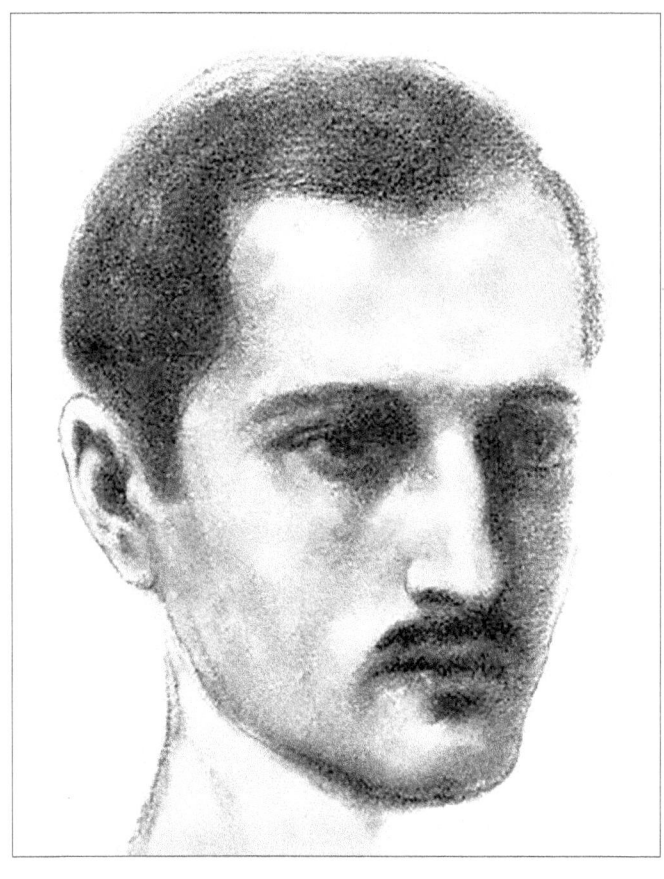

Mikhail Naimy (1889-1988) was a protégé of Gibran and while skilled in literary areas that Gibran never tackled (notably literary criticism), his opus reflects the powerful early influence of Gibran. Like Gibran's *The Prophet*,

Naimy produced *The Book of Mirdad*, a book of spiritual meditations and discourse imbued with eastern themes and style. Naimy also contributed an early translation of *The Prophet* to Arabic, marred somewhat by elaborate stylistic embellishments. He participated with Gibran in supplying the periodical *al-Funun* with material, and the two collaborated in the revival of *The Pen League* after the First World War.

Naimy is credited with the first book length biography of Gibran, a work blemished by fictitious accounts and fanciful recreations of events and scenes Naimy could have known about only through hearsay.

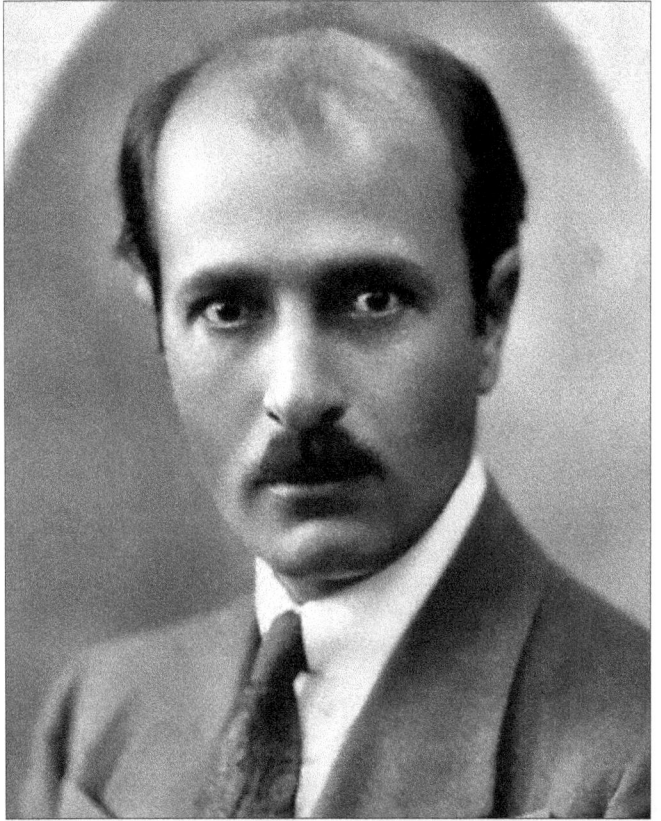

NASIB ARIDA

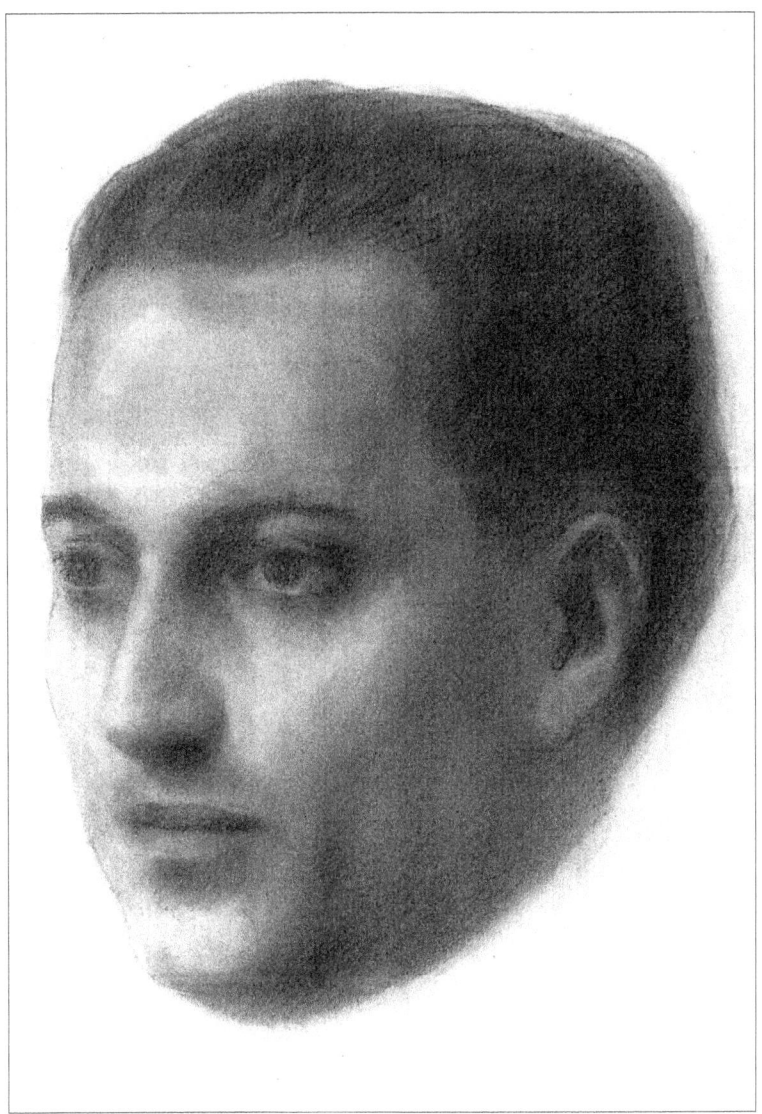

Nasib Arida (1887–1946) was another Syrian writer and poet that Gibran drew. Arida was part of the founding group of the literary society *The Pen League* along with Gibran and Mikhail Naimy.

He was also the publisher of the periodical *al-Funun* to which Gibran contributed regularly in prose and in drawings. Indeed, it was on the pages of *al-Funun* that Gibran published a series of imaginary portraits of major figures of Arabic literature and history.

Silent Faces

Despite extensive efforts to secure identification of the subjects in the extant portraits in hand, there remains a number of them that resisted our attempt! These are offered herein with the dual purpose of completing the documentation of the scope of portraitures by Gibran, and to allow others to contribute to the identification process.

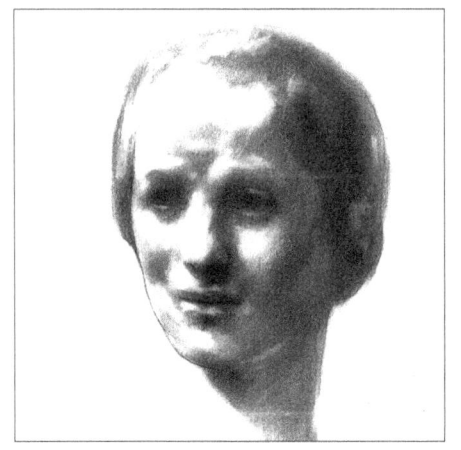
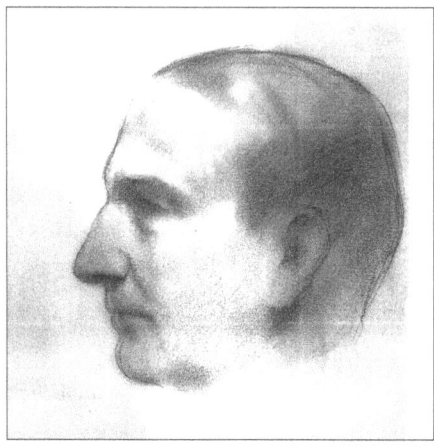
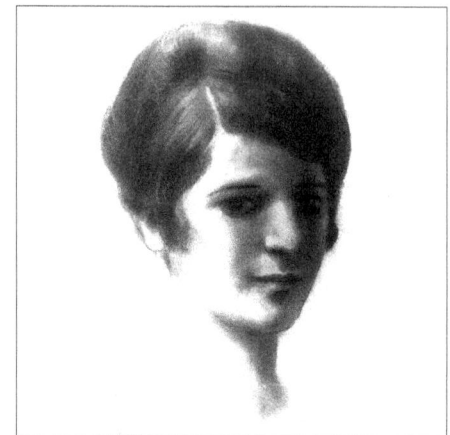
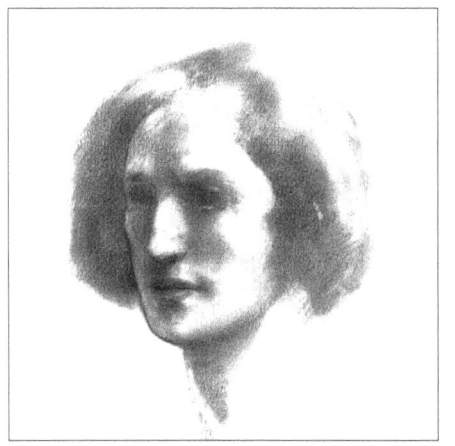
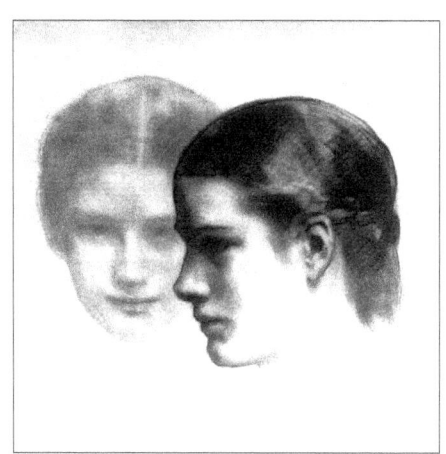
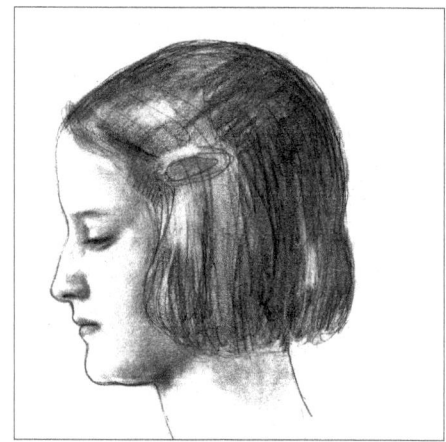
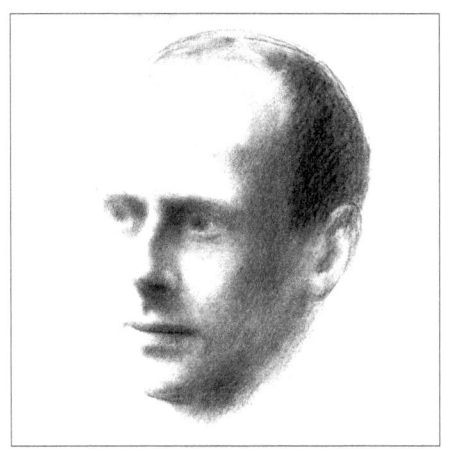
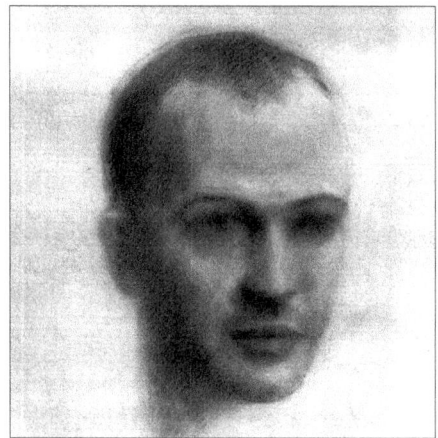
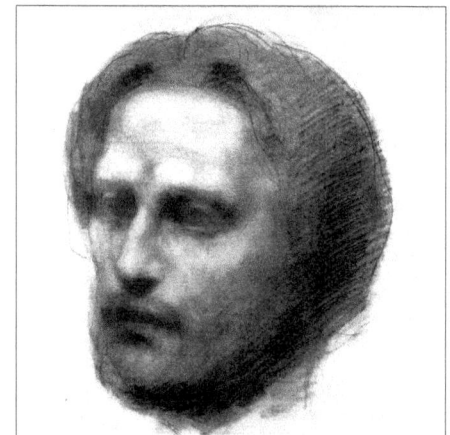

Lost Shadows

In addition to the extant portraits discussed above, there are portraits that remain to be found. Of the latter is the portrait of the playwright *Alice Bradley* (1875-1946). Gibran met her when he attended her play *The Governor's Wife* at the Belasco Theater in December of 1912. Gibran's friends encouraged him to draw her, which he did, but the whereabouts of the portrait are unknown.[20] Similarly, the portrait of Jack Barrymore mentioned by Mercedes de Acosta could not be located. Gibran drew the portrait of the American poet and writer Madeline Mason-Manheim (1898-1990) with whom he appears to have had an amorous relationship judging from the letters she had sent him.

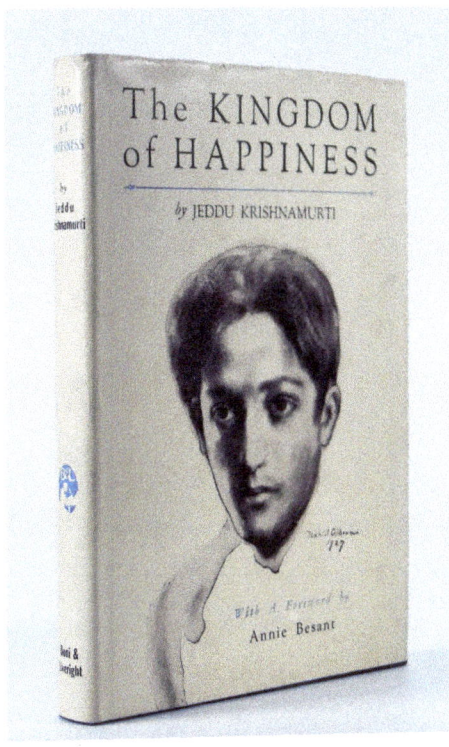

Gibran had also contributed five drawings to her poetry collection,[21] and she was the first to translate *The Prophet* to French.[22] The whereabouts of that portrait are unknown. Gibran's portrait of Jeddu Krishnamurti appeared on the cover of the latter's book *The Kingdom of Happiness*, but we could not locate the original.

In his correspondence with Mary Haskell, Gibran repeatedly mentions contacts with individuals he intends to draw, among them some famous individuals such as Edison and Belasco, and some less famous such as Margaret Wilson (1886-1944), the daughter of President Wilson,[23] and the British poet Alice Buckton (1867-1944) who was close to the Baha'i faith.[24] There is no proof, however, that Gibran drew either women and we could not match them to any of the unidentified portraits in his opus. Gibran had also tried through his friendship with Corinne Roosevelt Robinson (1861-1933) to obtain an appointment with her brother President Roosevelt, but was unsuccessful.[25]

---

20 *Letters of Kahlil Gibran*, page 221.
21 Madeline Mason-Manheim, *Hill Fragments*. Brentano's Publishers, New York, 1925.
22 *Le Prophète*, par Kahlil Gibran. Traduction de Madeline Mason-Manheim, Éd. du Sagittaire, Paris, 1926.
23 *Letters of Kahlil Gibran*, page 236.
24 *Letters of Kahlil Gibran*, page 177.
25 *Letters of Kahlil Gibran*, page 549.

Speaking in Color

THE DYING LIONESS - KAMILEH GIBRAN

When Syria was gripped with a terrible famine during the First World War as a result of the Allied sea blockade and Turkish oppressive policies, Gibran published in the journal *al-Funun* a drawing of the face of a woman expressing great suffering. He titled it "The Face of my Mother, The Face of my Nation!" Indeed, it seemed that Kamileh Gibran and Syria were fated to suffer the woes of life and history.

Kamileh Gibran had married young, divorced her first husband after she had her first son (Peter, born 1881), and married Khalil Gibran, our artist's father. The marriage though unhappy resulted in the birth of Gibran (1883) and his two sisters, Sultana (1887) and Marianna (1885), or Annie and Mary, as they were known in the US after their immigration. Kamileh was a woman of strength and determination. Dissatisfied with the life she had in the Lebanon mountain, with a man of modest means and even more modest ambition, she gathered her four children and headed to the New World. The squalor of their early years in Boston may have betrayed her dreams, but her singular decision to leave Syria for a better life was prophetic for her youngest son, if not for his siblings.

Kamileh, although illiterate, was very protective of the young Kahlil and fostered his progress into a career in literature and the arts as far as she could. She did not live to see him succeed as she died in June of 1903 from a cancer of the mesentery and intestines. She was buried next to her first son Peter who had died only a few months before from pulmonary tuberculosis (March 12, 1903), and her daughter Sultana who had died from a more disseminated form of the same disease known as miliary tuberculosis in April of 1902. Gibran commented that his mother had "buried her heart twice in less than a year."

The suffering of the tenacious Kamileh was on his mind when he painted her portrait years later, one of the few executed in oil on canvas. In this portrait, Kamileh's life of pain is symbolized in the agony of the noble Assyrian lioness. Gibran saw the Assyrian bas-relief in the British Museum in the summer of 1910 when he visited London in the company of Ameen Rihani. The lioness is an apt symbol for Kamileh for she was the nurturing and protecting parent of her brood. Using a symbol from his own Syrian heritage was a suitable device to telescope Kamileh's life into one scene where the profusion of arrows piercing the body of the lioness

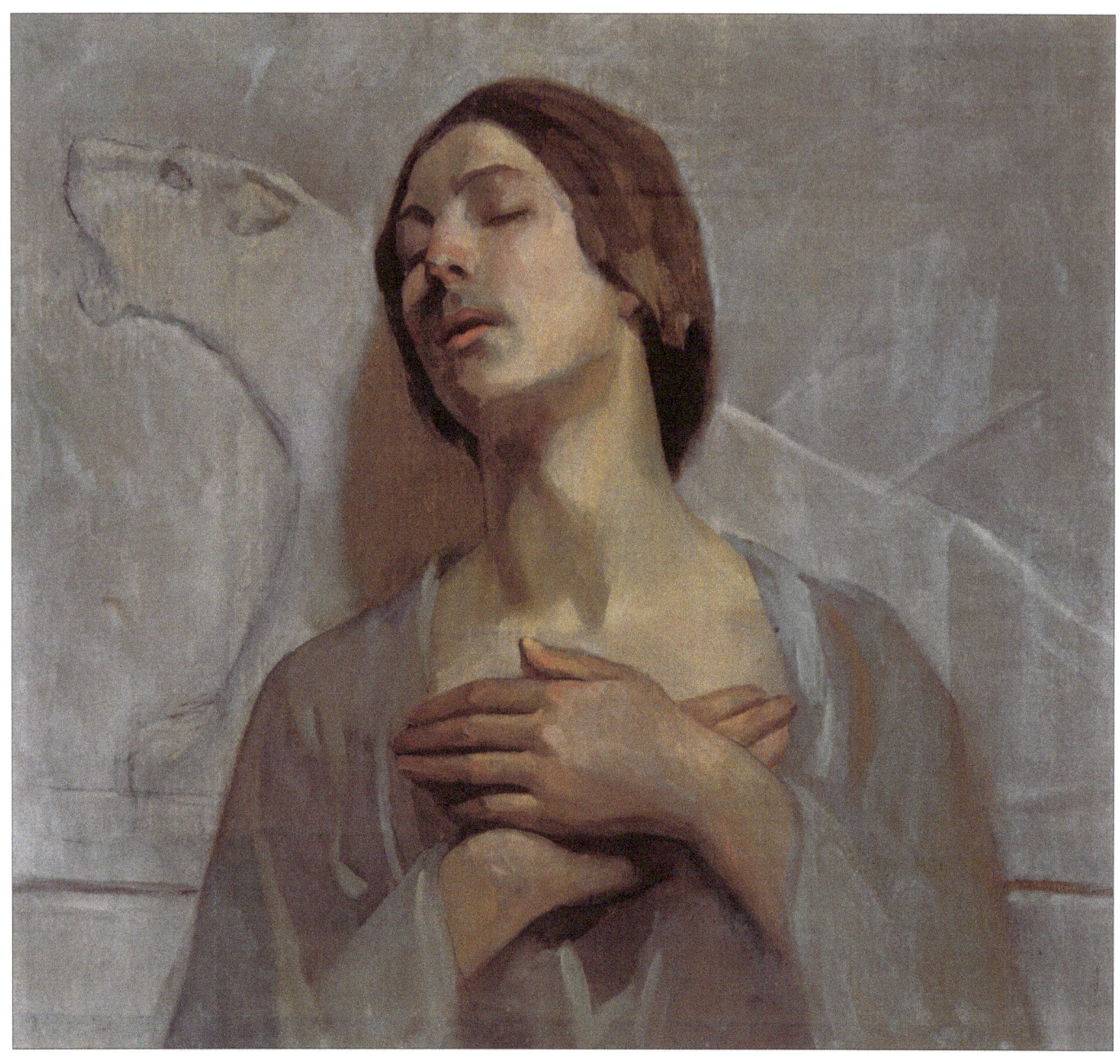

represents the recurrent tragedies of Kamileh's life. In the end, the lioness is paralyzed by an arrow that severed her spine, just like the death of her first born, Peter, had sapped Kamileh's resolve as she struggled with her fatal disease.

Having expressed the tragic element in his mother's life in the depiction of the wounded and dying lioness, Gibran could turn now to idealizing the woman who begot him in depicting her in a serene posture of blessed silence, almost like the accepting Holy Madonna. Her tilted head, closed eyes, and crossed arms are the emblems of beatification of the courageous and suffering mother who incessantly sacrificed for her children. The portrait executed at least ten years after Kamileh's death bears very little resemblance to her actual features. Gibran

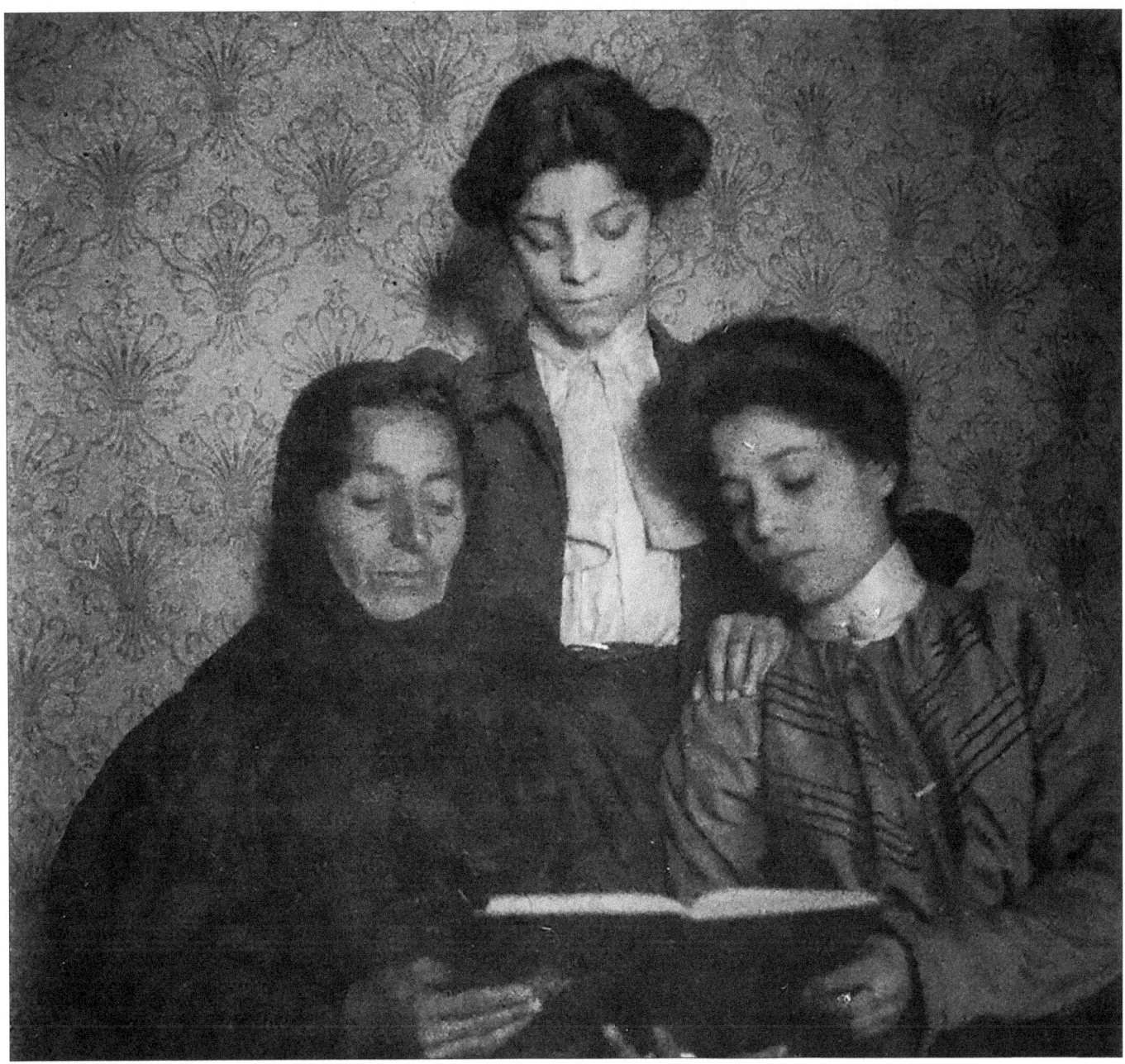

considerably softens the facial contours of his mother, likely evoking his idealized view of a more youthful woman than the one we know from photographs taken by his mentor Day in 1898. Consistent with the beatification of her face, Gibran erases the effects of hard labor from her hands which are no longer gnarled and arthritic. The portrait is a depiction of the image Gibran created about his mother and the narrative he presented to the world and to Mary Haskell in particular. Her diary entries are populated with numerous stories Gibran related about the wisdom and strength of his mother, her true noble character and her invented noble pedigree. The woman in the portrait, in her serene beauty and muted colored clothing appears more as a noble pre-Raphaelite woman than a suffering immigrant living a wretched life in a Boston tenement.

The Sad Mona Lisa - Sultana Gibran

Gibran's portrait of his sister Sultana (Annie) is equally filled with pathos. The young Sultana (1885-1902) had died while Gibran was overseas earning an education in a high school in Beirut. Sultana died in April, Gibran returned to America in May of 1902. He had left four years prior so in his mind he retained the image of an even younger sister. He depicts her seated, likely guided by a few photographs he had of her, against a dark and somber background that exacerbates her pallor and fragility. The darkness of fading memory and death seems to engulf the fragile child. She appears demure against the engulfing darkness and her seated position accentuates her vulnerability. Gibran modified her hair from the Western style we see in her pictures to a traditional flowing hair, as she would have worn as a child in Syria, along with the dress and garb of a Syrian young girl.

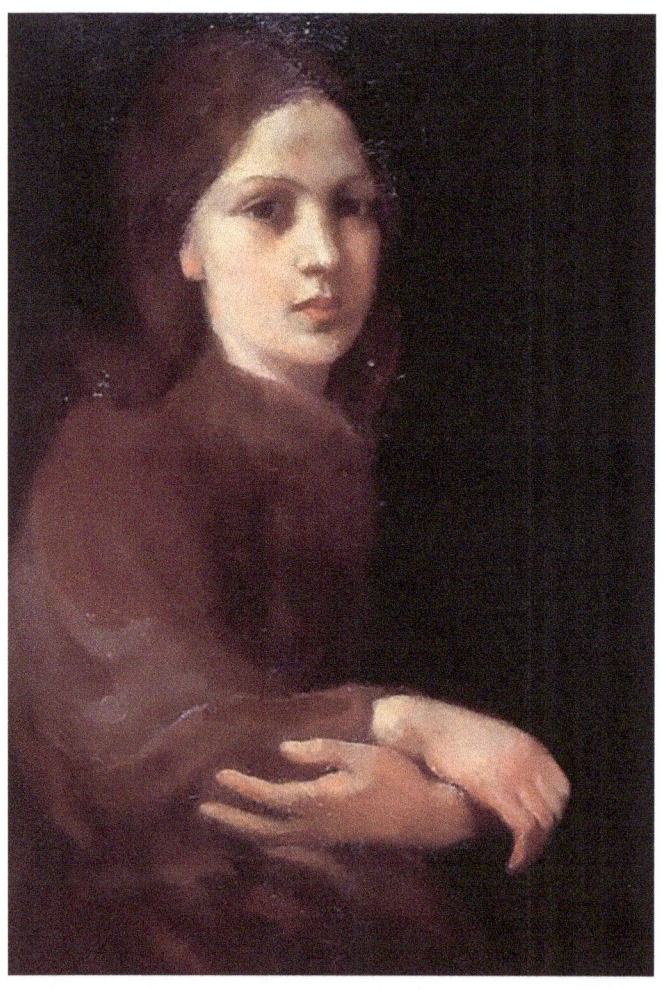 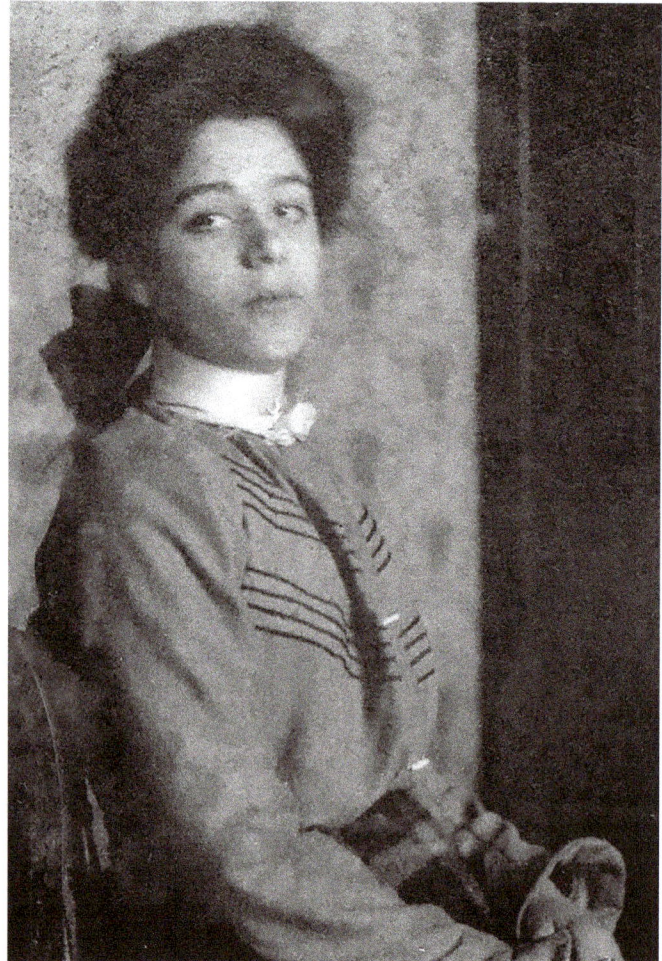

Speaking in Color

THE SUFFERING MARY - MARIANNA GIBRAN

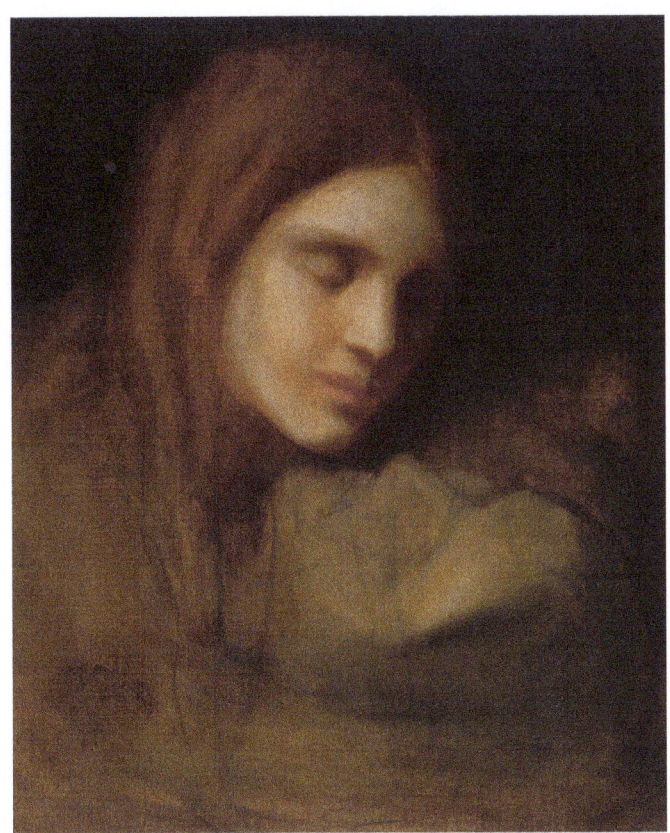
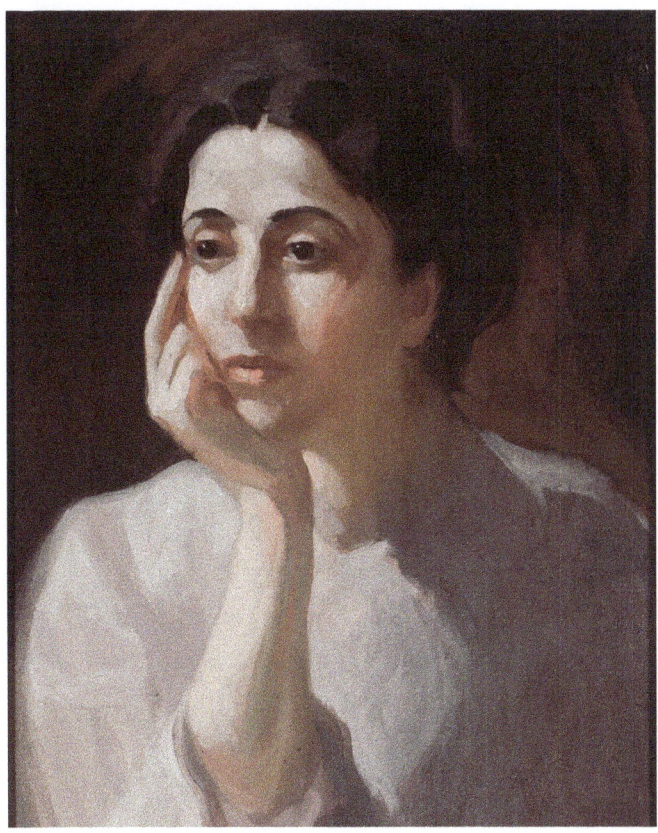

Of the two oil portraits of Marianna, the symbolic one encapsulates her life experiences. Marianna was fated to be the caretaker of the suffering family, recurrently confronting the death of a loved one. When Sultana died, Gibran was in Syria. He equally absented himself when his brother Peter died, and when his mother succumbed to her illness, finding refuge and consolation at the house of his muse Josephine Preston Peabody. Marianna was left at home alone face to face with loss and suffering. In the portrait, Marianna is tenderly facing the ghost of loved ones, dead or dying. Her features betray no horror or fear, just the resignation of someone long used to suffering. Her closed eyes retain the image of the loved one unblemished by the effects of death. She is calm in her deep sorrow and loneliness. Indeed, loneliness is Marianna's lot in life. After the family was decimated by successive deaths, she lived alone self-supporting while Gibran travelled to Paris for two years, and when he moved to live in New York permanently, enjoying his occasional visits and doting on him. On his death, she became the ill-prepared and unwitting guardian of his legacy, soon derailed into unfortunate decisions.

The second portrait of Marianna is, in contrast to the first, a reflection of a better time. The playful gaze of the young woman from her photographs is reflected in the mood of the portrait.

INVENTED SELF

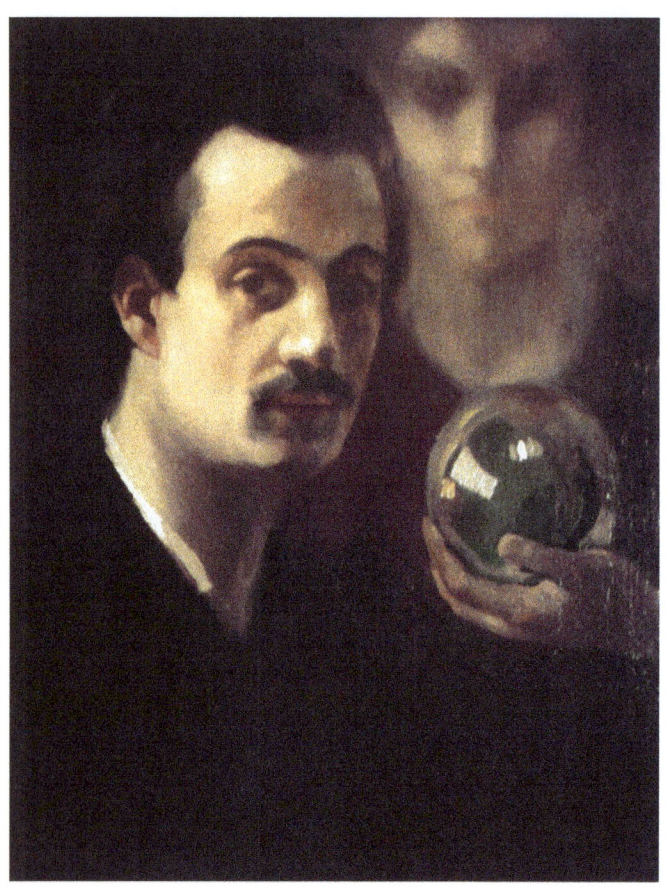 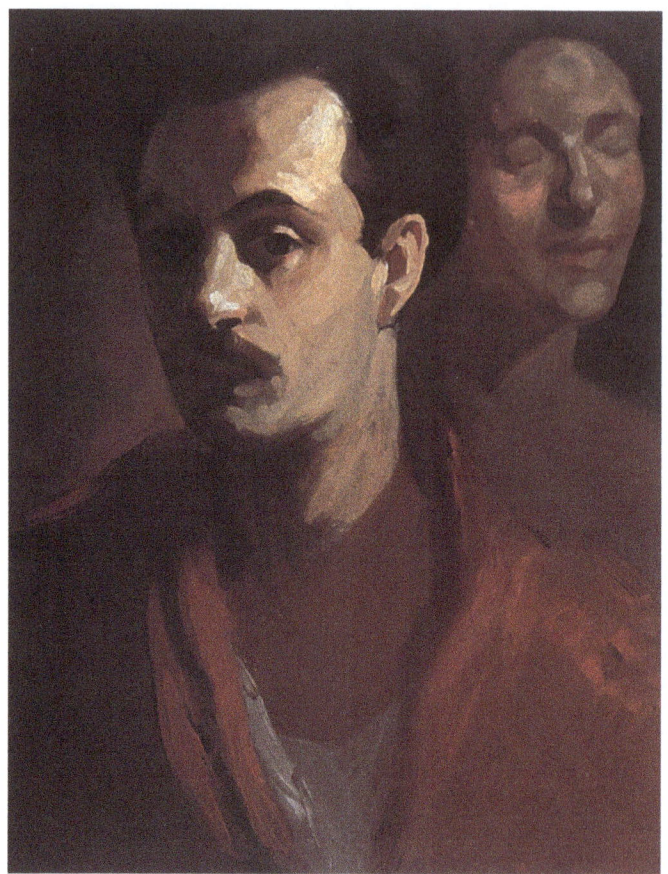

In addition to numerous self-portraits in pencil, Gibran executed two in oil. He introduced in both allegorical elements to create an aura for the persona he is trying to project. In both portraits, he depicts himself looking at the observer from the side with a determined gaze. His features in both portraits are also "beautified" just like his wont with the portraits of others or his representation of his models. Indeed, it is difficult to find an ugly face in Gibran's entire opus!

Speaking in Color

L'Amante - Micheline Emily Michel

Gibran must have executed Micheline's oil portrait while they lived together for a few months in Paris at the beginning of his sojourn in the French capital. The portrait has a Parisian feel to it with the decorative wallpaper used as background, reminiscent of many indoor French paintings of the period. The young woman is depicted as a dreamy lover, calmly sensuous, in repose and contentment. The Micheline of the painting is the same woman Naimy, speaking for Gibran, describes in his biography of the latter:

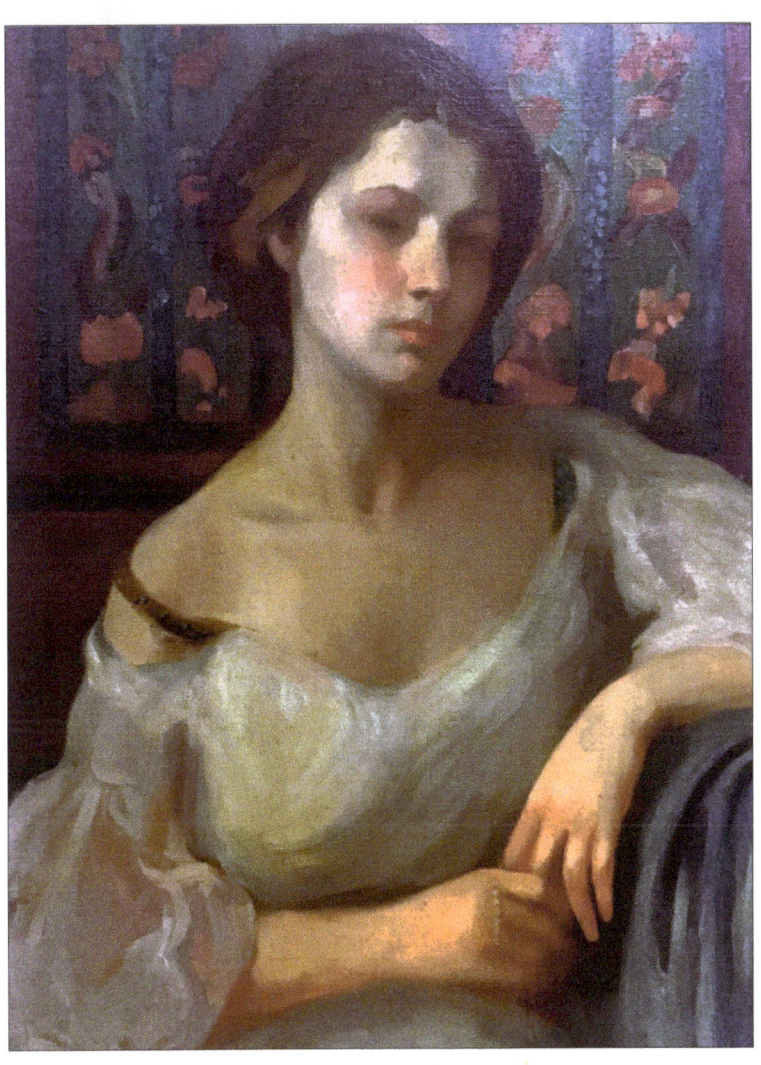

"In her dark hair alone is a sheen that fascinates the eye and electrifies the hands to the extent that the looker can barely restrain the impulse to touch it and stroke it. In her large, black eyes sparkles a light teeming with the budding desires and innocent dreams of healthful, energetic, self-confident youth. In her complexion is an ivory tinge suffused with the red of the poppy. Her smile has the modesty and innocence of a child's smile. Her laughter is the gurgling of a running brook; she seldom smiles or laughs. Perhaps her twenty years have taught her that equanimity is Beauty's strong shield, while too much laughing leaves Beauty open to many poisoned shafts. At times, she prattles like a child; at others, she utters things full of poetry and wisdom."[1]

Micheline (Emily Michel) first met Gibran in Boston while she taught French at Mary Haskell's school. Mary seems to be recurrently pairing Gibran with one or another of her young women protégés, first with Micheline, and a few years later with Charlotte Teller. The latter attempt was rapidly stifled by Charlotte's unequivocal and vehement refusal: "Not even if he was the last man on earth!"

---

1 Mikhail Naimy: *Kahlil Gibran: a Biography*, Philosophical Library, NY, 1950, page 65.

The Francophone young man, a rarity in Boston, charmed Micheline. Their romance continued when they both travelled to France and lived together in Paris. Gibran seems to have tired then of the sweet teacher as his life experience in the art world of Paris exposed him to strikingly beautiful women like Ms. Marie Doro whose portrait he also drew. The romance with Micheline died by neglect. Micheline later returned to America, married and lived in New York. She would dutifully attend Gibran's exhibitions, and meet him whenever Mary Haskell visited the great metropolis.

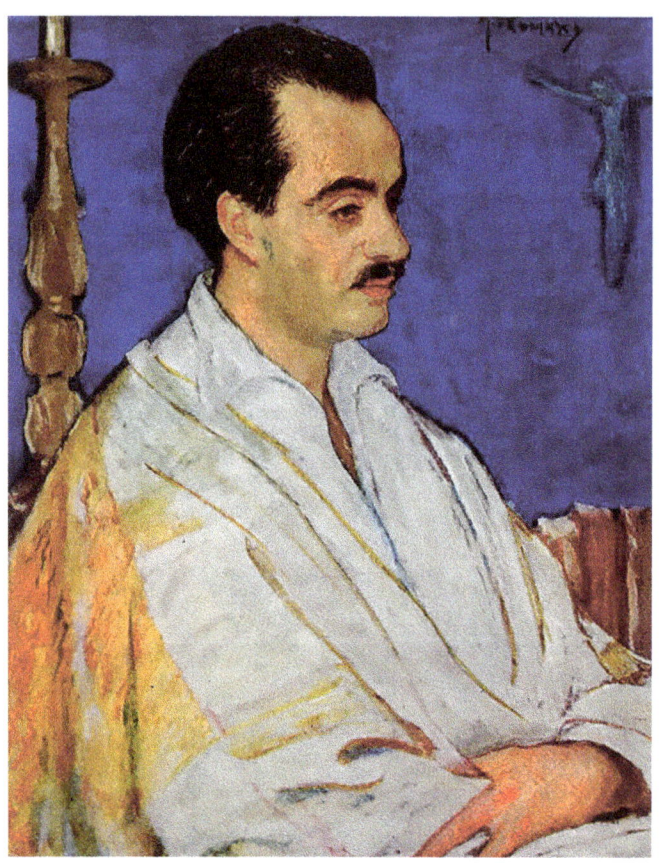

Portrait of Gibran by Maurice Fromkes

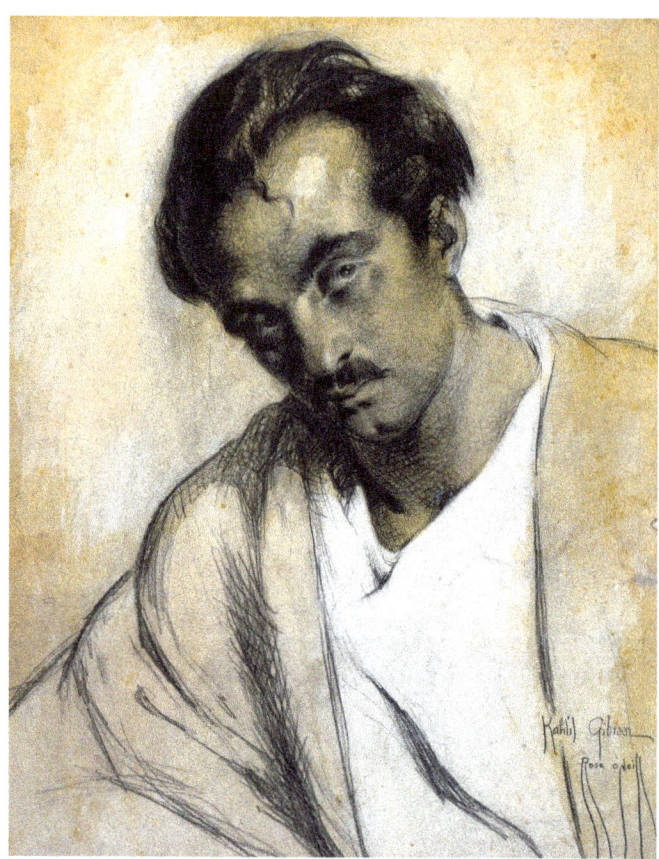

Portrait of Gibran by Rose Cecil O'Neill

Speaking in Color

Not Even If... - Charlotte Teller

Charlotte Teller was one of Mary Haskell's brilliant protégés. A woman of strong character and vibrant energy, she seemed indefatigable. She wrote novels, plays, political essays, parables, short stories, art reviews, and expositions of psychoanalytic theory with equal facility, while simultaneously contributing regular newspaper fare! Gibran was taken by her from their first encounter in Boston in 1908. He saw her in Paris a year later where she was trying to stage her play 'Mirabeau'. When he felt constrained in Boston, she offered him the use of her apartment in New York while she was on tour with a theatre company.

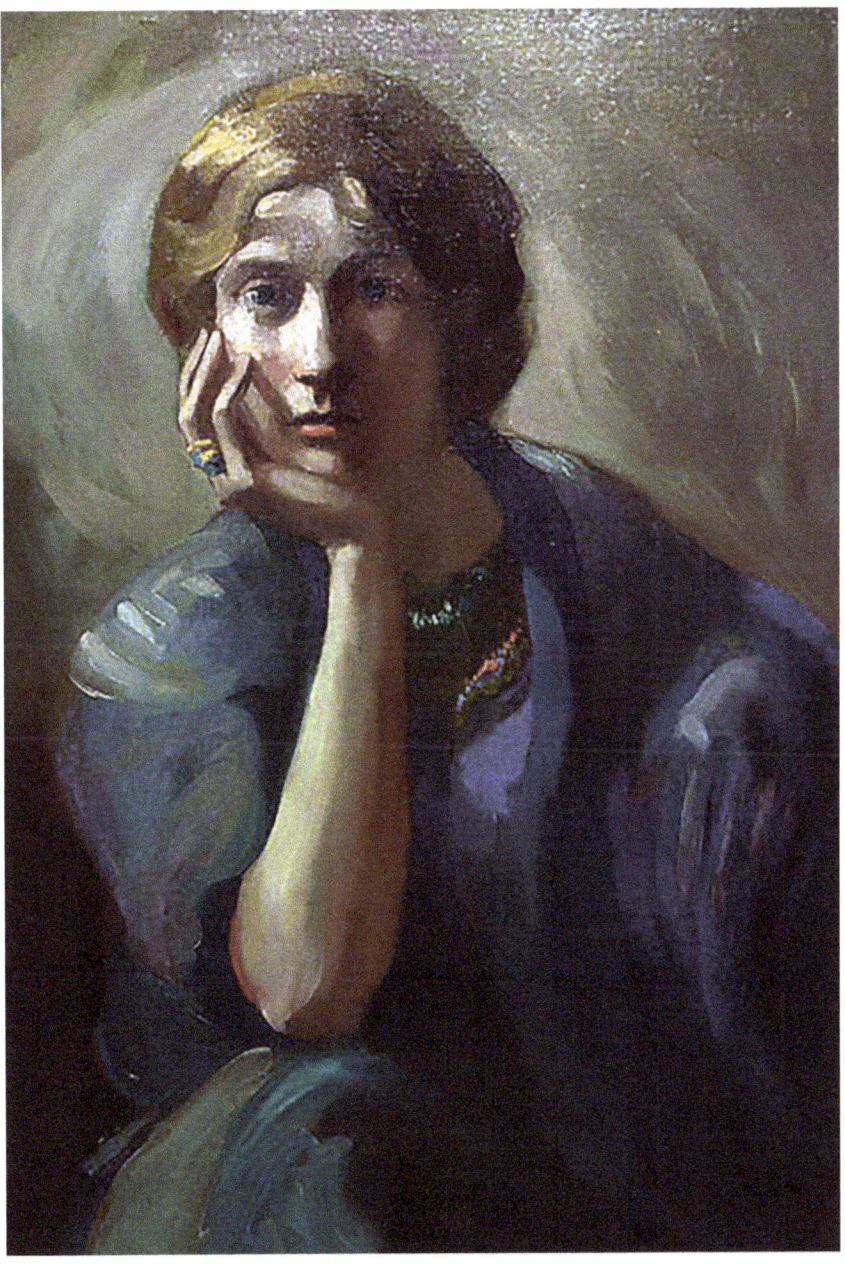

Charlotte helped Gibran settle in New York by networking with the political and intellectual elite of the city that she knew very well. This she did as an act of gratitude to Mary Haskell with whom she had an unconsummated amorous liaison. She gradually grew tired of Mary's excessive adulation of Gibran and Mary's blindness to his greatest flaws. This likely contributed to the final breach in their special friendship.

The oil portrait of Charlotte belongs to the early days of Gibran's stay in New York. We find celebratory mention of it in Gibran's letters to Mary and in her diary entries for the weeks she visited the pair, when she usually stayed with Charlotte. It was originally titled 'Isis' with jewels and robes worked into it. There is epistolary evidence of Gibran incessantly revising and modifying the portrait into the form we have before us today.

COLORFUL, BUT SILENT

As with the case of the pencil portraits, Gibran's opus in oil contains several portraits that remain unidentified. They span the period from his stay in Paris to the beginning of the First World War after which he abandoned oils and used washes as his preferred medium.

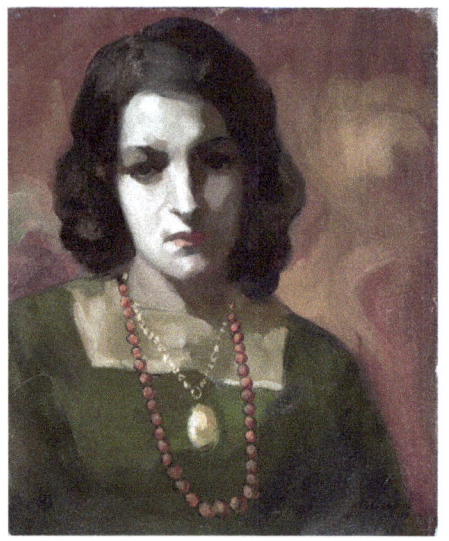
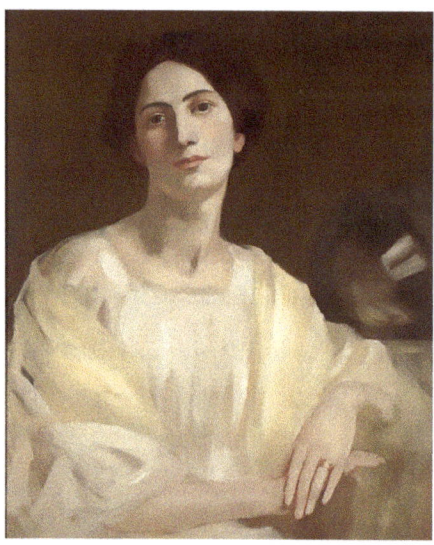
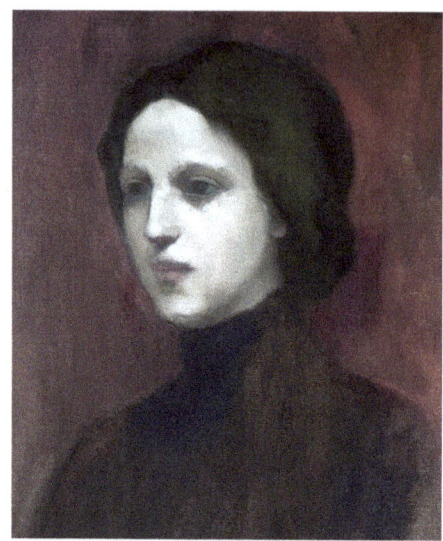
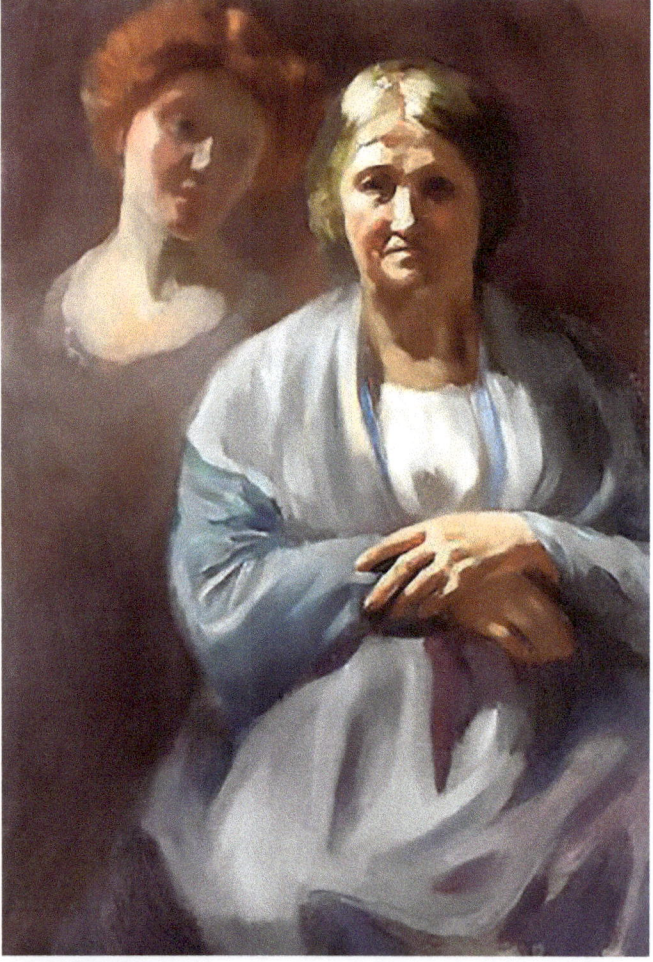
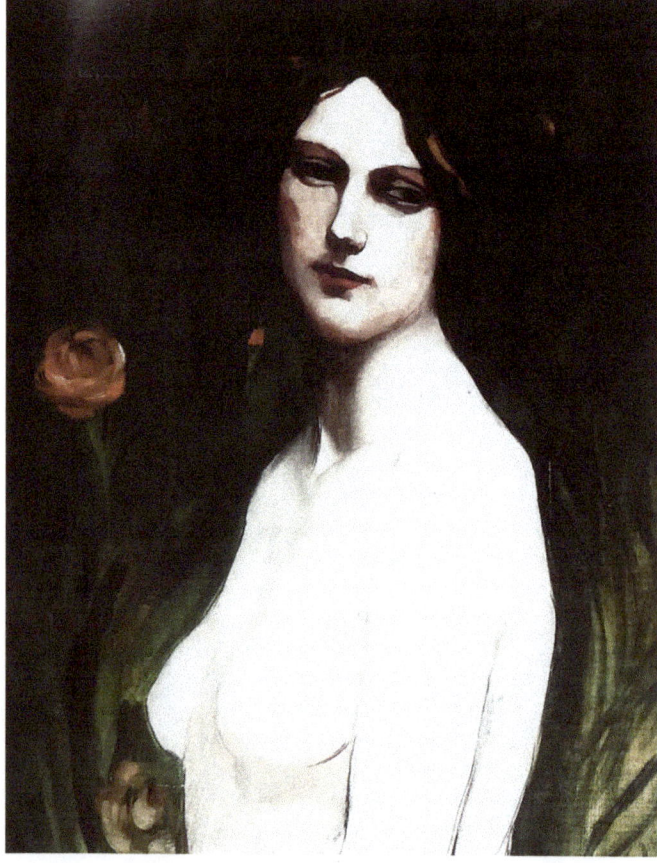

Speaking in Color

A Gallery Of Heads

As we examine the series of portraits that Gibran produced between 1910 and his death, we find a preponderance of writers and poets, and to a lesser extent, painters and musicians. The endeavor that started originally as an attempt to capture the greatest living artists gradually became a mixed collection of great men and women, but also commissioned works.[2] Gibran's portraits were praised whenever he exhibited them,[3] and appeared as illustrations of articles about the people he drew.

Gibran, however, never completed the project by the publication of a separate book or portfolio as he originally intended. Most of the portraits discussed above were found in his studio at the time of his death and most have now found their way to his museum in Lebanon, except for a few at the Metropolitan Museum in New York and the Newark Museum in New Jersey. Many reasons can be invoked to explain Gibran's failure in carrying the project to its planned conclusion. He may have not gathered a representative enough sample of the great men and women of the period, or the stature of those he drew was so heterogeneous and disparate that the common link was growing weaker. Alternatively, the stature of the people he drew waned with time, and a few may have become obscure by the time he may have considered publishing his portfolio.

Whatever the reasons for the non-publication of this collection in Gibran's lifetime, two conclusions are clear: the first is Gibran's exceptional skill in drawing portraits that are truly representative of the character of his subject; the second is the richness of the social and cultural environment in which Gibran lived and the opportunities he had to interact with truly exceptional and fascinating people.

Gibran's portraits stand apart from his avocation as a painter as a self-contained group of character studies. Over the years, he evolved a graceful technique that we encounter first in his Rodin portrait, further amplified in the portrait of Ryder, and finally forcefully expressed in the portrait of Bojer. In parallel, he seems to have retained a Leonardo like delicacy in portraying his friends (Bynner, Watson, Crofts) and a unique sensitivity to the fatal beauties of Elinor Wylie and Rita de Acosta.

---

2   Mikhail Naimy: *Kahlil Gibran: a Biography*, page 182.
3   *New York Tribune*, 20 December 1920, page 21.

Bibliography

BOOKS

Mercedes de Acosta: *Here Lies the Heart: A Tale of My Life,* Reynal, New York, 1960.

Jack Anderson: *Art Without Boundaries,* University of Iowa Press, Iowa City, 1997.

Elizabeth Broun: *Albert Pinkham Ryder,* Smithsonian Institution, Washington DC, 1989.

Suheil Bushrui, Joe Jenkins: *Kahlil Gibran: Man and Poet,* Oneworld Publications, Oxford, 1998.

Ruth Butler: *Rodin: The Shape of Genius,* Yale University Press, New haven, 1993.

Witter Bynner: *Caravan.* Alfred A. Knopf, publisher, New York, 1925.

Witter Bynner: *Take Away the Darkness.* Alfred A. Knopf, New York, 1947.

Witter Bynner: *Selected Poems,* edited with a critical introduction by Richard Wilbur. Farrar, Straus and Giroux, publishers, New York, 1977.

Judith Cladel: *Rodin: The Man and His Art, With Leaves From His Notebooks*, The Century Company, New York, 1917, translated from the French.

Laura Claridge: *The Lady With the Borzoi: Blanche Knopf.* Farrar, Straus and Giroux, New York, 2016.

Nathalie Sedgwick Colby, *Remembering,* Little, Brown and company, Boston, 1938.

Howard Willard Cook, *Our Poets of Today,* Moffat, Yard & company, New York, 1923.

Margaret Lee Crofts: *Armed With Light.* Doubleday, Doran and Co., Garden City, New York, 1937.

Carl Gad: *Johan Bojer, The Man and His Works,* Moffat, Yard and co., New York, 1920.

Mary Tudor Garland: *The Potter's Clay,* Published by G. P. Putnam's Sons, New York, 1917.

Mary Tudor Garland: *The Winged Spirit,* Published by G. P. Putnam's Sons, New York, 1918.

Mary Tudor Garland: *The Marriage Feast,* Published by G. P. Putnam's Sons, New York, 1920.

Kahlil Gibran: *Twenty Drawings,* Alfred A. Knopf, New York, 1919.

Jean Gibran and Kahlil Gibran: *Kahlil Gibran: His Life and World,* Interlink Books, New York, 1998.

Arthur Gold and Robert Fizdale: *The Divine Sarah: A Life Of Sarah Bernhardt,* Alfred A. Knopf, New York, 1991.

Robert Gottlieb: *Sarah: The Life Of Sarah Bernhardt,* Yale University Press, New Haven, 2010.

Frederic Grunfeld: *Rodin: A Biography,* Henry Holt and Company, New York, 1987.

Virginia Hilu (Editor): *Beloved Prophet: The Love Letters Of Kahlil Gibran And Mary Haskell, And Her Private Journal,* 1972.

William Homer and Lloyd Goodrich: *Albert Pinkham Ryder: Painter Of Dreams,* Harry N. Abrams, Inc., New York, 1989.

Elaine Lacroix Hopson: *Abdul Baha' In New York: The City Of The Covenant,* New Vista Design, New York, 1999.

Norman Jeffares: *W.b. Yeats: A New Biography,* Farrar Straus Giroux, New York, 1988.

D. H. Lawrence. *The Plumed Serpent.* Alfred A. Knopf, New York, 1926.

LeGallienne, Richard: *The Burial of Romeo and Juliette.* The Blue Skye Press, 1904.

Richard Londraville, Janis Londraville: *Dear Yeats, Dear Pound, Dear Ford: Jeanne Robert Foster And Her Circle Of Friends,* Syracuse University Press, 2001.

William McElwee Miller: *The Baha'i Faith: Its History and Teachings,* William Carey Library Publishers, 2000.

Percy McKaye: *Saint Louis, A Civic Masque,* Edition de Luxe, limited to 300 copies, signed by the Author: Frontispiece portrait-drawing of the Author by Kahlil Gibran; Doubleday, 1914.

Madeline Mason-Manheim, *Hill Fragments.* Brentano's Publishers, New York, 1925.

Madeline Mason-Manheim, *Le Prophète,* par Kahlil Gibran. Traduction de Madeline Mason-Manheim, Éd. du Sagittaire, Paris, 1926.

Mikhail Naimy: *Kahlil Gibran: A Biography,* Philosophical Library, New York, 1950.

Rose Cecil O'Neill, Miriam Formanek-Brunell: *The Story of Rose O'Neill: An Autobiography,* University of Missouri Press, Columbia, 1997.

Annie Salem Otto (Editor): *The Letters of Kahlil Gibran and Mary Haskell; Visions of Life as Expressed by The Author of The Prophet,* 1970.

Alice Raphael: *The Fulfillment,* Sturgis and Walton, New York, 1910.

Alice Raphael. *Faust; A Tragedy: In a Modern Translation,* Johann Wolfgang von Goethe; The Heritage club, New York, 1928.

Bibliography

Alma Reed, Michael Schluessleer: *Peregrina: Love and Death In Mexico,* University of Texas Press, 2007.

Alma Reed: *Orozco,* Oxford University Press, 1956.

Joanna Richardson: *Sarah Bernhardt and Her World,* Published by G. P. Putnam's Sons, New York, 1977.

George W. Russell: *The Living Torch,* The Macmillan Company, New York, 1938.

Aram Saroyan: *Kahlil Gibran: Paintings & Drawings,* 1905-1930. Vrej Baghoomian Gallery, New York, 1989.

Carl Schreiber: *A Note on Faust Translations.* Jonathan Cape and Harrison Smith, New York, 1930.

Ruth St Denis: *The Independent Art of the Dance.* In *Theatre: Essays on the Arts of the Theatre*, edited by Juliet Rich Isaacs, Books for Libraries Press, New York, 1927.

Warren & Putnam, New York, 1932.

Robin Waterfield: *Prophet: The Life and Times of Kahlil Gibran*, St Martins Press, New York, 2000.

Anzia Yezierska: *All I Could Never Be,* Brewer,

Barbara Young: *This Man From Lebanon*, Alfred A. Knopf, New York, 1945.

ARCHIVES

Smithsonian American Art Museum photo archives, Washington, DC.

Witter Bynner Papers. Rio Grande Historical Collections. New Mexico State University Library, Las Cruces, NM.

Mary Haskell Diary, in the Minis Family Papers #2725, Southern Historical Collection, The Wilson Library, University of North Carolina Library, Chapel Hill, NC, USA.

Rose Pastor Stokes Papers, General Correspondence, Manuscripts and Archives, Yale University Library, New Haven, CT, USA.

Margaret Lee Crofts correspondence, Library of Congress Manuscript Division, Washington, DC.

PERIODICALS

American Monthly Review of Reviews
The Argonaut
The Baltimore Sun
The Birmingham News
The Bookman
Boston Globe
Boston Post
The Brooklyn Citizen
The Brooklyn Daily Eagle
The Brooklyn Times
Buffalo Courier
The Buffalo Times
The Century
Chicago Tribune
The Cincinnati Inquirer
Current Opinion
Daily News
The Dial
The Drama
The Equinox
The Escanaba Daily Press
The Evening Mail
The Evening News
The Evening World
Green Bay Press – Gazette
Harvard Library Bulletin
Indianapolis Star
Intelligencer Journal
The International Journal of Psychoanalysis
The La Crosse Tribune
LA Times
The Missoulian
Montgomery Advertiser
Musical America
The Nation
The New Music Review and Church Music Review
The New Republic
The New York Herald
The New York Press
The New York Tribune,
The New York Times
The News – Herald
The Ogden Standard Examiner
The Ottawa Citizen
The Philadelphia Enquirer
Poetry
The San Francisco Call
The San Francisco Chronicle
The San Francisco Examiner
The Seven Arts
The South Bend Tribune
The Springfield News Reader Star Tribune
St Louis Dispatch
St. Louis Globe-Democrat
The Sun
The Tennessean
Times Colonist
Unity
The Yale Review